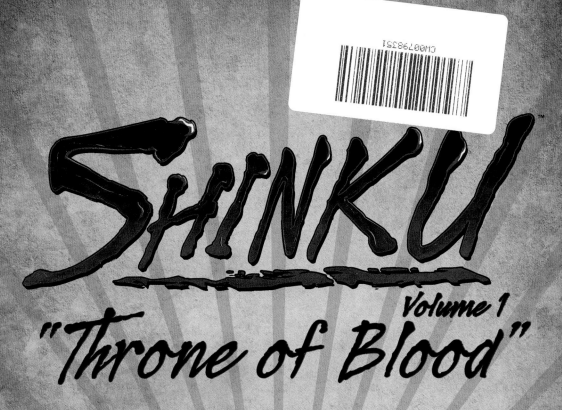

SHINKU™

Volume 1
"Throne of Blood"

published by
Image Comics, Berkeley

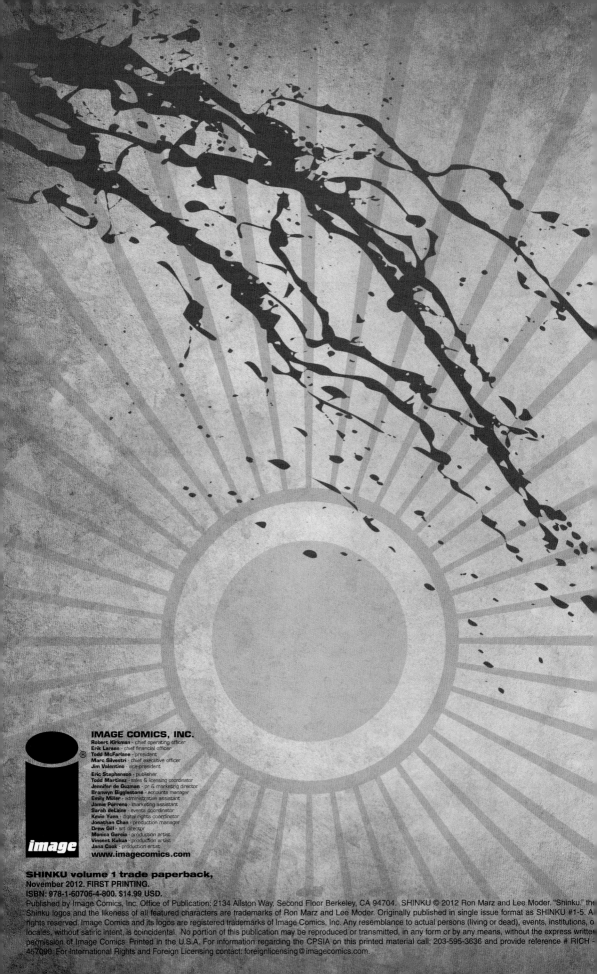

IMAGE COMICS, INC.

Robert Kirkman - chief operating officer
Erik Larsen - chief financial officer
Todd McFarlane - president
Marc Silvestri - chief executive officer
Jim Valentino - vice-president

Eric Stephenson - publisher
Todd Martinez - sales & licensing coordinator
Jennifer de Guzman - pr & marketing director
Branwyn Bigglestone - accounts manager
Emily Miller - administrative assistant
Jamie Parreno - marketing assistant
Sarah deLaine - events coordinator
Kevin Yuen - digital rights coordinator
Jonathan Chan - production manager
Drew Gill - art director
Monica Garcia - production artist
Vincent Kukua - production artist
Jana Cook - production artist
www.imagecomics.com

SHINKU volume 1 trade paperback,
November 2012. FIRST PRINTING.
ISBN: 978-1-60706-4-800. $14.99 USD.

SHINKU

Volume 1
"Throne of Blood"

SHINKU CREATED BY
RON MARZ & LEE MODER

••••

WRITTEN BY RON MARZ
PENCILS BY LEE MODER
INKS BY MATTHEW WAITE
COLORS BY MICHAEL ATIYEH
LETTERS BY TROY PETERI

••••

COVER BY LEE MODER, MATTHEW WAITE
& MICHAEL ATIYEH

••••

LOGO, DESIGN & EDITS BY PHIL SMITH
PRODUCTION BY JANA COOK

Chapter 1

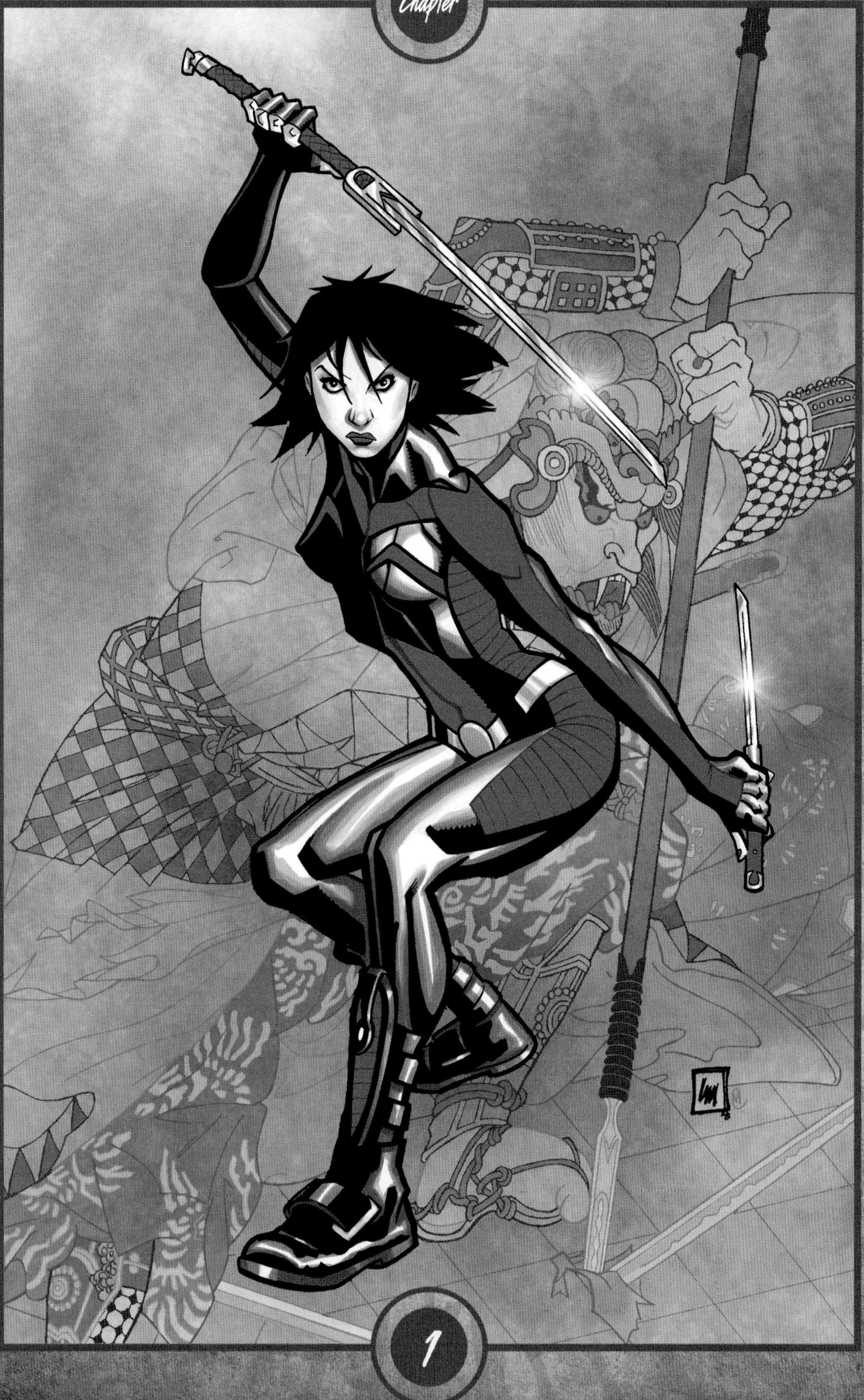

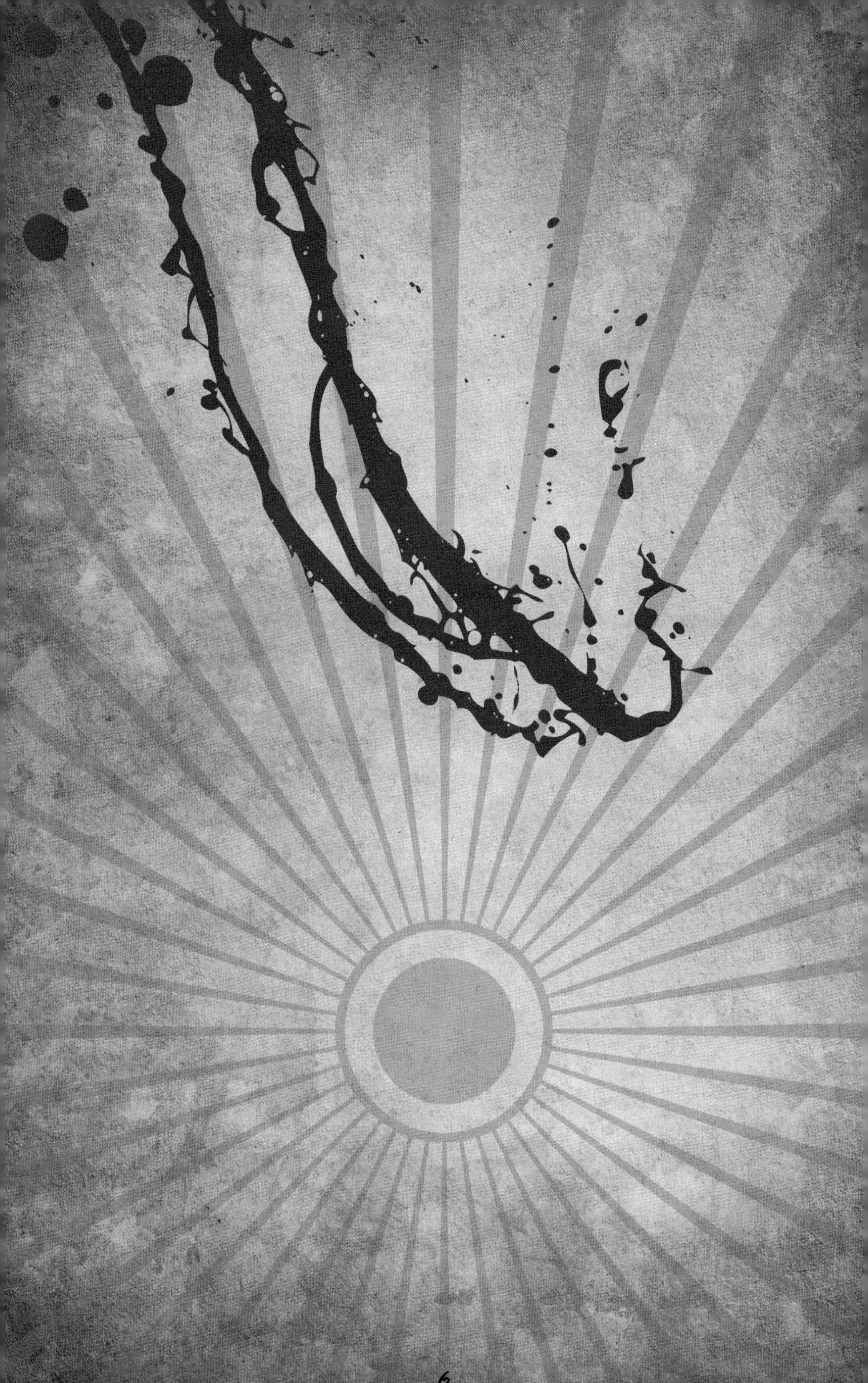

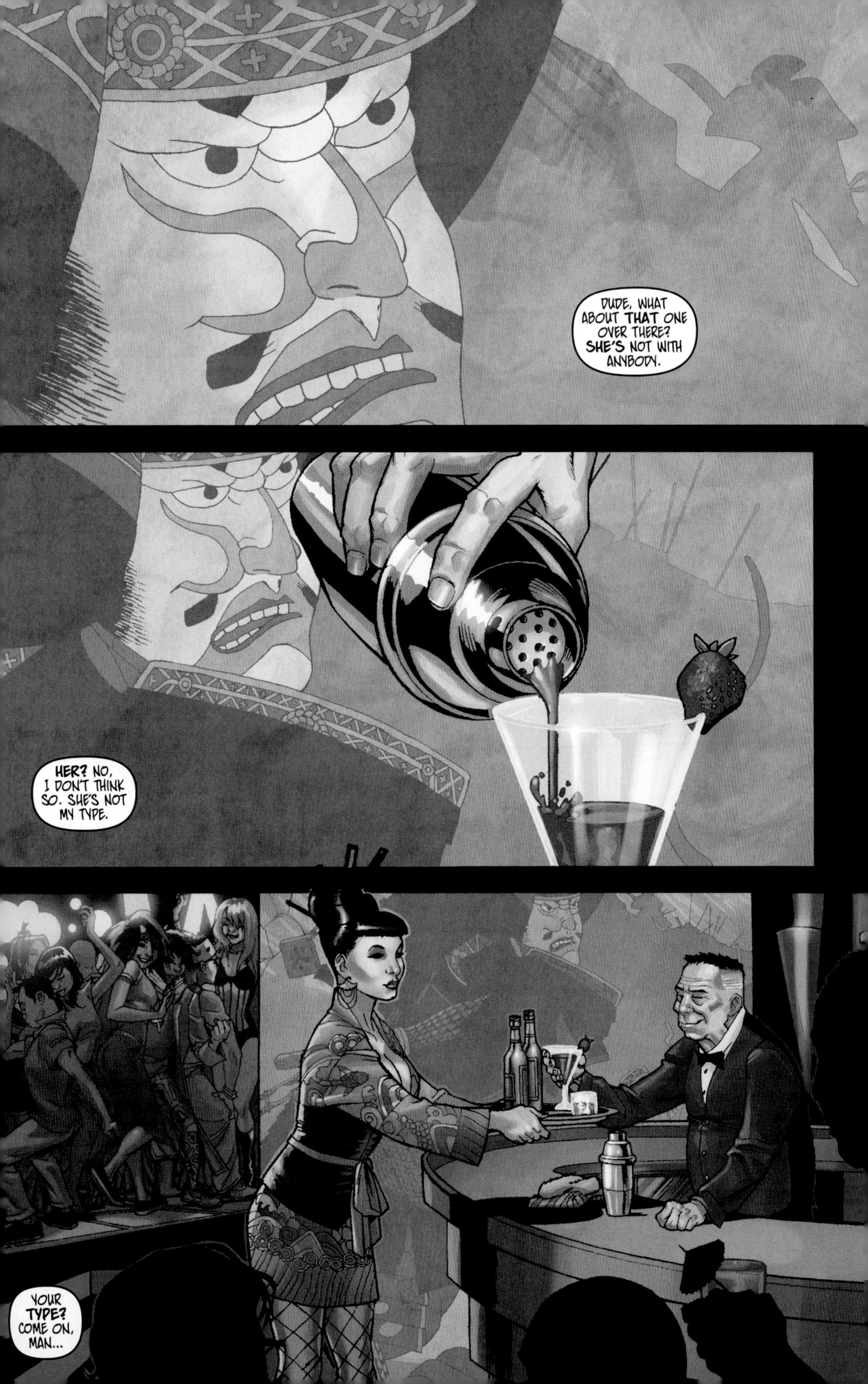
DUDE, WHAT ABOUT THAT ONE OVER THERE? SHE'S NOT WITH ANYBODY.
HER? NO, I DON'T THINK SO. SHE'S NOT MY TYPE.
YOUR TYPE? COME ON, MAN...

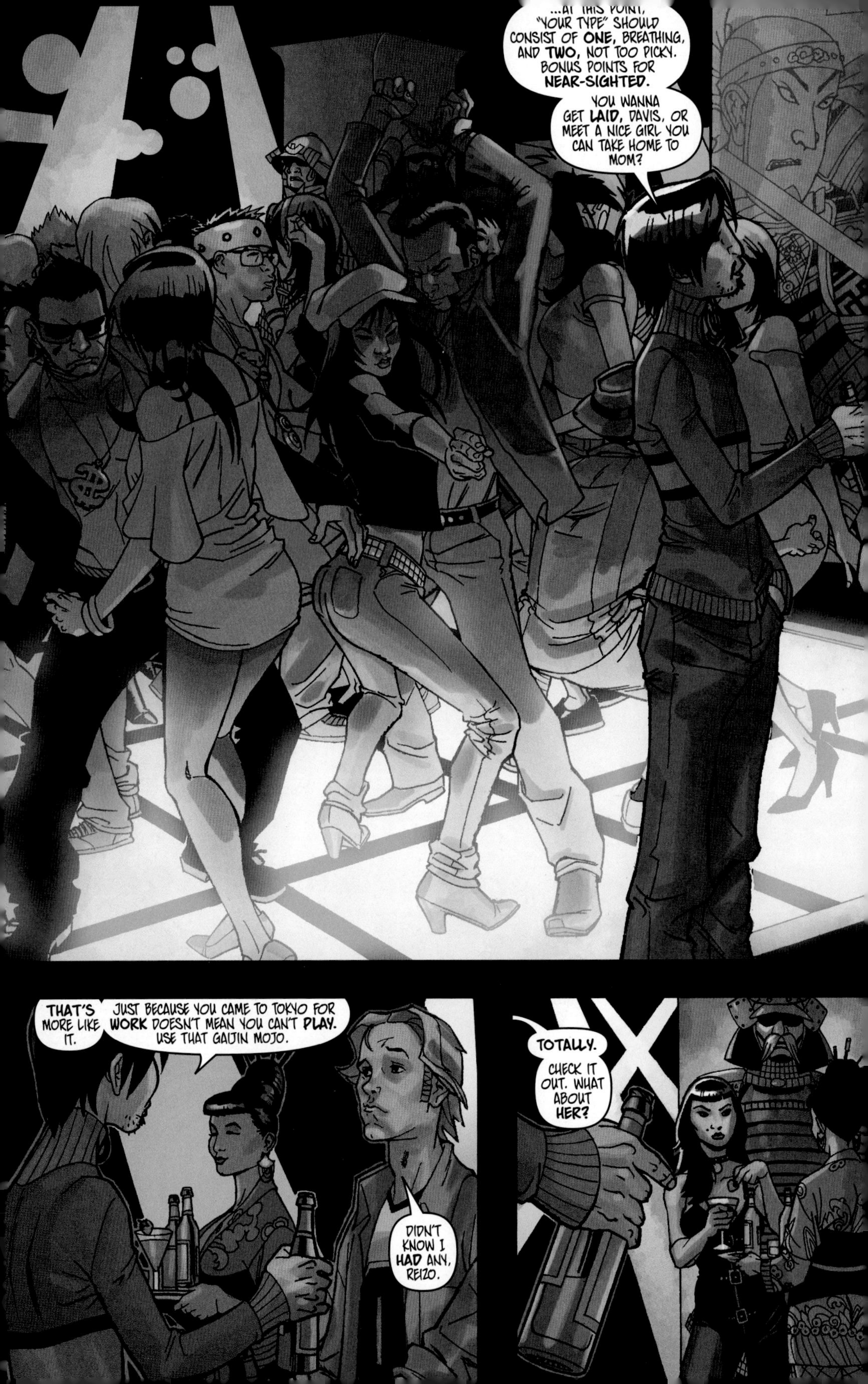
...AT THIS POINT, "YOUR TYPE" SHOULD CONSIST OF **ONE**, BREATHING, AND **TWO**, NOT TOO PICKY. BONUS POINTS FOR **NEAR-SIGHTED**.
YOU WANNA GET **LAID**, DAVIS, OR MEET A NICE GIRL YOU CAN TAKE HOME TO MOM?
THAT'S MORE LIKE IT.
JUST BECAUSE YOU CAME TO TOKYO FOR **WORK** DOESN'T MEAN YOU CAN'T **PLAY**. USE THAT GAIJIN MOJO.
DIDN'T KNOW I **HAD** ANY, REIZO.
TOTALLY.
CHECK IT OUT. WHAT ABOUT **HER?**

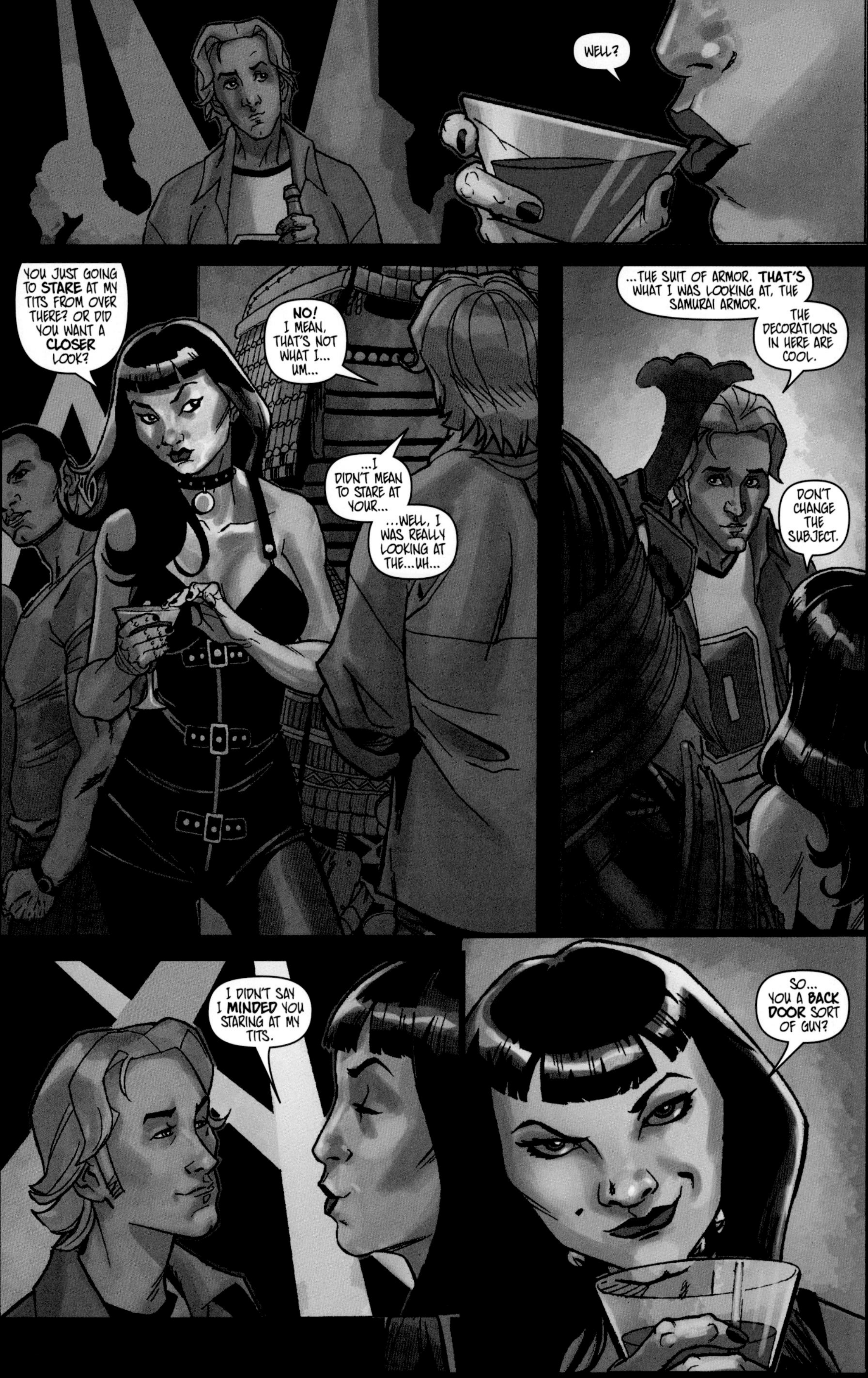
WELL?
YOU JUST GOING TO STARE AT MY TITS FROM OVER THERE? OR DID YOU WANT A CLOSER LOOK?
NO! I MEAN, THAT'S NOT WHAT I... UM...
...I DIDN'T MEAN TO STARE AT YOUR...
...WELL, I WAS REALLY LOOKING AT THE...UH...
...THE SUIT OF ARMOR. THAT'S WHAT I WAS LOOKING AT, THE SAMURAI ARMOR.
THE DECORATIONS IN HERE ARE COOL.
DON'T CHANGE THE SUBJECT.
I DIDN'T SAY I MINDED YOU STARING AT MY TITS.
SO... YOU A BACK DOOR SORT OF GUY?

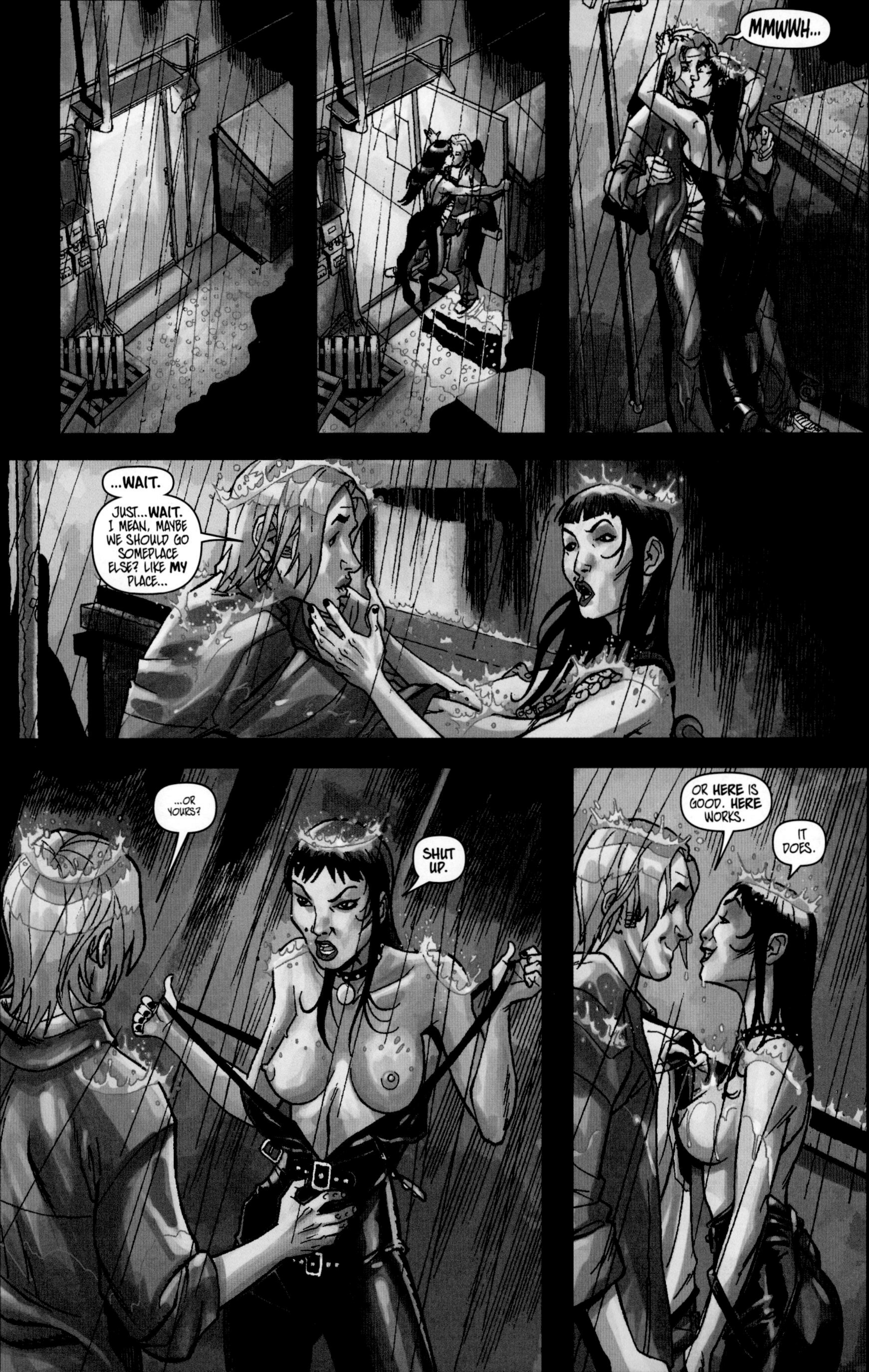
MMWWH...
...WAIT.
JUST...WAIT. I MEAN, MAYBE WE SHOULD GO SOMEPLACE ELSE? LIKE MY PLACE...
...OR YOURS?
SHUT UP.
OR HERE IS GOOD. HERE WORKS.
IT DOES.

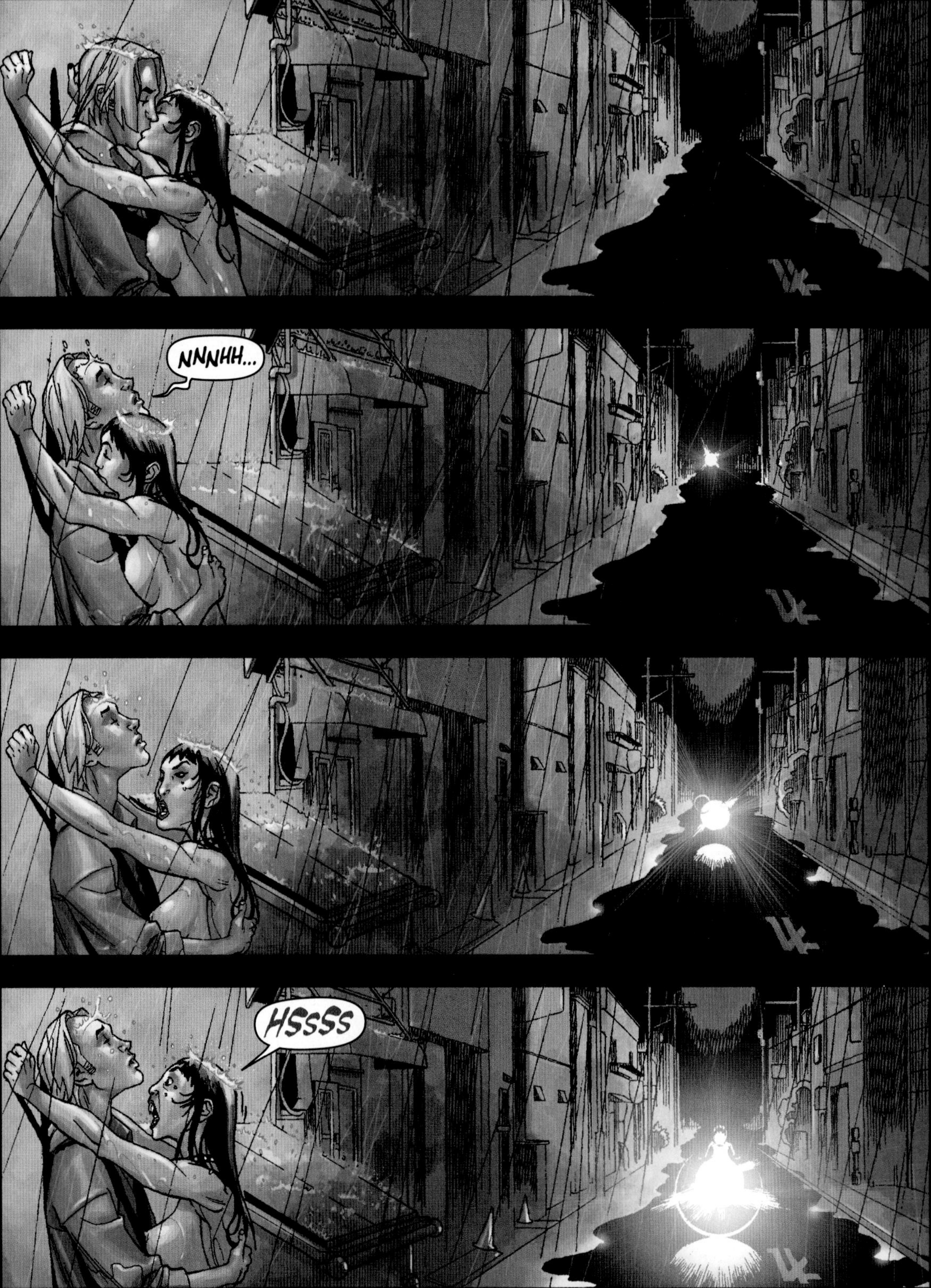
NNNHH...
HSSSS

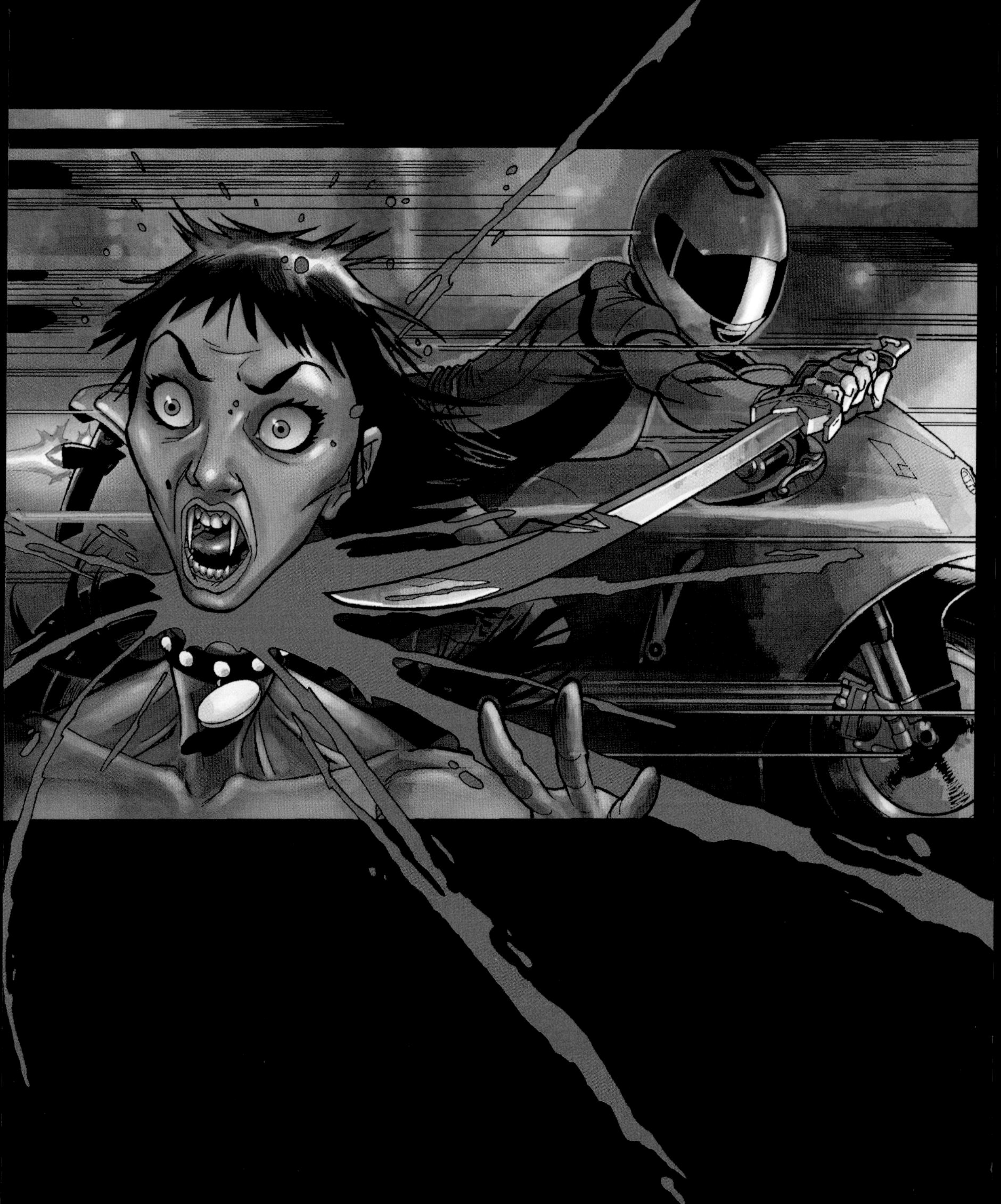

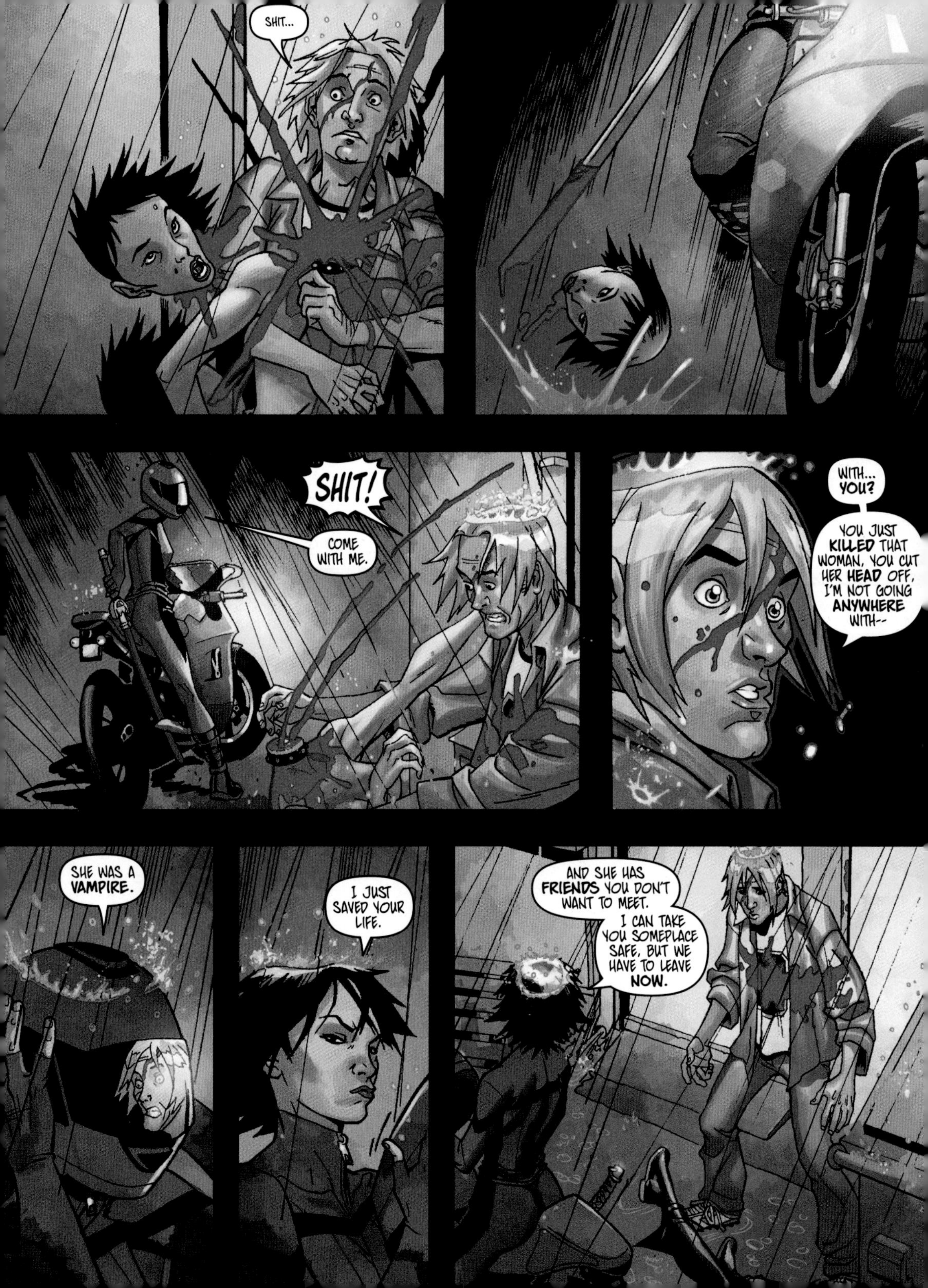
SHIT...
SHIT!
COME WITH ME.
WITH... YOU?
YOU JUST KILLED THAT WOMAN, YOU CUT HER HEAD OFF, I'M NOT GOING ANYWHERE WITH--
SHE WAS A VAMPIRE.
I JUST SAVED YOUR LIFE.
AND SHE HAS FRIENDS YOU DON'T WANT TO MEET.
I CAN TAKE YOU SOMEPLACE SAFE, BUT WE HAVE TO LEAVE NOW.

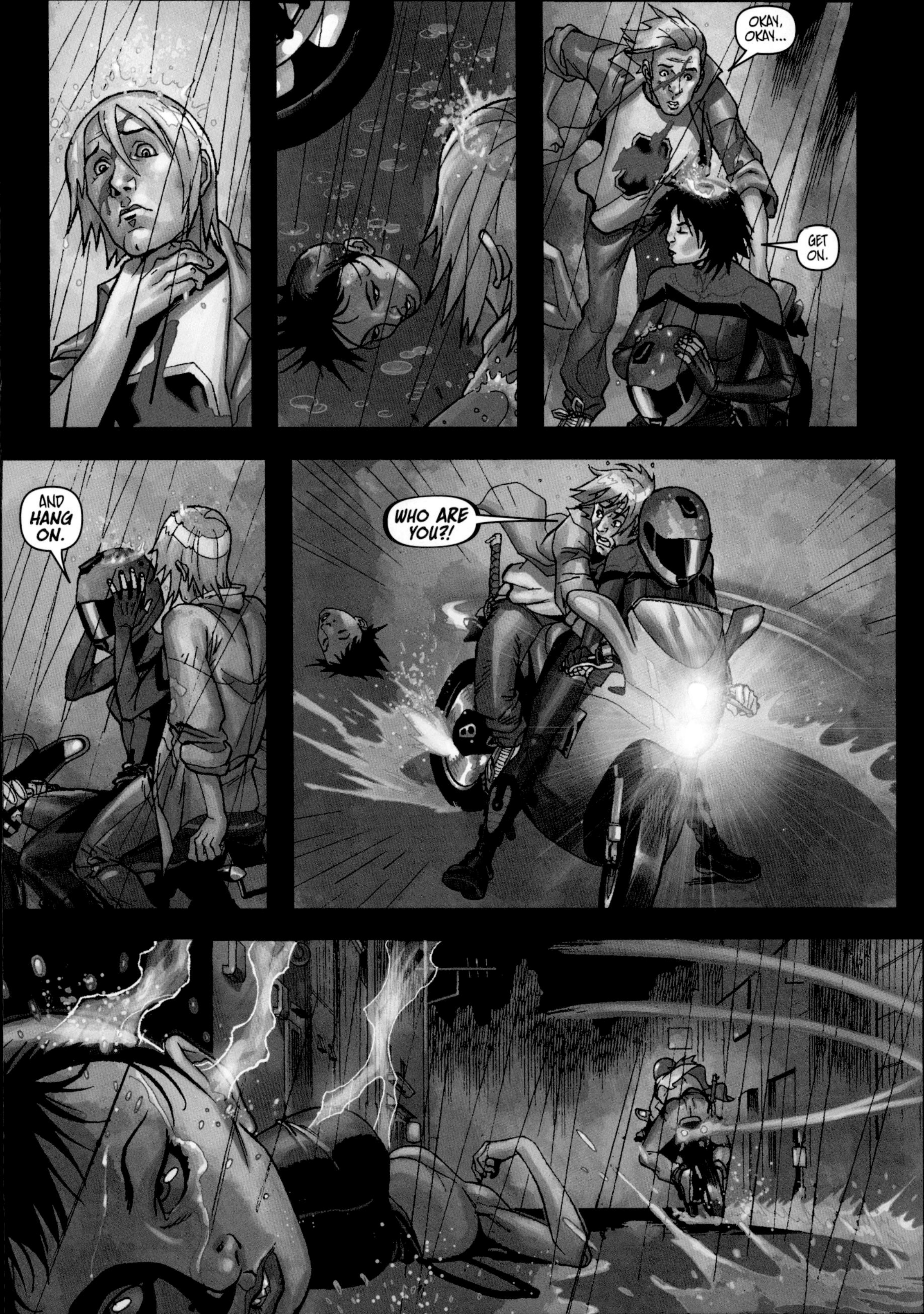
OKAY, OKAY...
GET ON.
AND HANG ON.
WHO ARE YOU?!

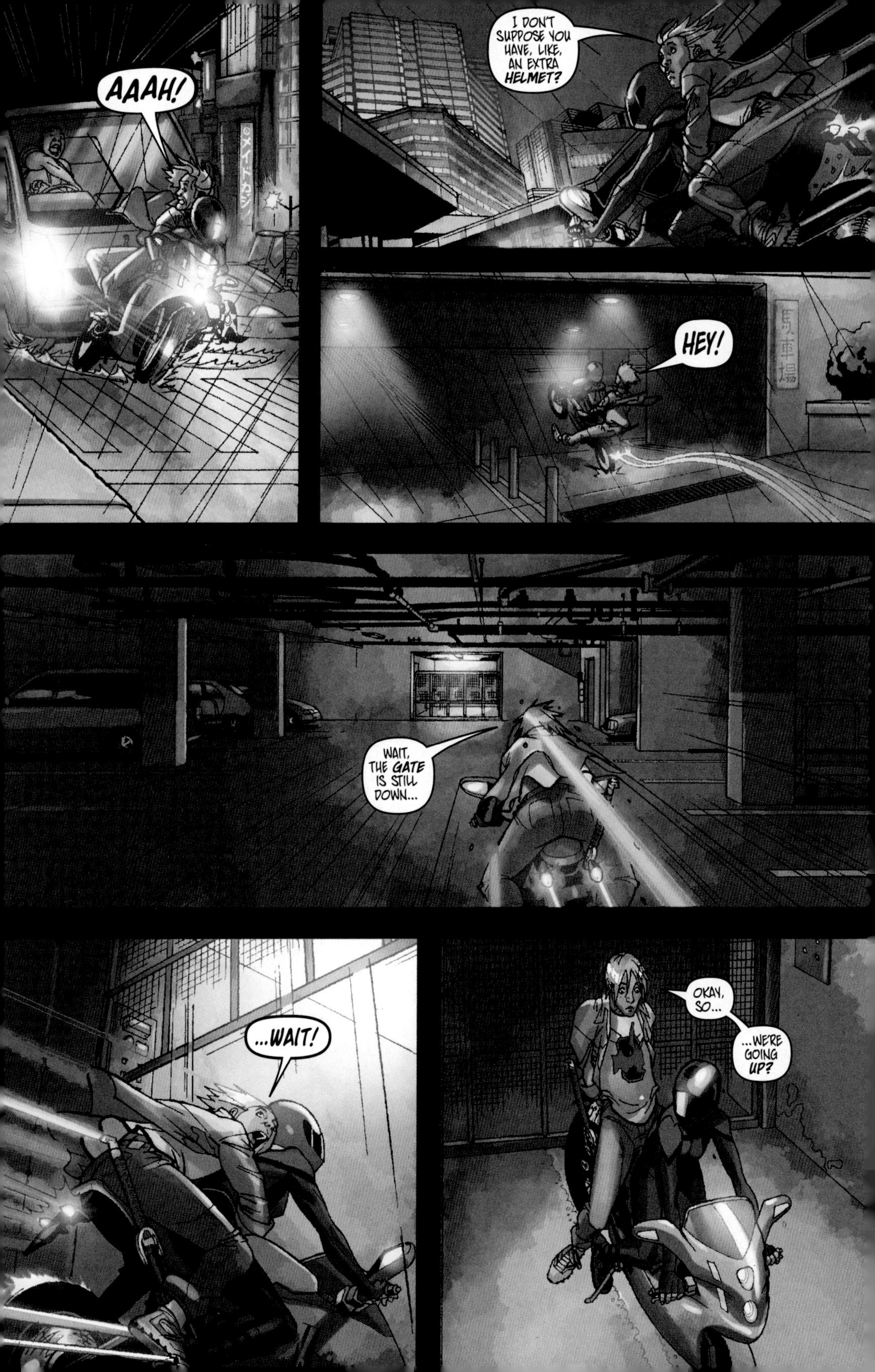
AAAH!
I DON'T SUPPOSE YOU HAVE, LIKE, AN EXTRA HELMET?
HEY!
WAIT, THE GATE IS STILL DOWN...
...WAIT!
OKAY, SO...
...WE'RE GOING UP?

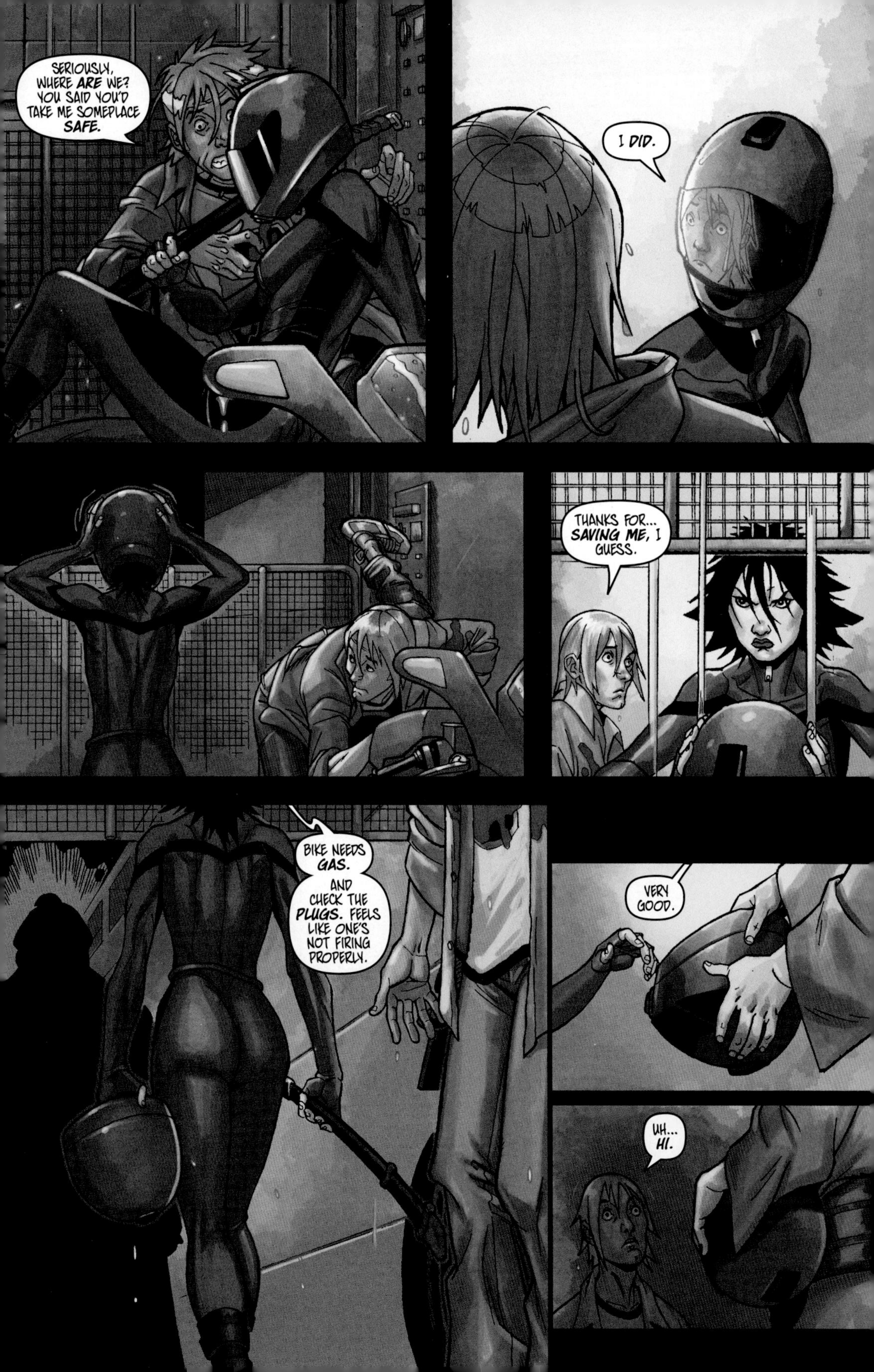
SERIOUSLY, WHERE ARE WE? YOU SAID YOU'D TAKE ME SOMEPLACE SAFE.
I DID.
THANKS FOR... SAVING ME, I GUESS.
BIKE NEEDS GAS.
AND CHECK THE PLUGS. FEELS LIKE ONE'S NOT FIRING PROPERLY.
VERY GOOD.
UH... HI.

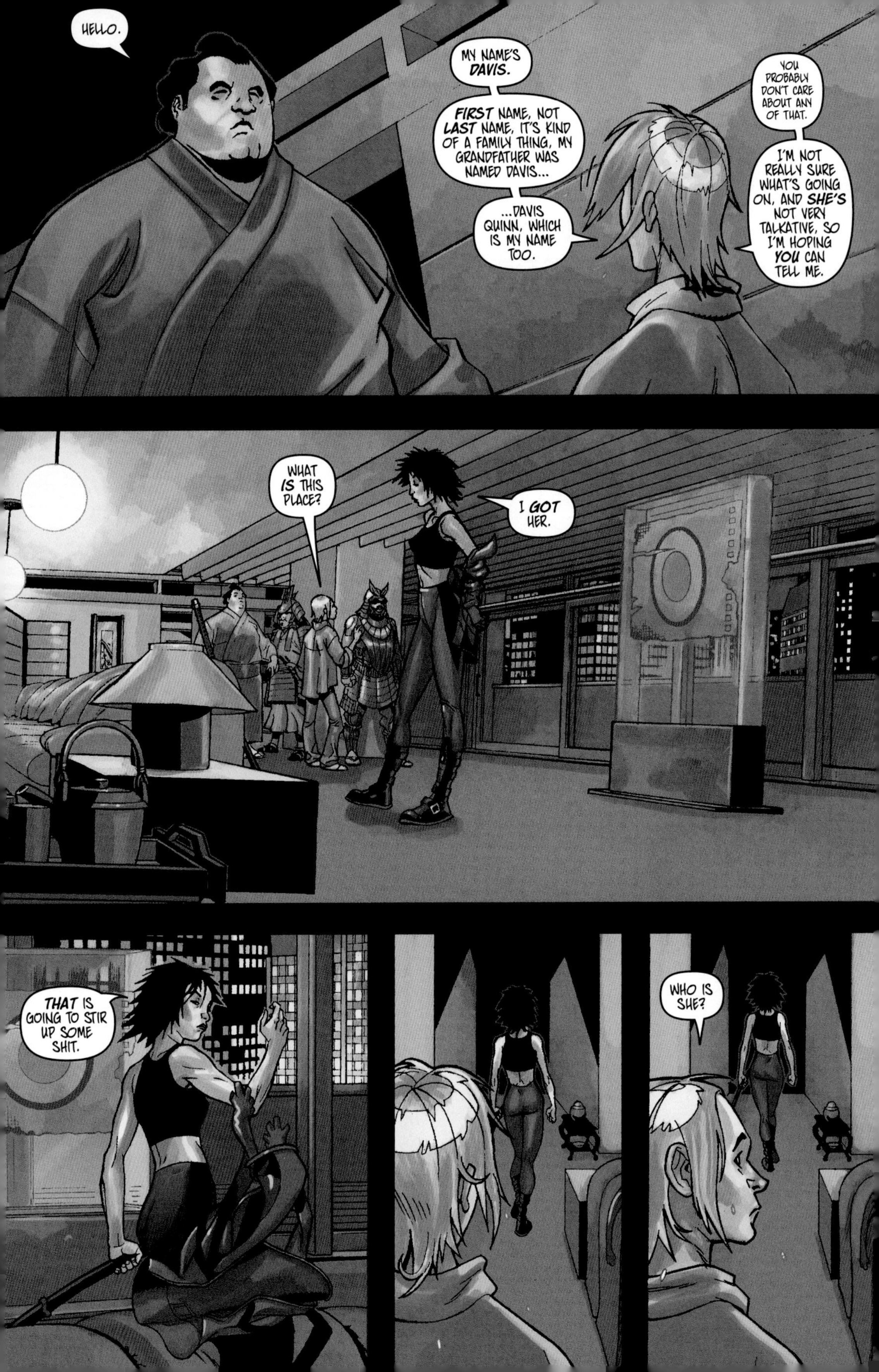
HELLO.
MY NAME'S DAVIS.
FIRST NAME, NOT LAST NAME, IT'S KIND OF A FAMILY THING, MY GRANDFATHER WAS NAMED DAVIS...
...DAVIS QUINN, WHICH IS MY NAME TOO.
YOU PROBABLY DON'T CARE ABOUT ANY OF THAT.
I'M NOT REALLY SURE WHAT'S GOING ON, AND SHE'S NOT VERY TALKATIVE, SO I'M HOPING YOU CAN TELL ME.
WHAT IS THIS PLACE?
I GOT HER.
THAT IS GOING TO STIR UP SOME SHIT.
WHO IS SHE?

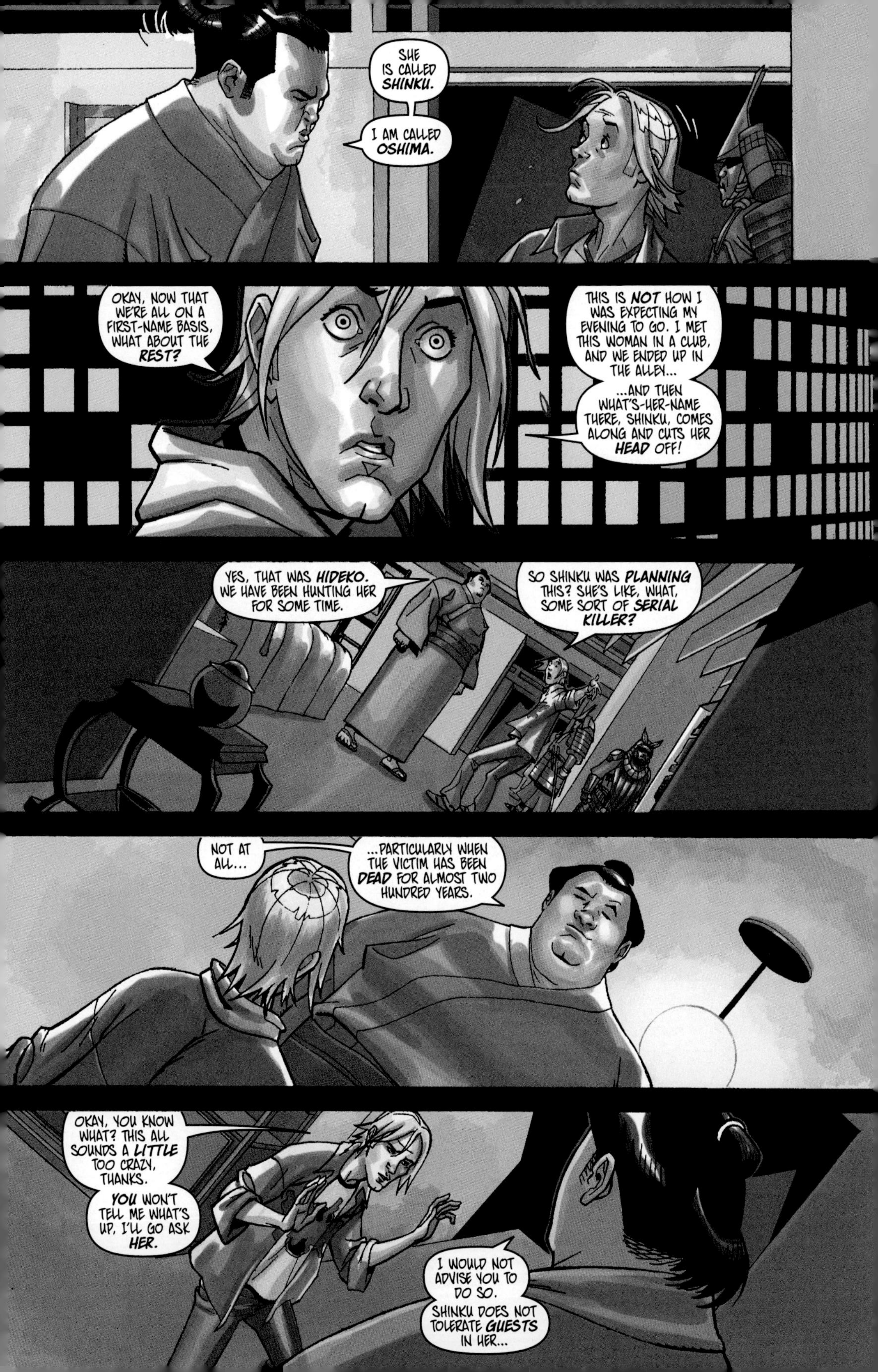
SHE IS CALLED **SHINKU.**
I AM CALLED **OSHIMA.**
OKAY, NOW THAT WE'RE ALL ON A FIRST-NAME BASIS, WHAT ABOUT THE **REST?**
THIS IS **NOT** HOW I WAS EXPECTING MY EVENING TO GO. I MET THIS WOMAN IN A CLUB, AND WE ENDED UP IN THE ALLEY...
...AND THEN WHAT'S-HER-NAME THERE, SHINKU, COMES ALONG AND CUTS HER **HEAD** OFF!
YES, THAT WAS **HIDEKO.** WE HAVE BEEN HUNTING HER FOR SOME TIME.
SO SHINKU WAS **PLANNING** THIS? SHE'S LIKE, WHAT, SOME SORT OF **SERIAL KILLER?**
NOT AT ALL...
...PARTICULARLY WHEN THE VICTIM HAS BEEN **DEAD** FOR ALMOST TWO HUNDRED YEARS.
OKAY, YOU KNOW WHAT? THIS ALL SOUNDS A **LITTLE** TOO CRAZY, THANKS.
YOU WON'T TELL ME WHAT'S UP, I'LL GO ASK **HER.**
I WOULD NOT ADVISE YOU TO DO SO.
SHINKU DOES NOT TOLERATE **GUESTS** IN HER...

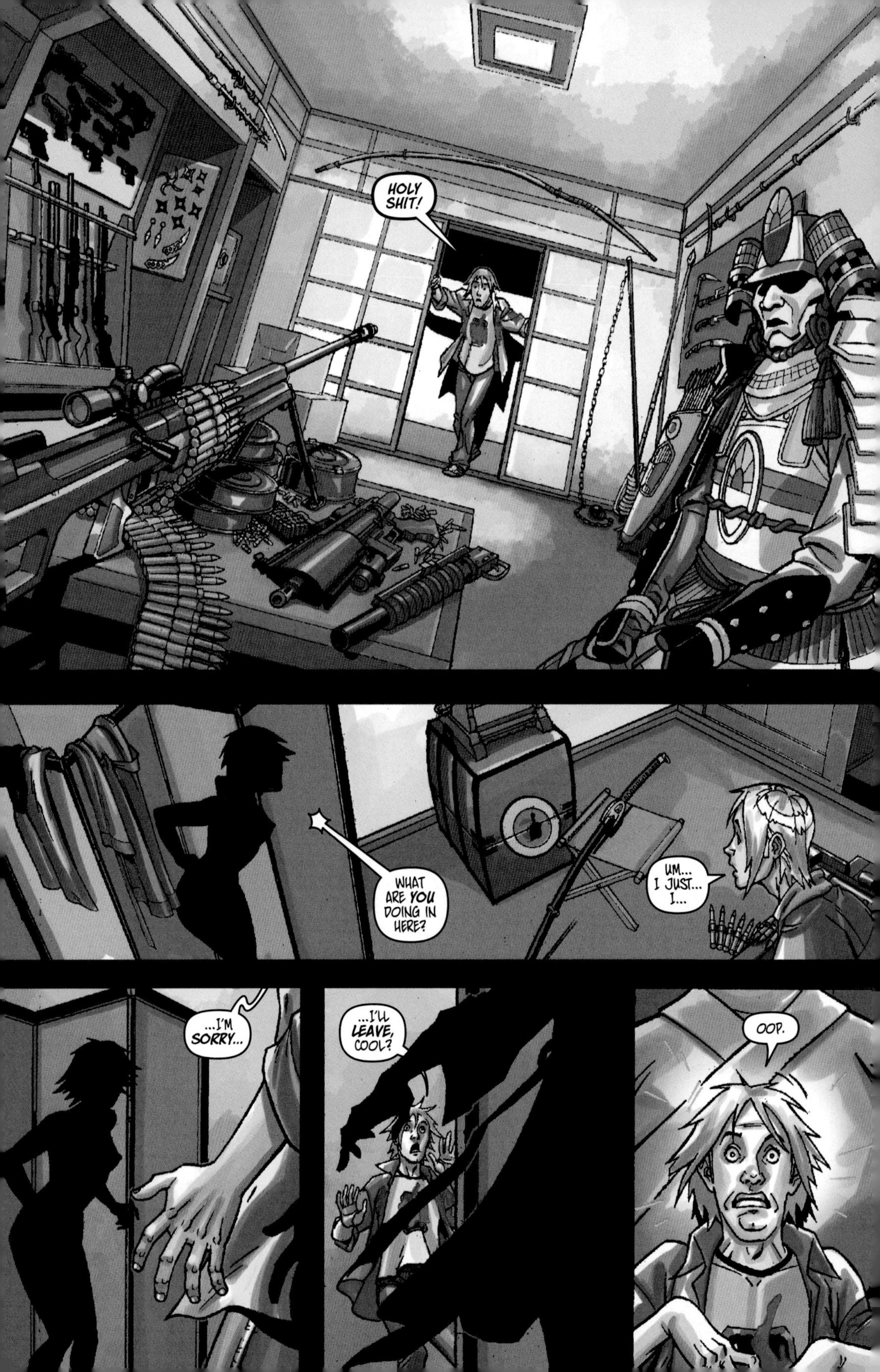
HOLY SHIT!
WHAT ARE YOU DOING IN HERE?
UM... I JUST... I...
...I'M SORRY...
...I'LL LEAVE, COOL?
OOP.

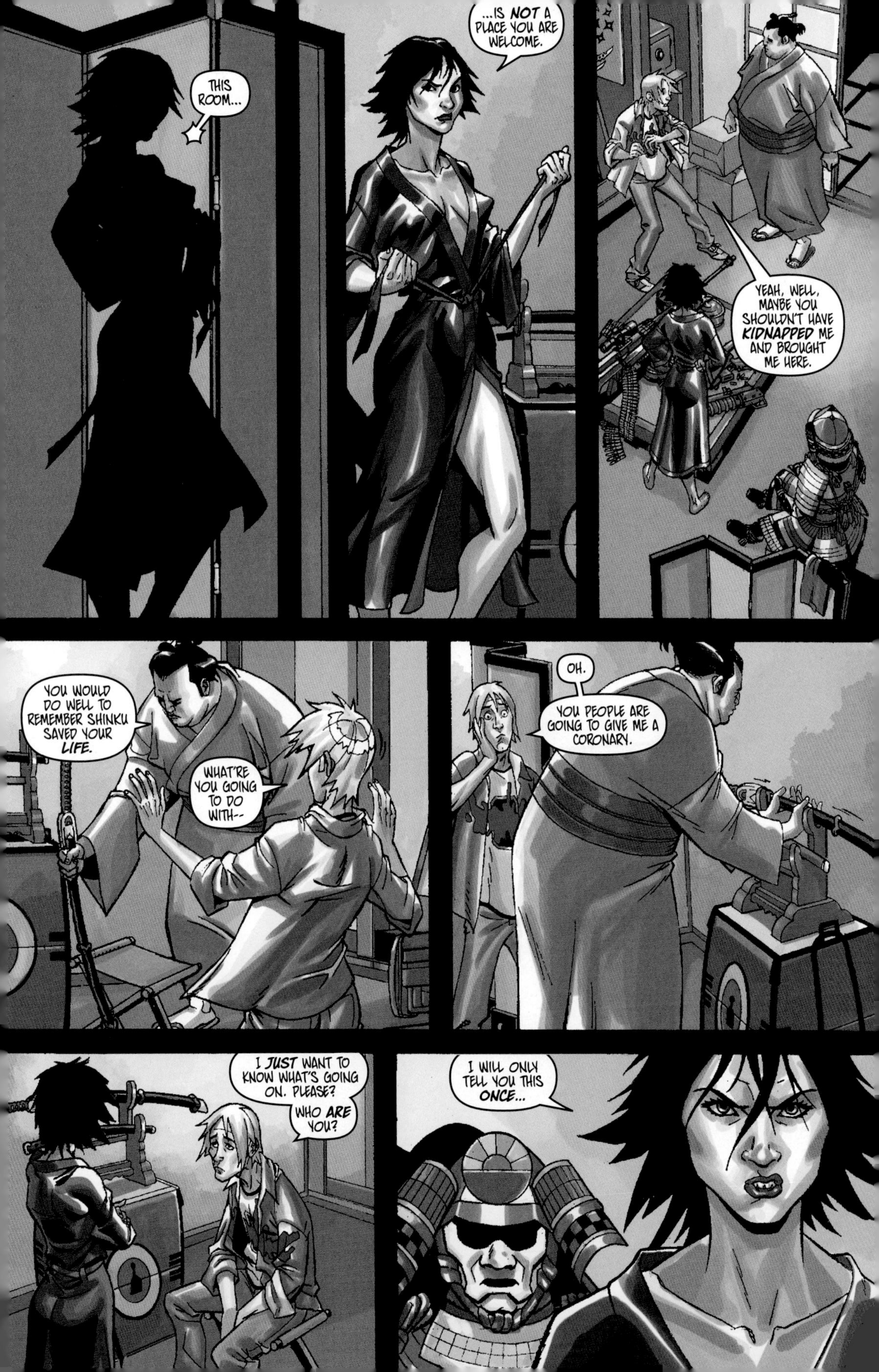
THIS ROOM...
...IS NOT A PLACE YOU ARE WELCOME.
YEAH, WELL, MAYBE YOU SHOULDN'T HAVE KIDNAPPED ME AND BROUGHT ME HERE.
YOU WOULD DO WELL TO REMEMBER SHINKU SAVED YOUR LIFE.
WHAT'RE YOU GOING TO DO WITH--
OH.
YOU PEOPLE ARE GOING TO GIVE ME A CORONARY.
I JUST WANT TO KNOW WHAT'S GOING ON. PLEASE?
WHO ARE YOU?
I WILL ONLY TELL YOU THIS ONCE...

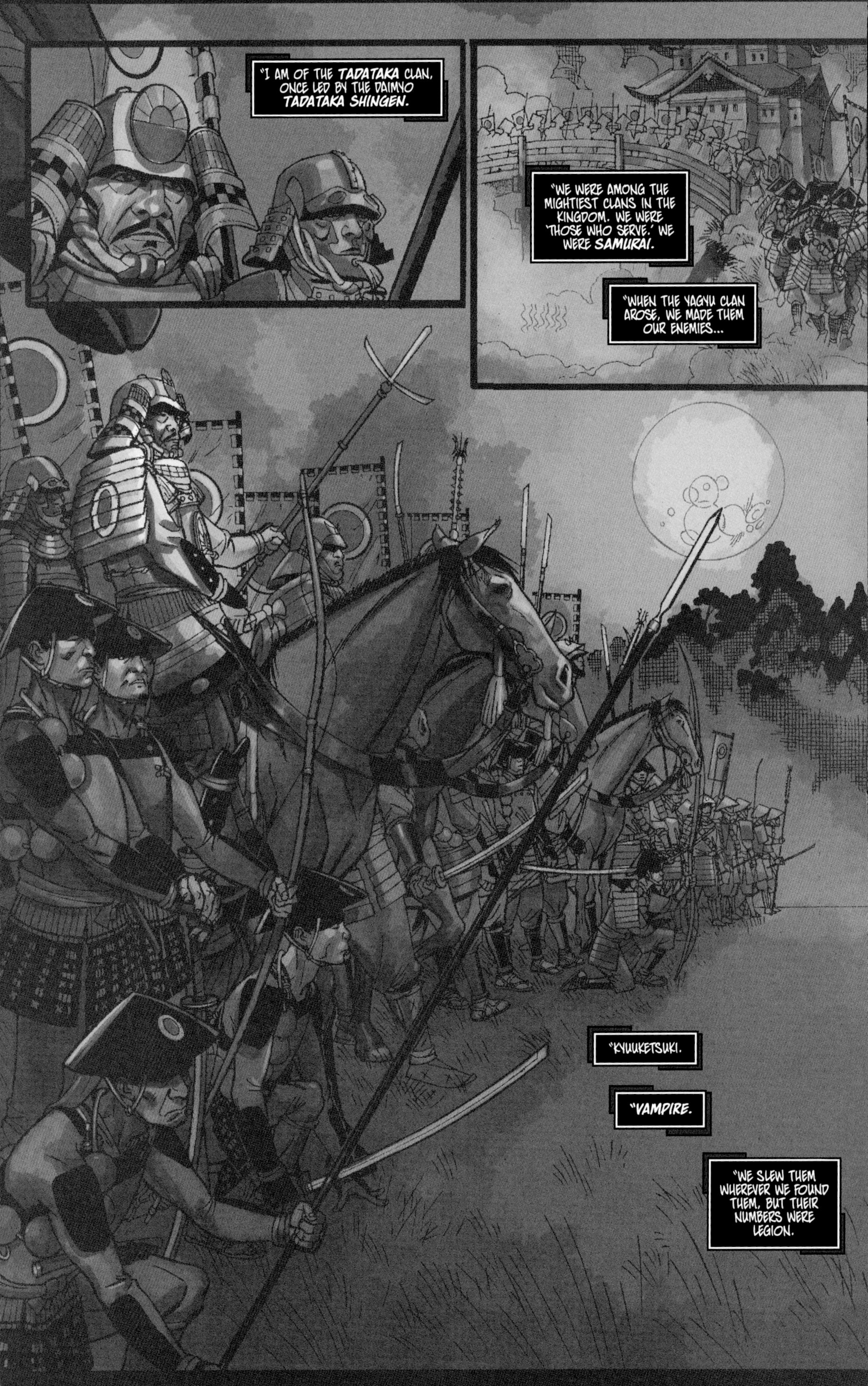
"I AM OF THE TADATAKA CLAN, ONCE LED BY THE DAIMYO TADATAKA SHINGEN.
"WE WERE AMONG THE MIGHTIEST CLANS IN THE KINGDOM. WE WERE 'THOSE WHO SERVE.' WE WERE SAMURAI.
"WHEN THE YAGYU CLAN AROSE, WE MADE THEM OUR ENEMIES...
"KYUUKETSUKI.
"VAMPIRE.
"WE SLEW THEM WHEREVER WE FOUND THEM, BUT THEIR NUMBERS WERE LEGION.

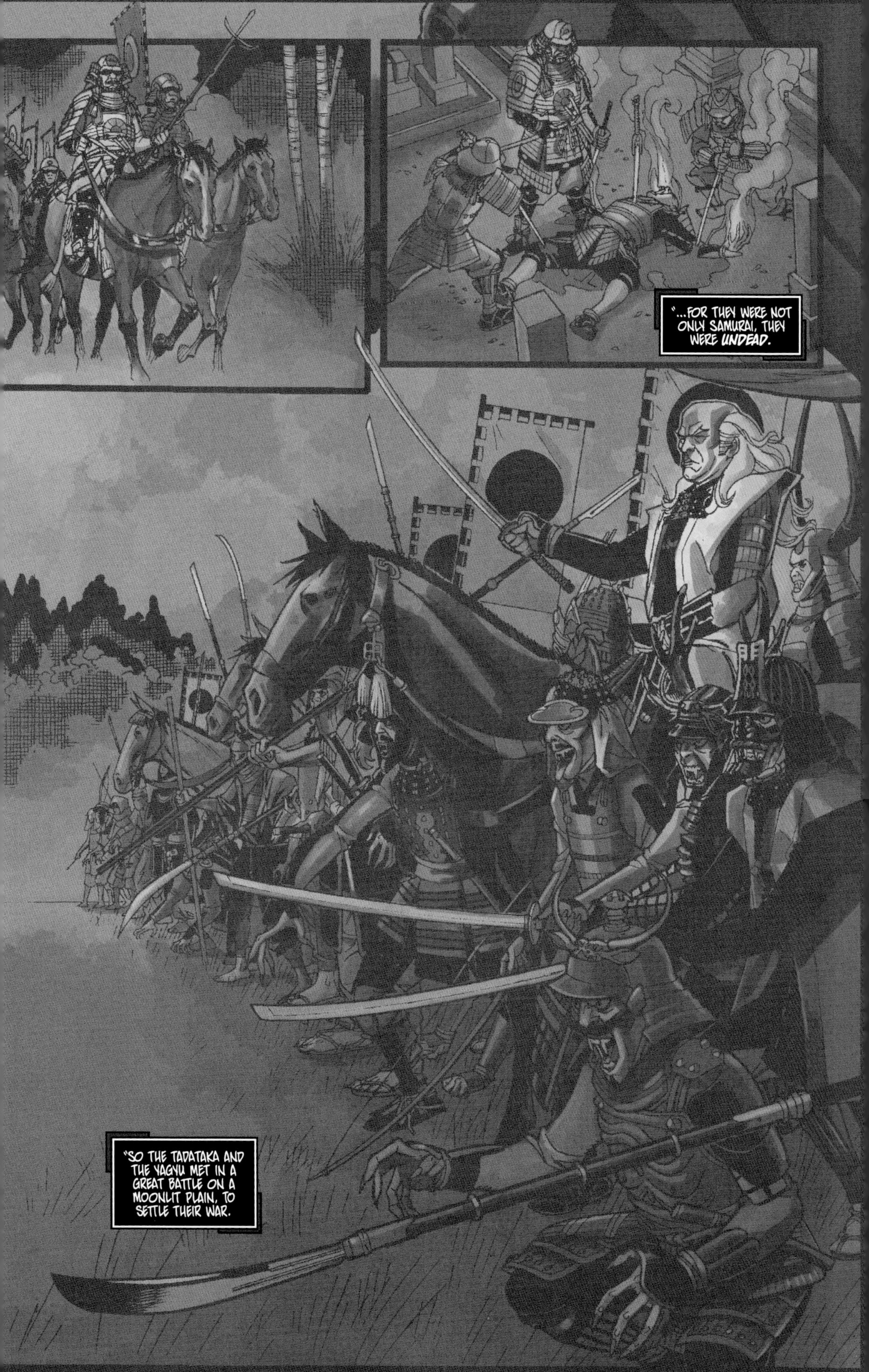
"...FOR THEY WERE NOT ONLY SAMURAI, THEY WERE UNDEAD.
"SO THE TADATAKA AND THE YAGYU MET IN A GREAT BATTLE ON A MOONLIT PLAIN, TO SETTLE THEIR WAR.

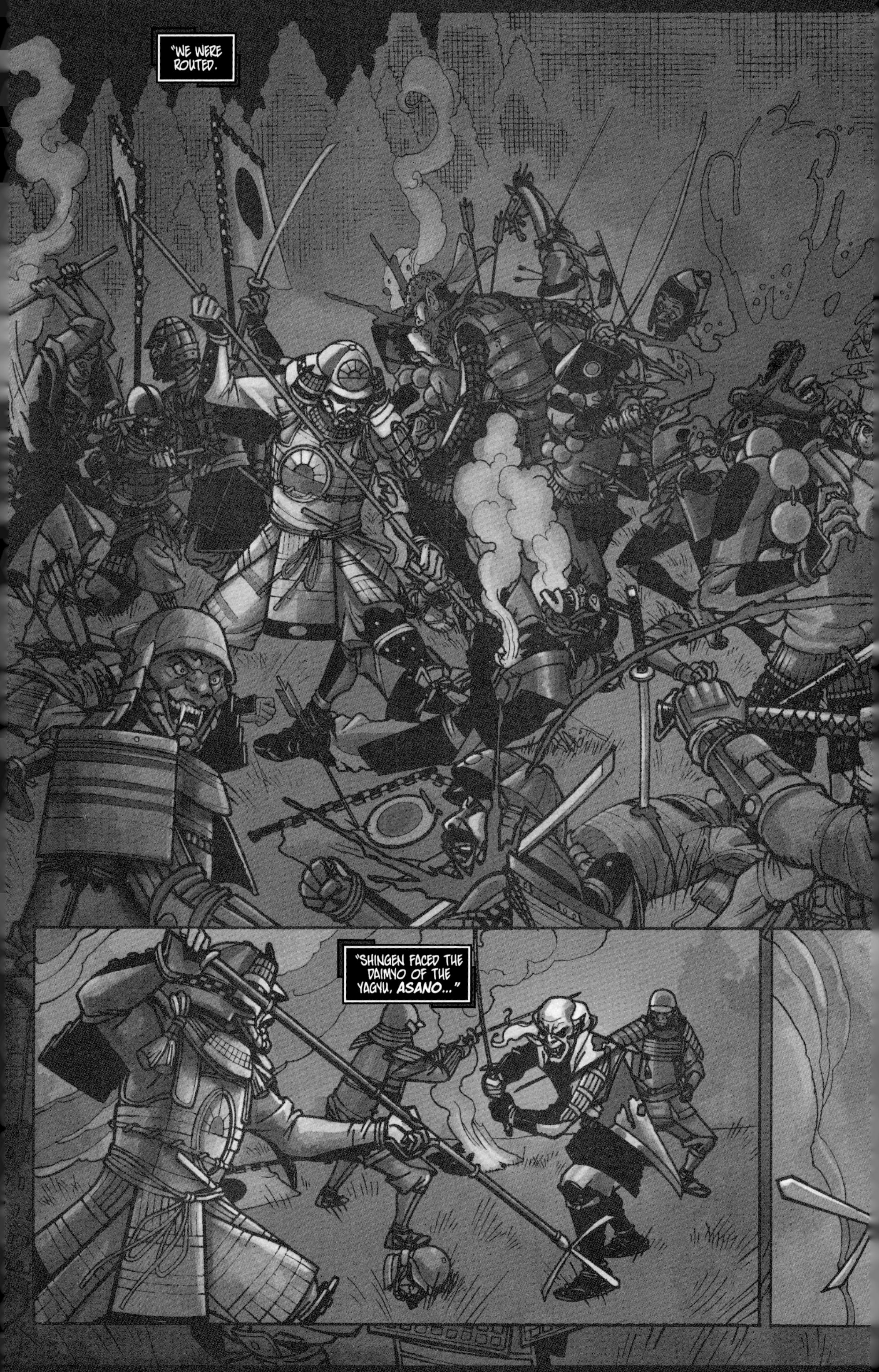
"WE WERE ROUTED.
"SHINGEN FACED THE DAIMYO OF THE YAGYU, **ASANO**..."

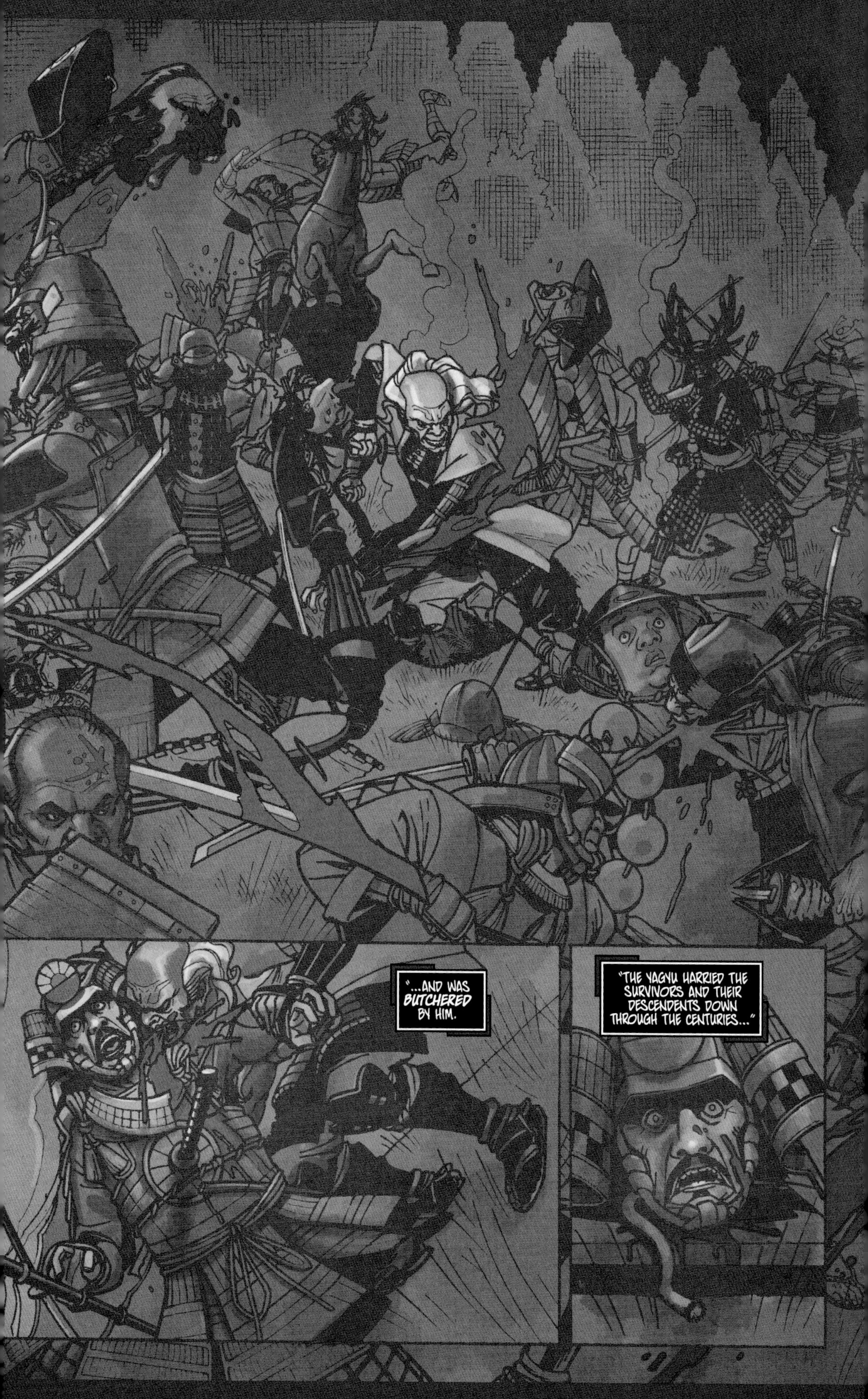
"...AND WAS BUTCHERED BY HIM.
"THE YAGYU HARRIED THE SURVIVORS AND THEIR DESCENDENTS DOWN THROUGH THE CENTURIES..."

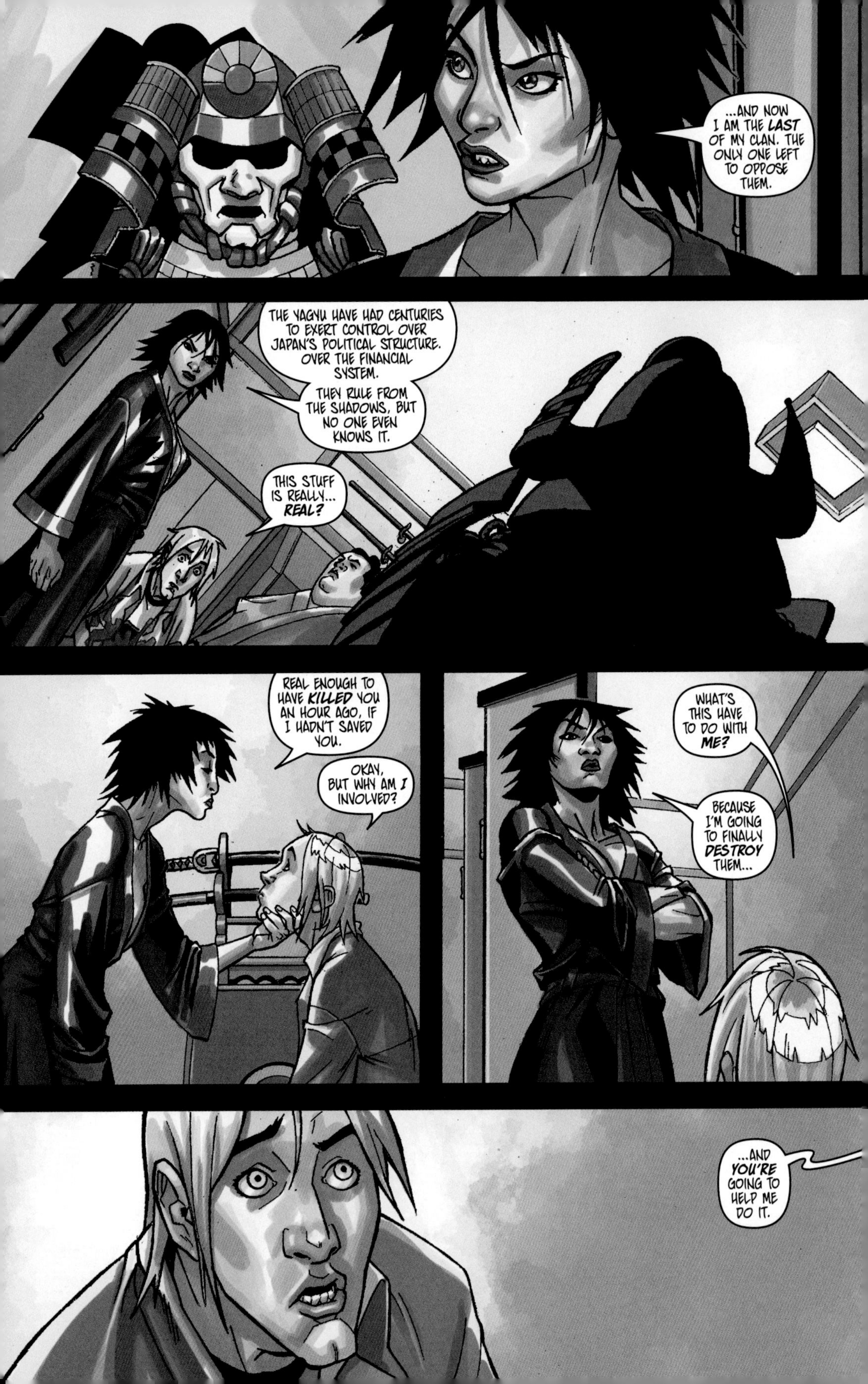
...AND NOW I AM THE LAST OF MY CLAN. THE ONLY ONE LEFT TO OPPOSE THEM.
THE YAGYU HAVE HAD CENTURIES TO EXERT CONTROL OVER JAPAN'S POLITICAL STRUCTURE. OVER THE FINANCIAL SYSTEM.
THEY RULE FROM THE SHADOWS, BUT NO ONE EVEN KNOWS IT.
THIS STUFF IS REALLY... REAL?
REAL ENOUGH TO HAVE KILLED YOU AN HOUR AGO, IF I HADN'T SAVED YOU.
OKAY, BUT WHY AM I INVOLVED?
WHAT'S THIS HAVE TO DO WITH ME?
BECAUSE I'M GOING TO FINALLY DESTROY THEM...
...AND YOU'RE GOING TO HELP ME DO IT.

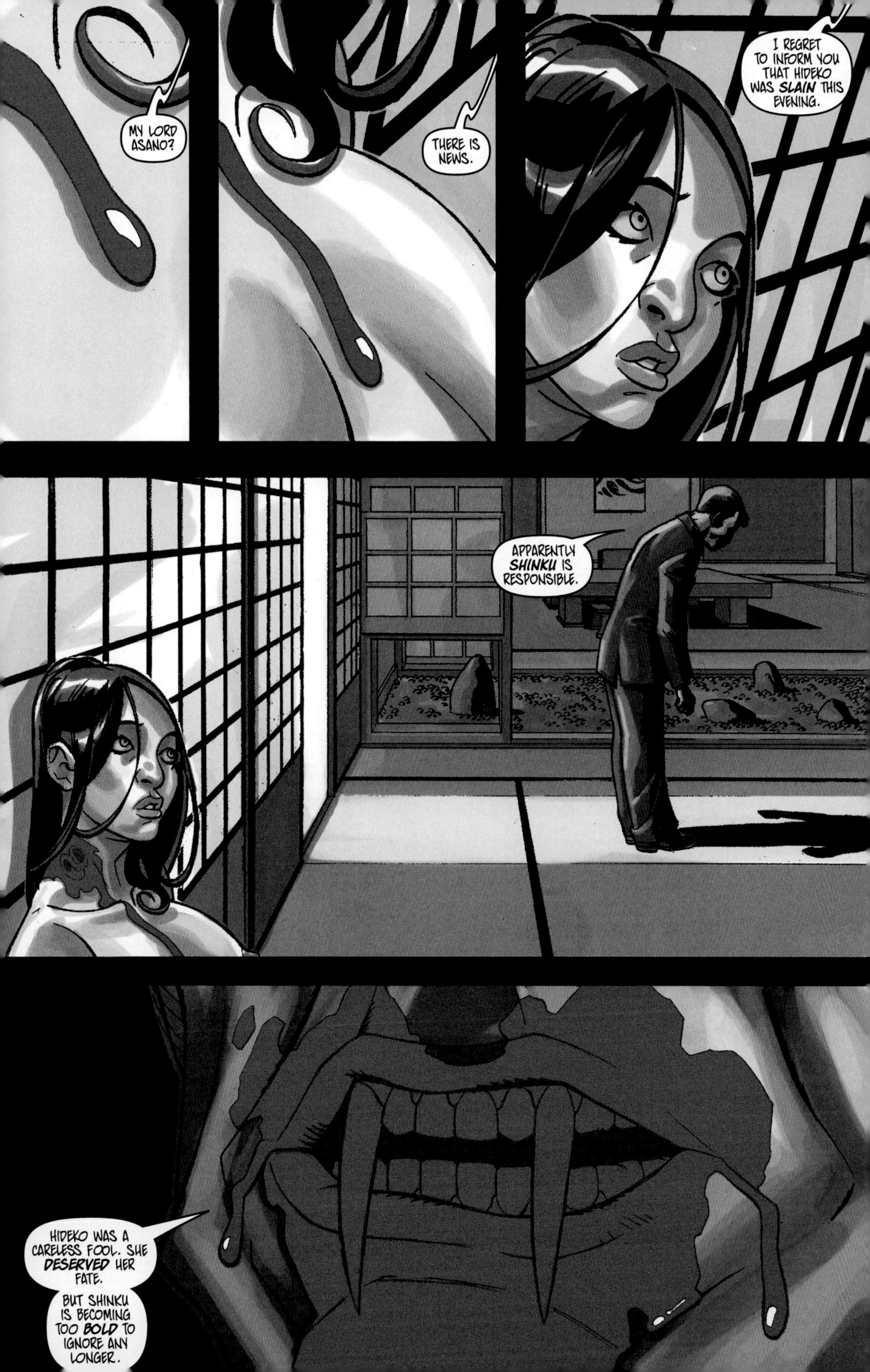
MY LORD ASANO?
THERE IS NEWS.
I REGRET TO INFORM YOU THAT HIDEKO WAS SLAIN THIS EVENING.
APPARENTLY SHINKU IS RESPONSIBLE.
HIDEKO WAS A CARELESS FOOL. SHE DESERVED HER FATE.
BUT SHINKU IS BECOMING TOO BOLD TO IGNORE ANY LONGER.

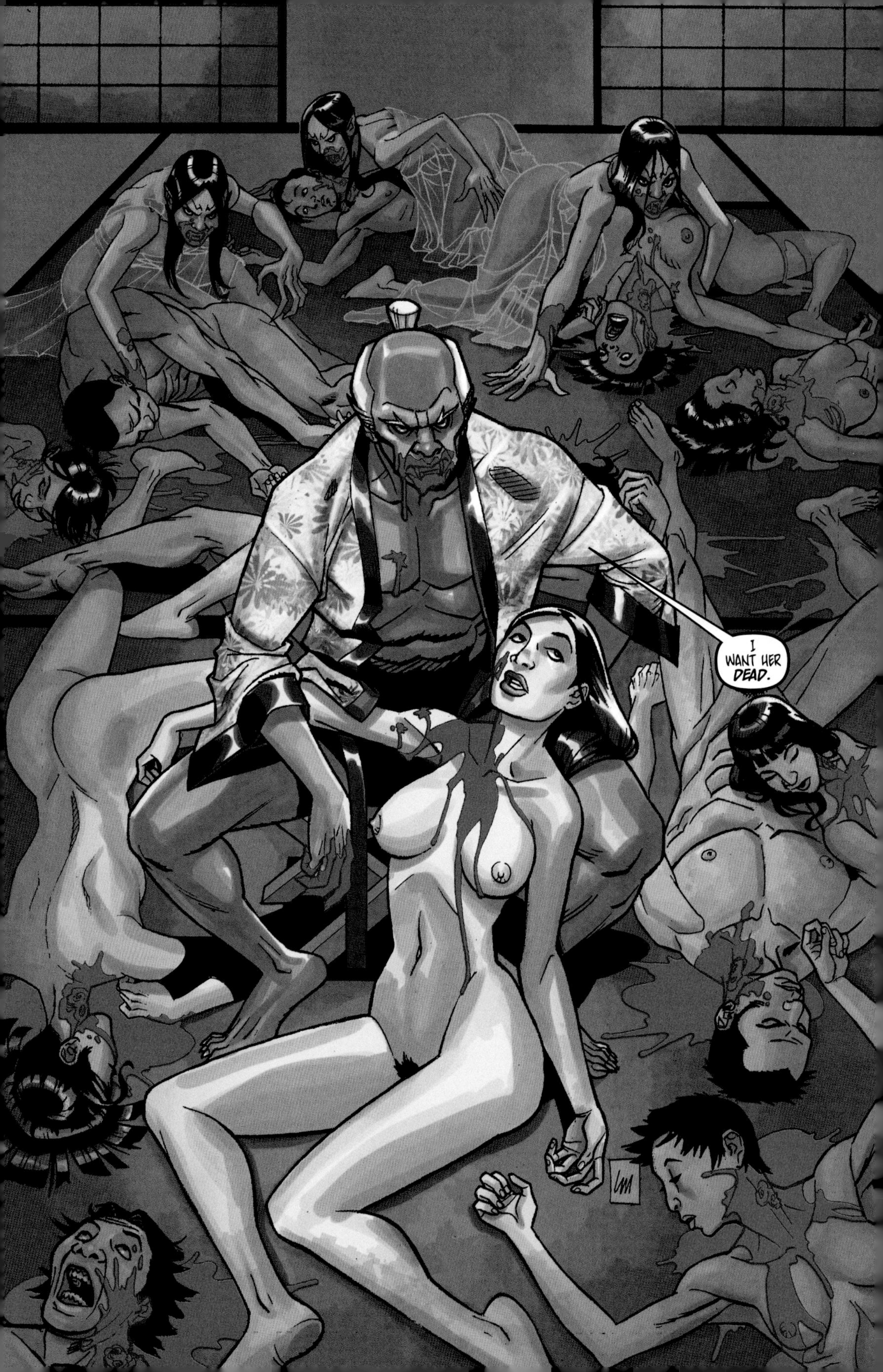
I WANT HER DEAD.

Chapter 2

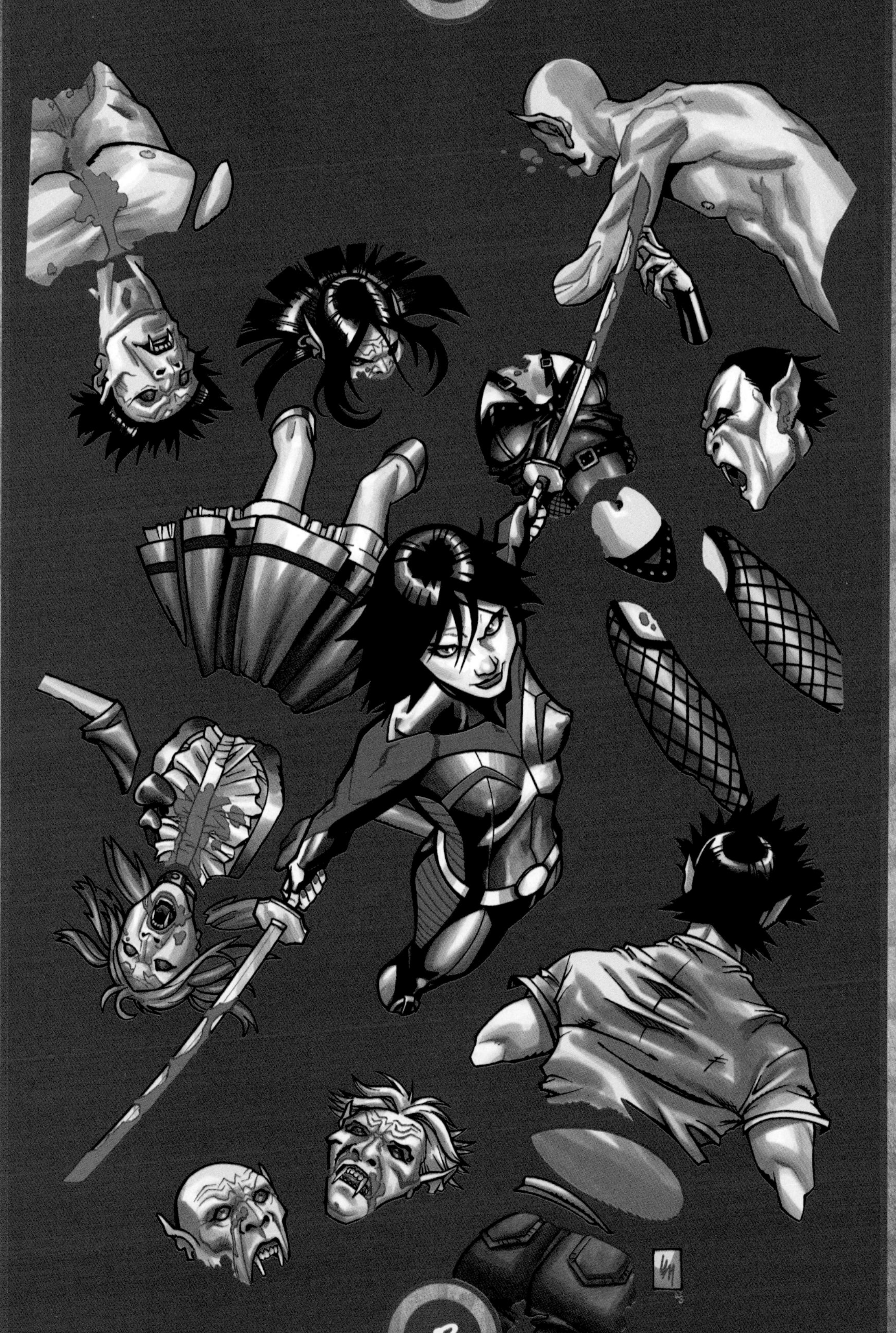

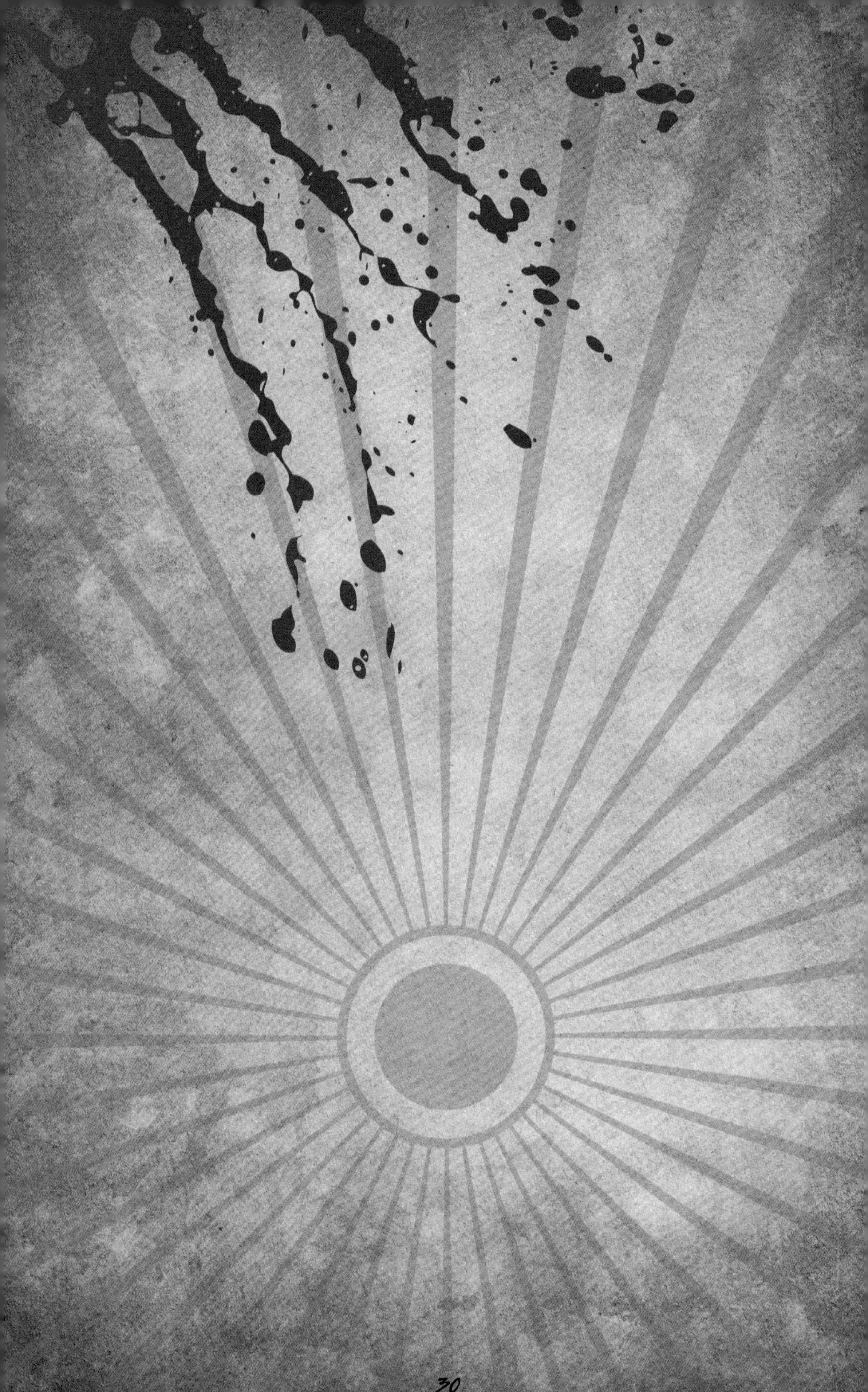

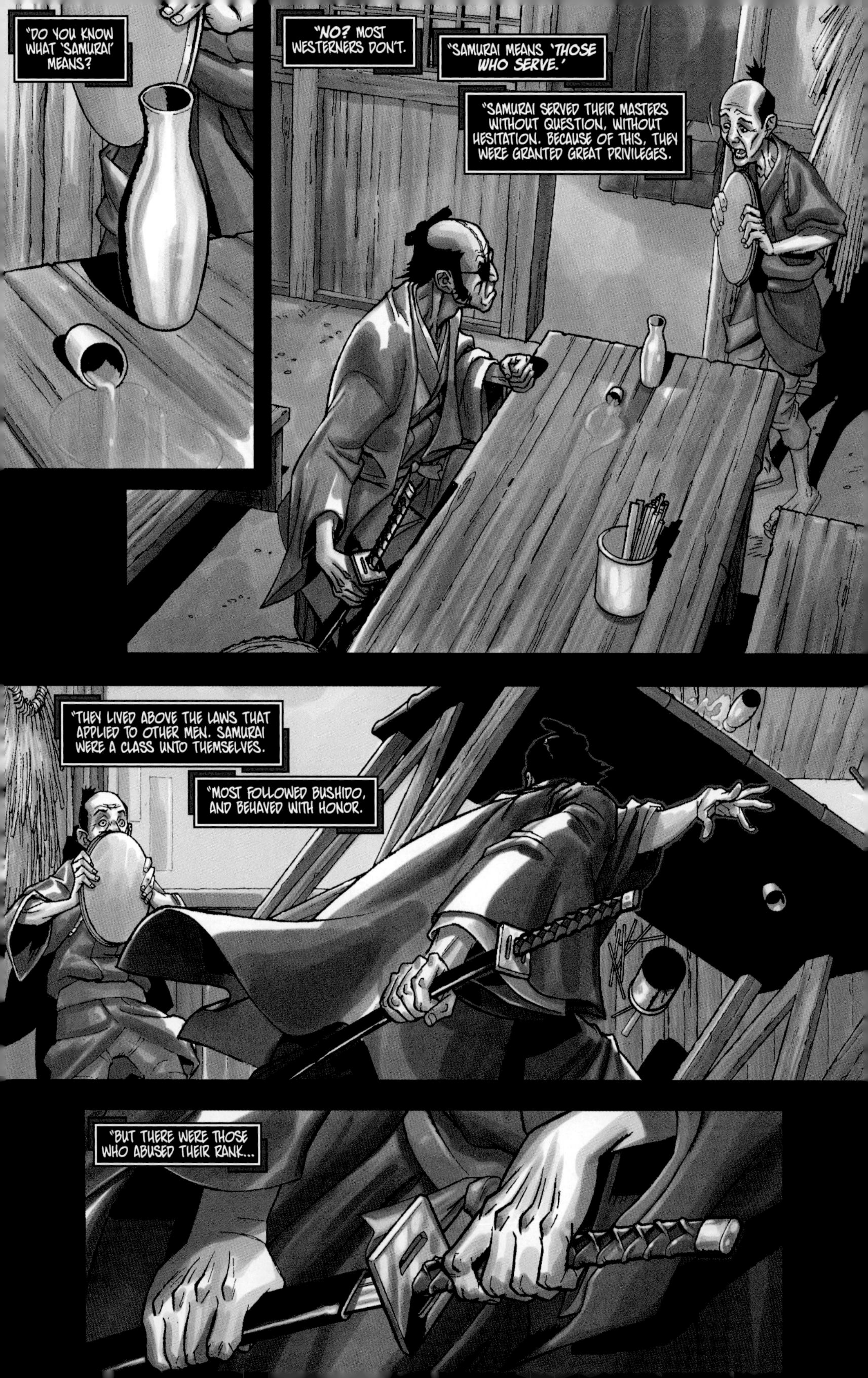
"DO YOU KNOW WHAT 'SAMURAI' MEANS?
"NO? MOST WESTERNERS DON'T.
"SAMURAI MEANS 'THOSE WHO SERVE.'
"SAMURAI SERVED THEIR MASTERS WITHOUT QUESTION, WITHOUT HESITATION. BECAUSE OF THIS, THEY WERE GRANTED GREAT PRIVILEGES.
"THEY LIVED ABOVE THE LAWS THAT APPLIED TO OTHER MEN. SAMURAI WERE A CLASS UNTO THEMSELVES.
"MOST FOLLOWED BUSHIDO, AND BEHAVED WITH HONOR.
"BUT THERE WERE THOSE WHO ABUSED THEIR RANK...

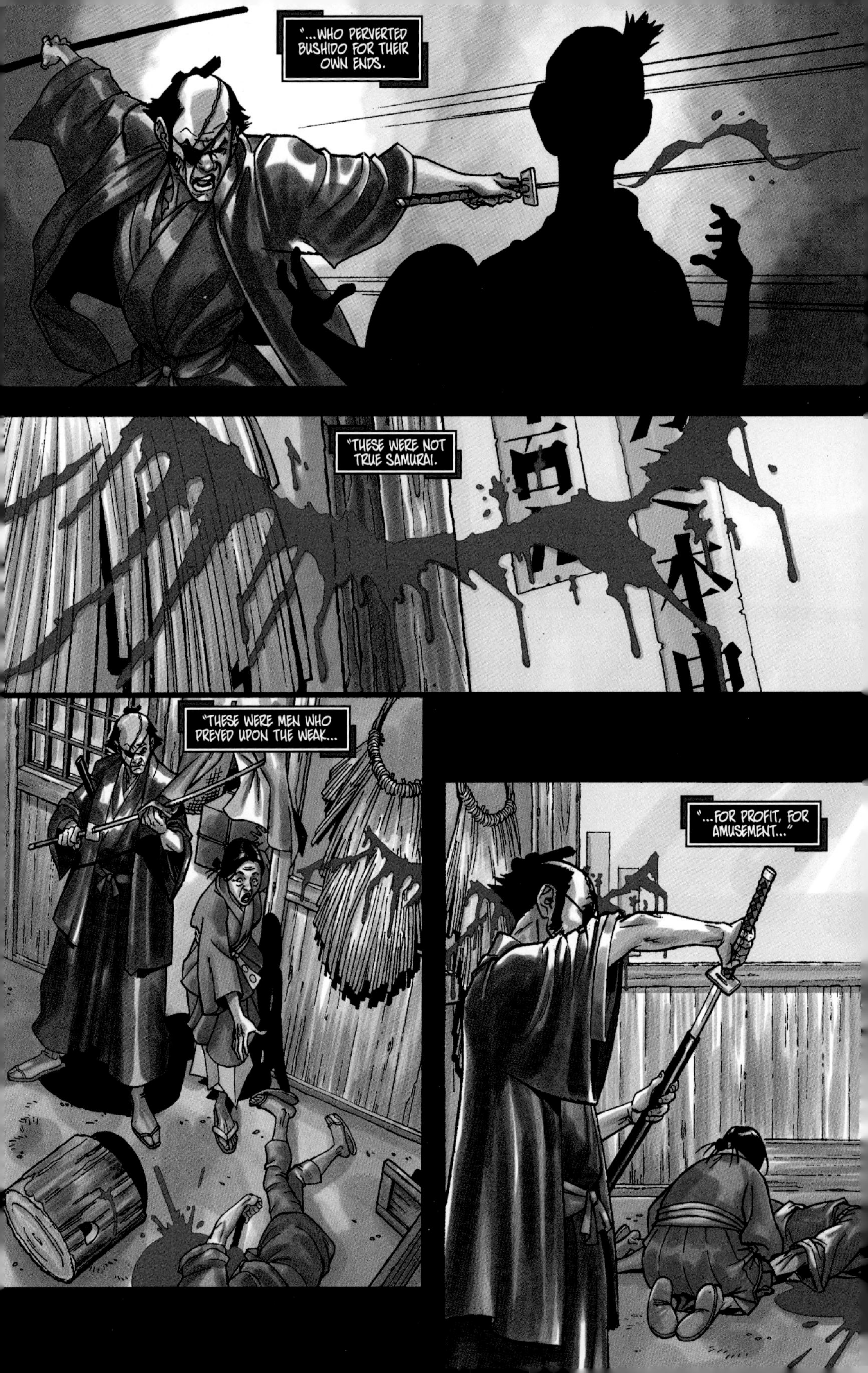
"...WHO PERVERTED BUSHIDO FOR THEIR OWN ENDS.
"THESE WERE NOT TRUE SAMURAI.
"THESE WERE MEN WHO PREYED UPON THE WEAK...
"...FOR PROFIT, FOR AMUSEMENT..."

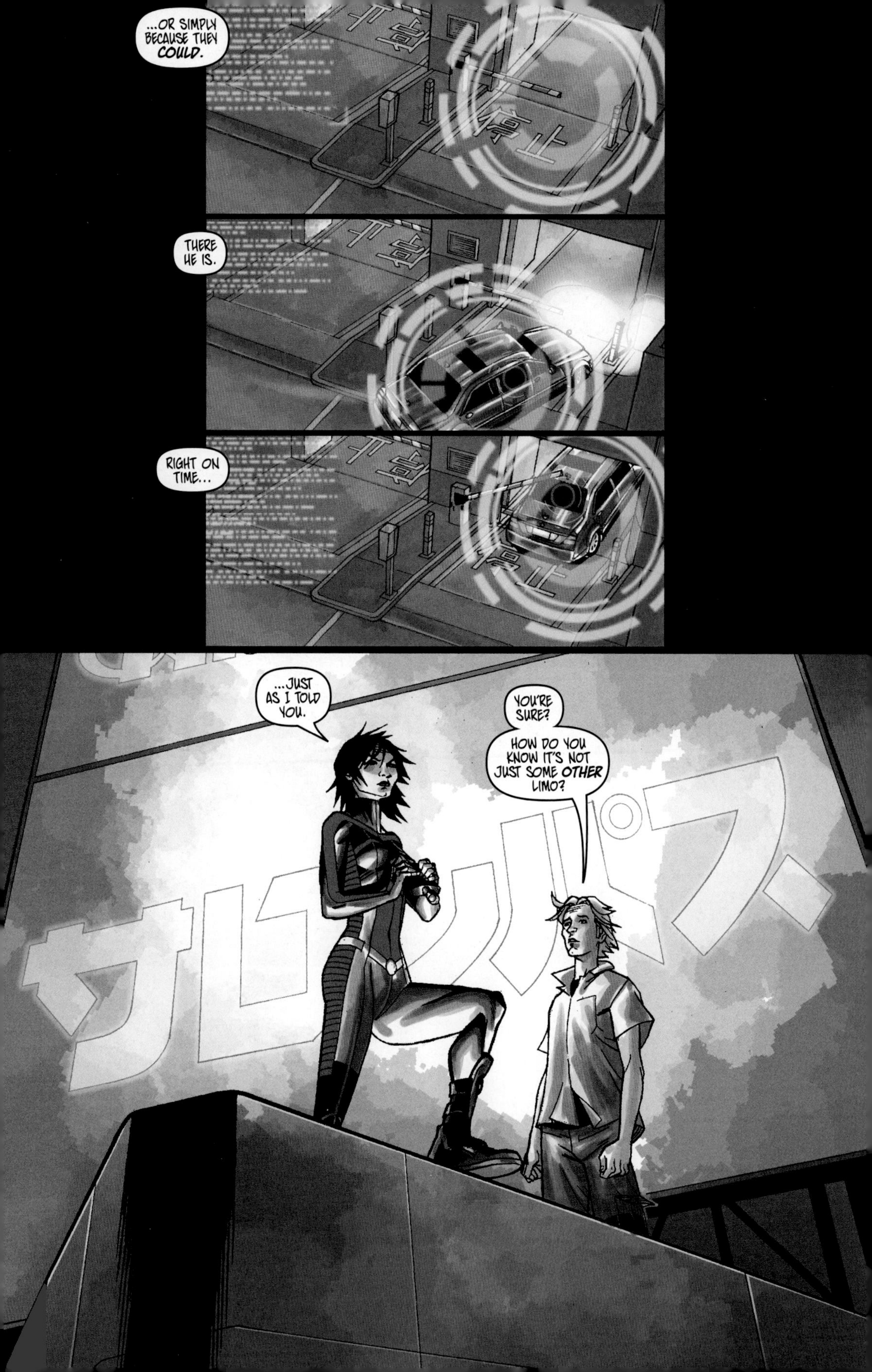
...OR SIMPLY BECAUSE THEY COULD.
THERE HE IS.
RIGHT ON TIME...
...JUST AS I TOLD YOU.
YOU'RE SURE?
HOW DO YOU KNOW IT'S NOT JUST SOME OTHER LIMO?
サレソパプ

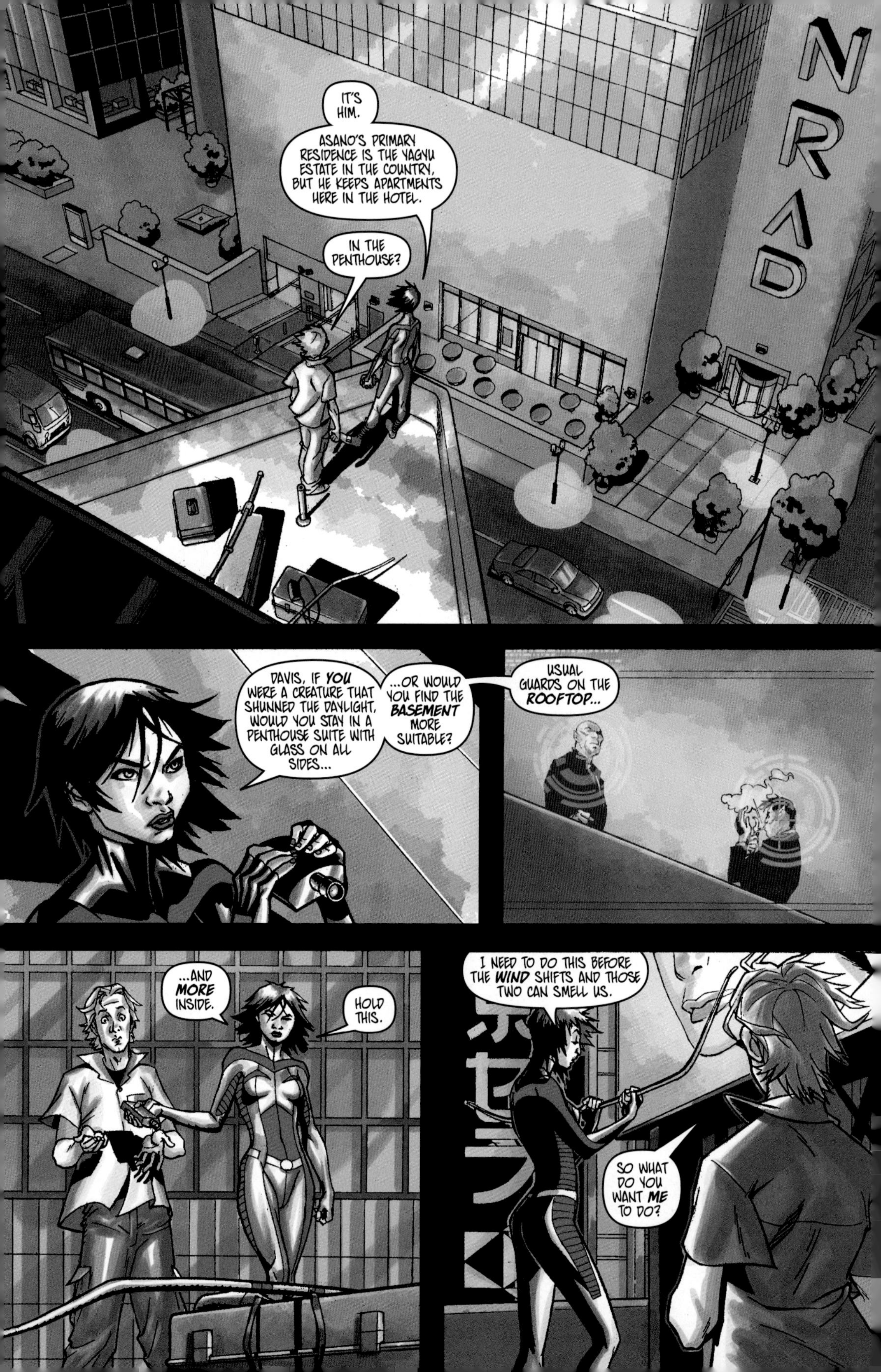
NRAD
IT'S HIM.
ASANO'S PRIMARY RESIDENCE IS THE YAGYU ESTATE IN THE COUNTRY, BUT HE KEEPS APARTMENTS HERE IN THE HOTEL.
IN THE PENTHOUSE?
DAVIS, IF YOU WERE A CREATURE THAT SHUNNED THE DAYLIGHT, WOULD YOU STAY IN A PENTHOUSE SUITE WITH GLASS ON ALL SIDES...
...OR WOULD YOU FIND THE BASEMENT MORE SUITABLE?
USUAL GUARDS ON THE ROOFTOP...
...AND MORE INSIDE.
HOLD THIS.
I NEED TO DO THIS BEFORE THE WIND SHIFTS AND THOSE TWO CAN SMELL US.
SO WHAT DO YOU WANT ME TO DO?

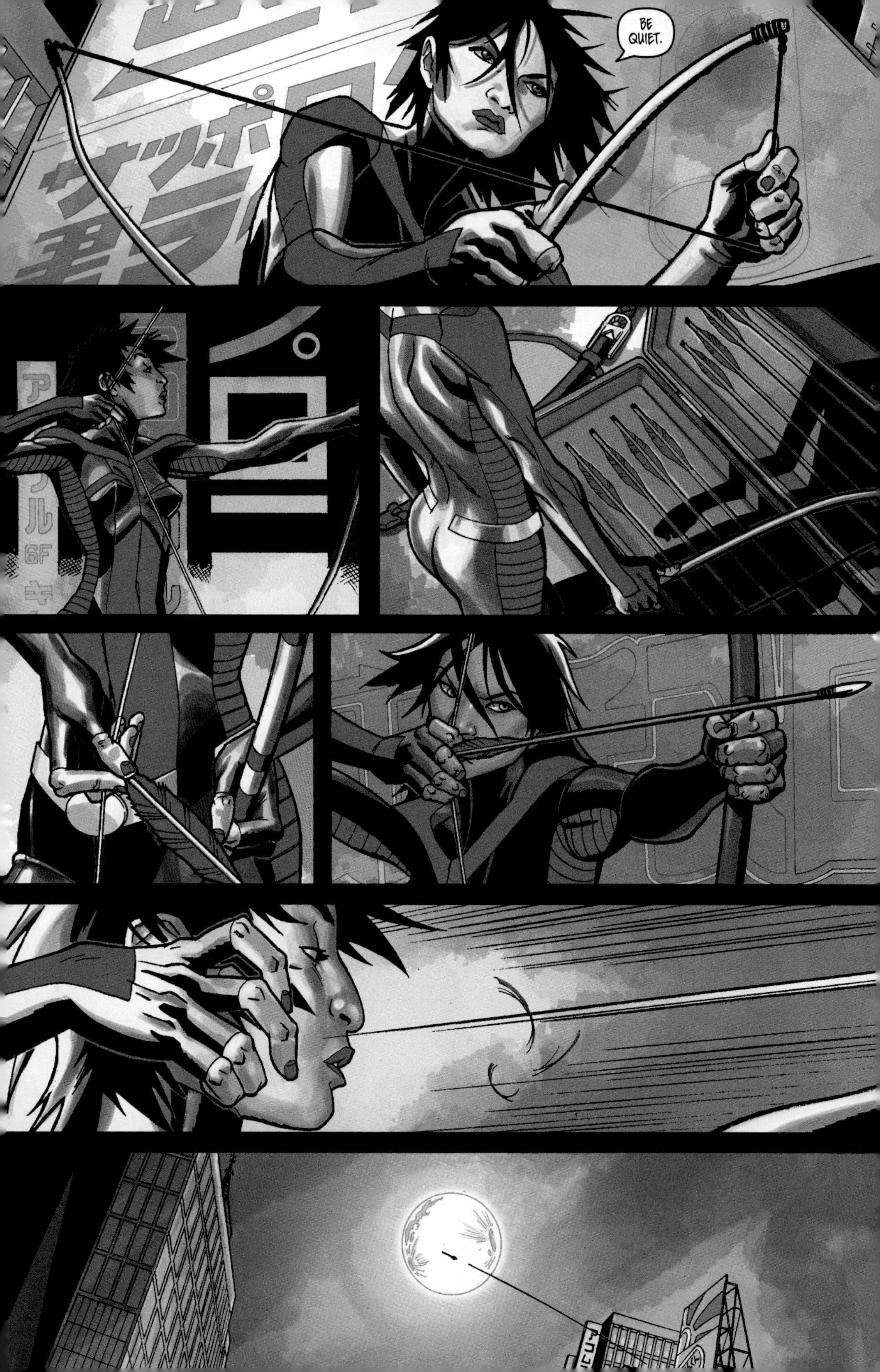
BE QUIET.

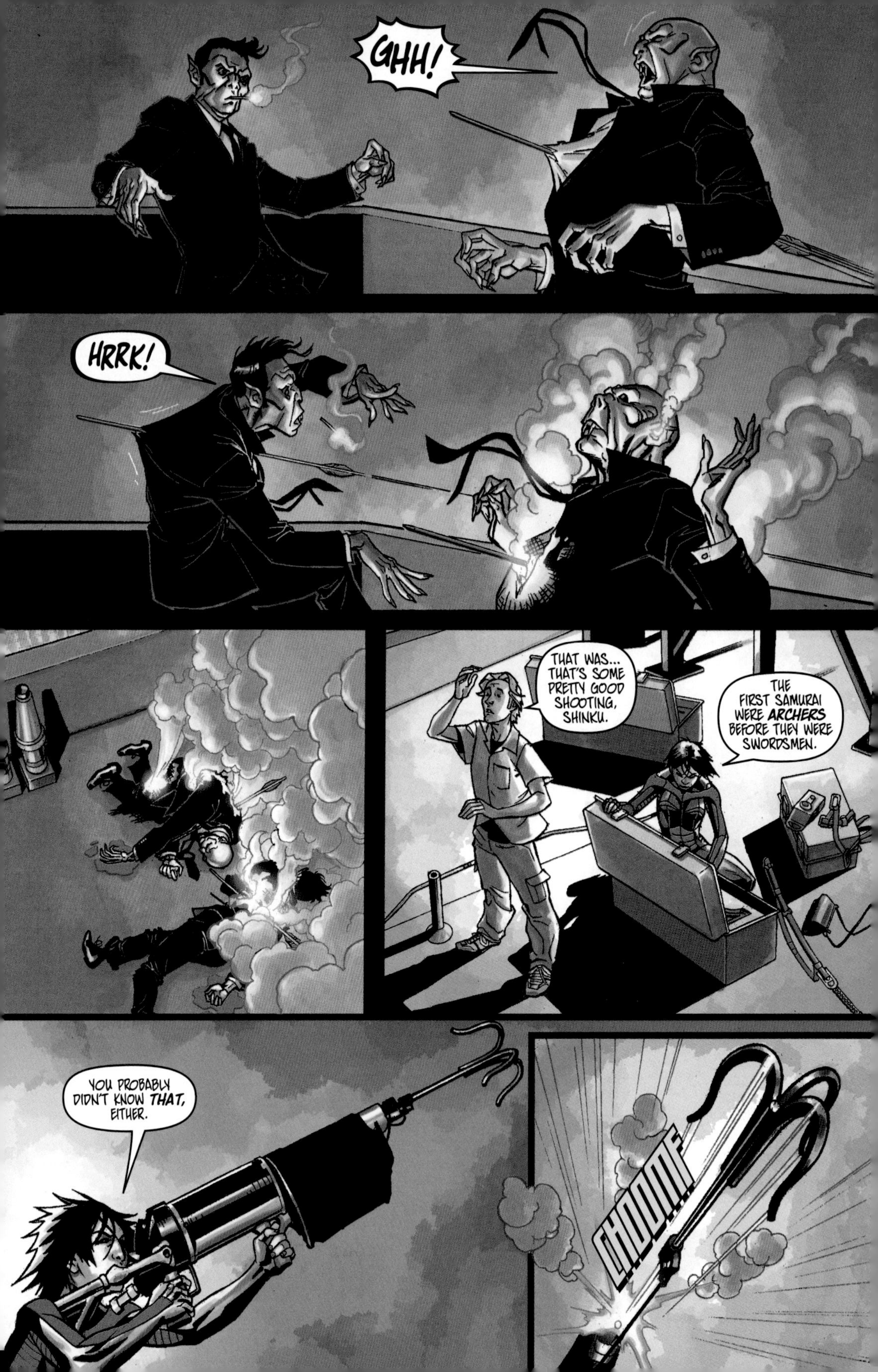
GHH!
HRRK!
THAT WAS... THAT'S SOME PRETTY GOOD SHOOTING, SHINKU.
THE FIRST SAMURAI WERE ARCHERS BEFORE THEY WERE SWORDSMEN.
YOU PROBABLY DIDN'T KNOW THAT, EITHER.
CHOOMF

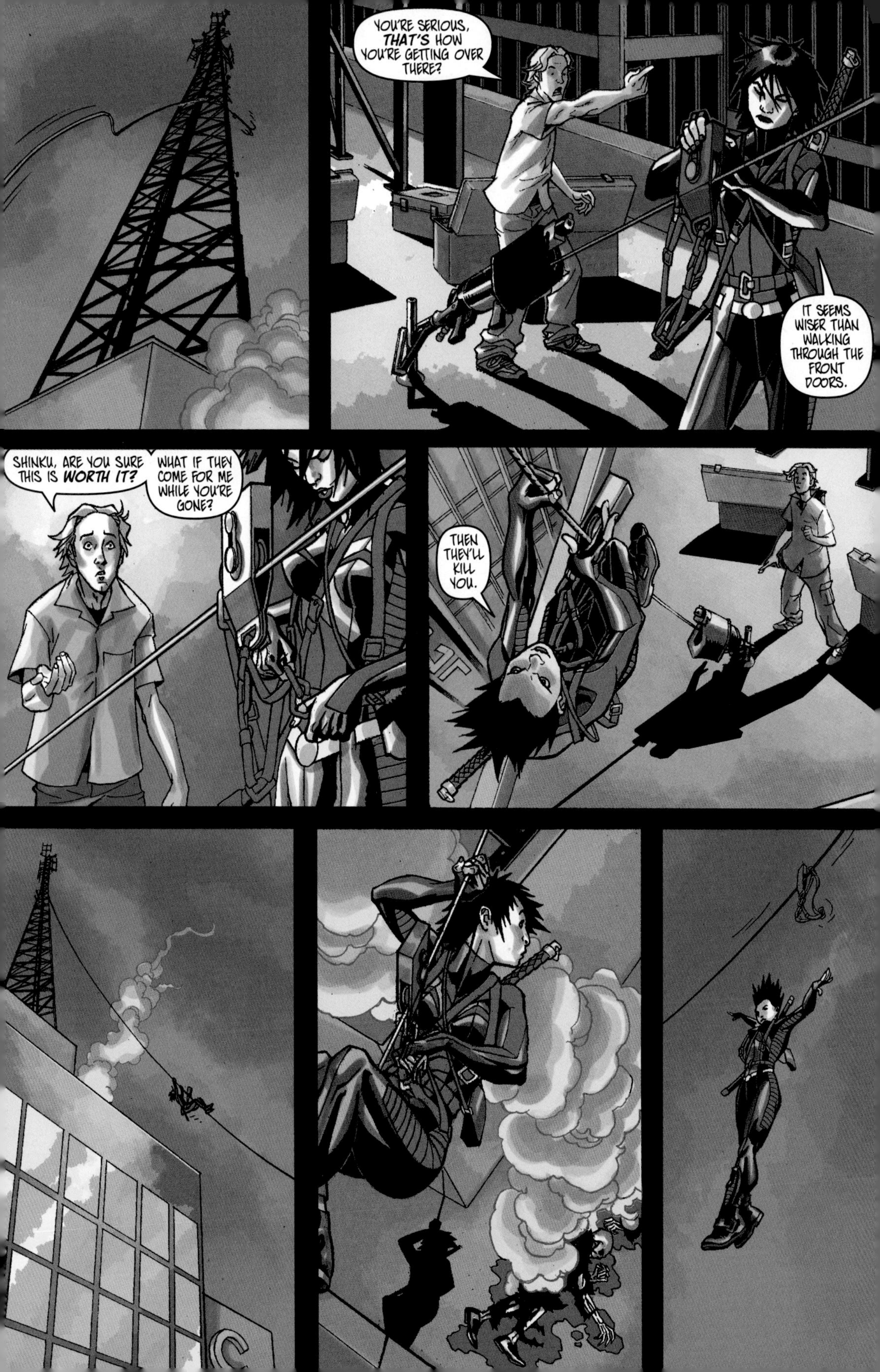
YOU'RE SERIOUS, THAT'S HOW YOU'RE GETTING OVER THERE?
IT SEEMS WISER THAN WALKING THROUGH THE FRONT DOORS.
SHINKU, ARE YOU SURE THIS IS WORTH IT?
WHAT IF THEY COME FOR ME WHILE YOU'RE GONE?
THEN THEY'LL KILL YOU.

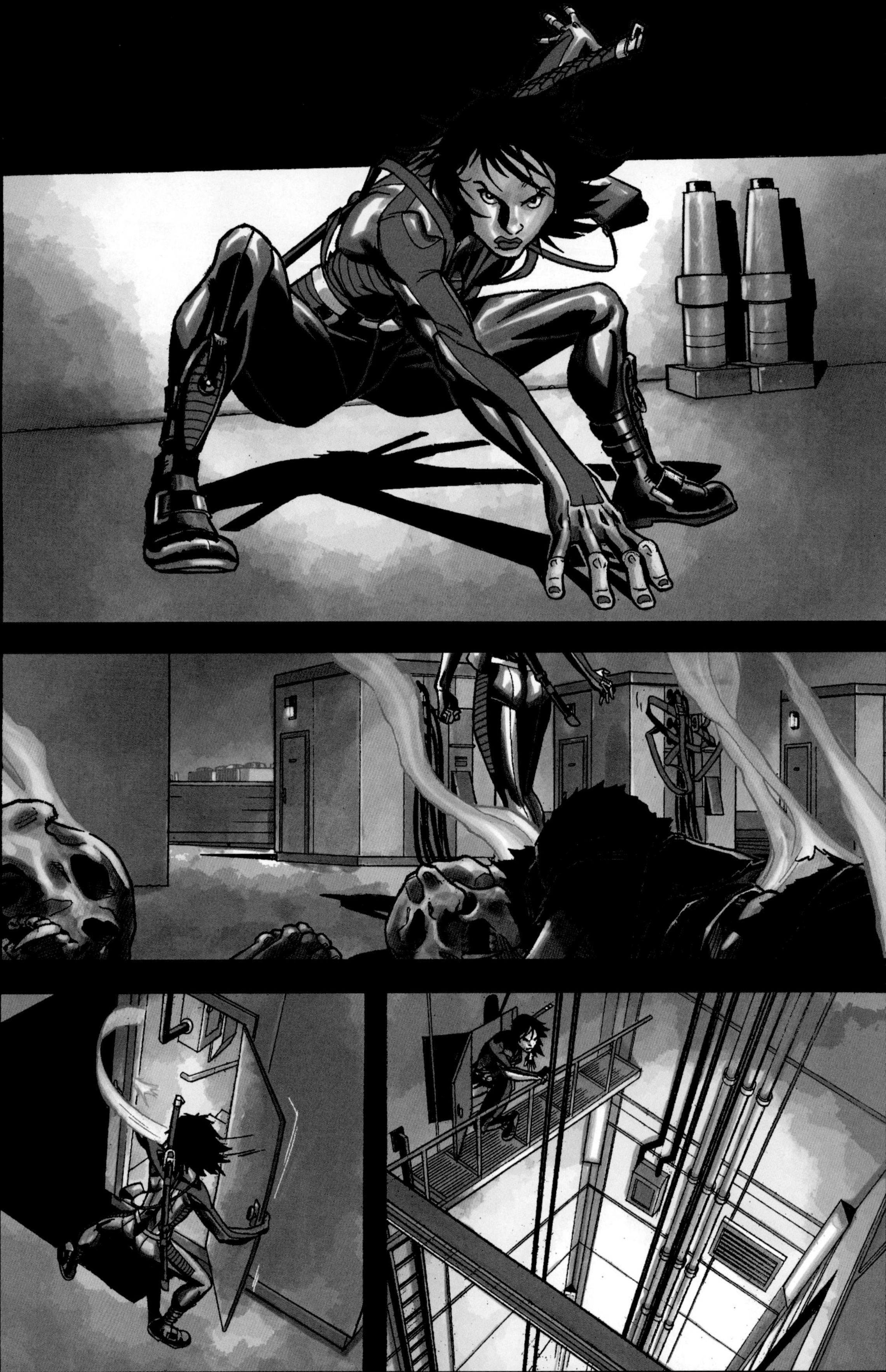

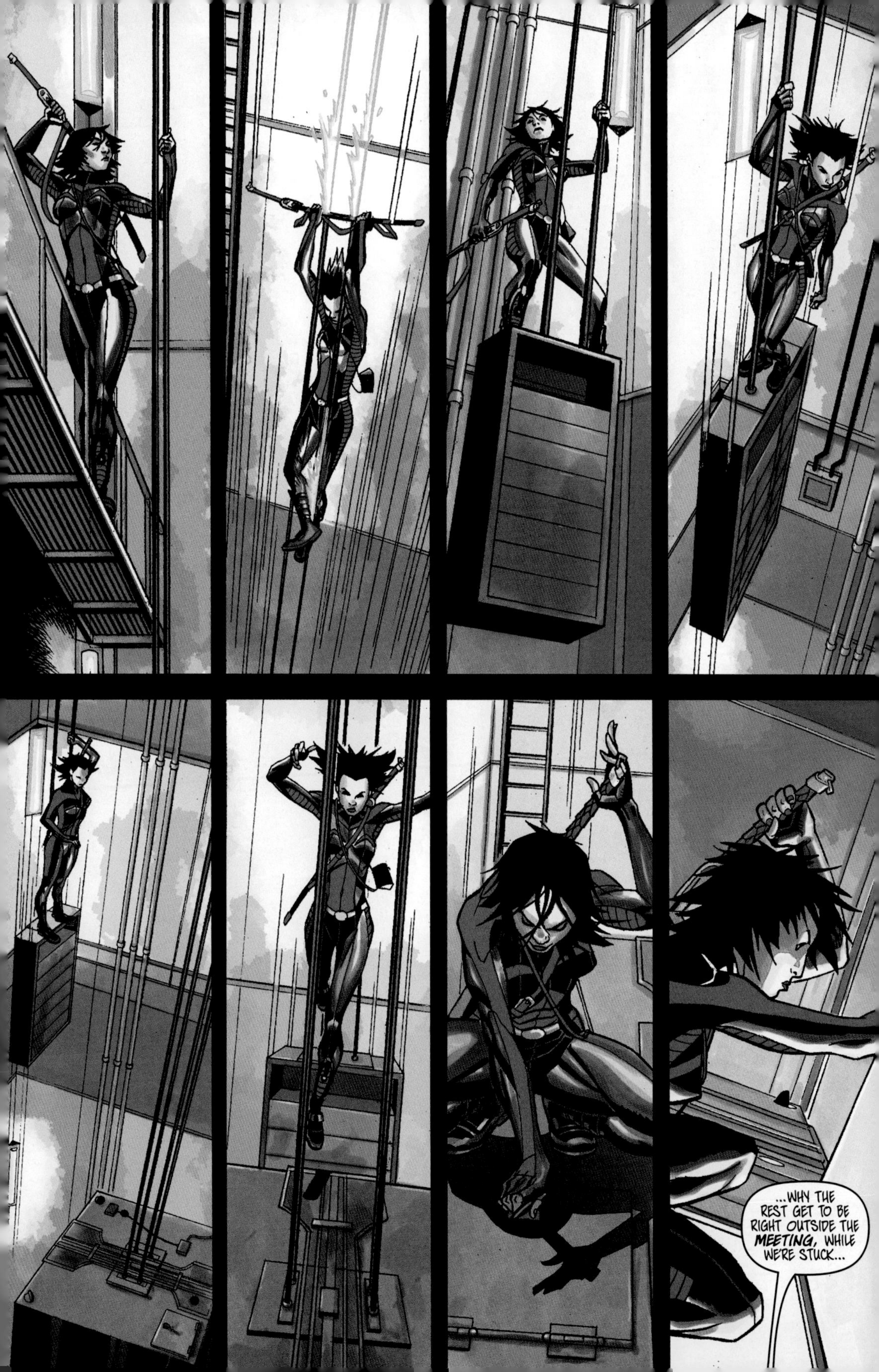
...WHY THE REST GET TO BE RIGHT OUTSIDE THE MEETING, WHILE WE'RE STUCK...

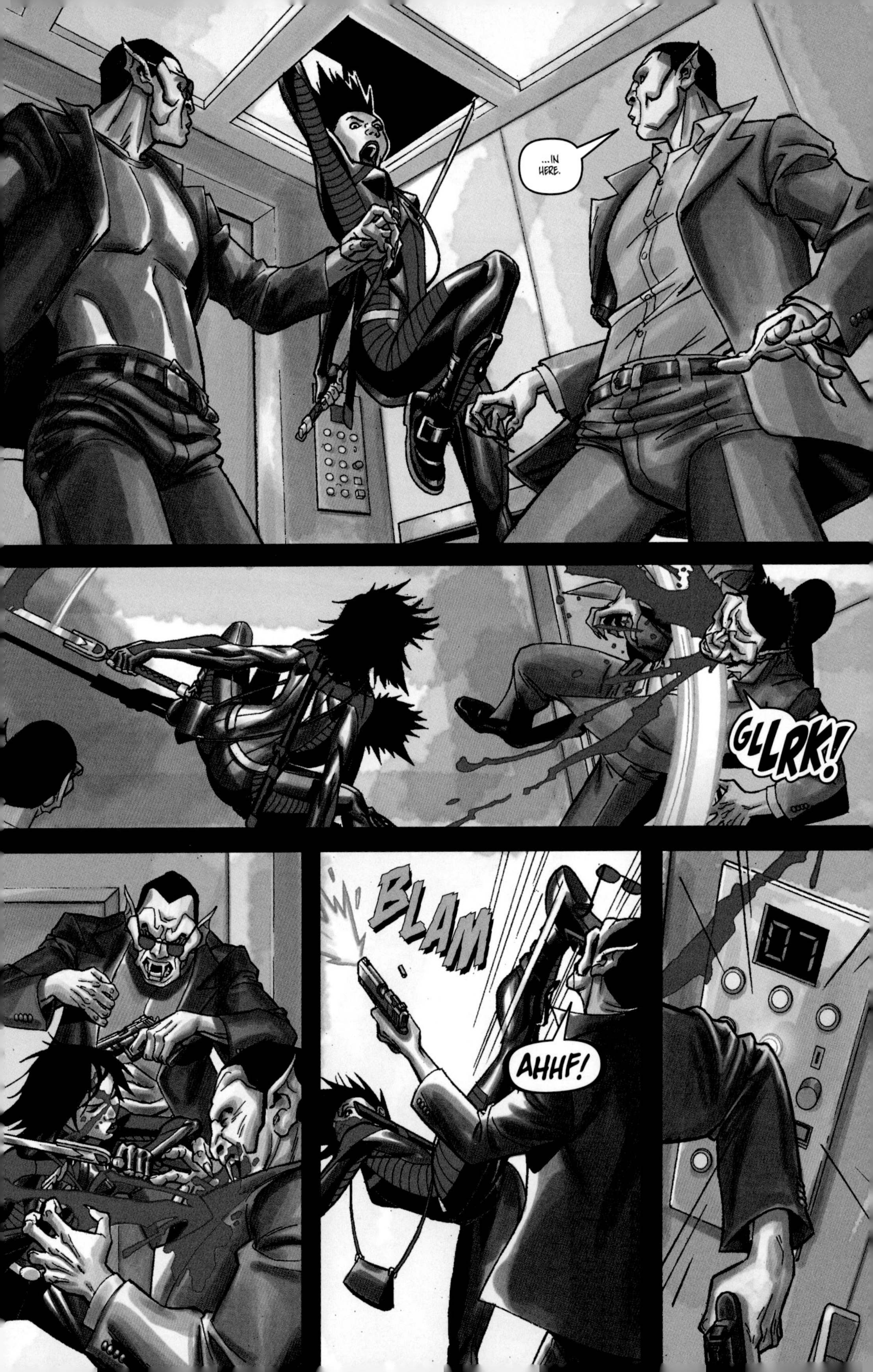
...IN HERE.
GLLRK!
BLAM
AHHF!

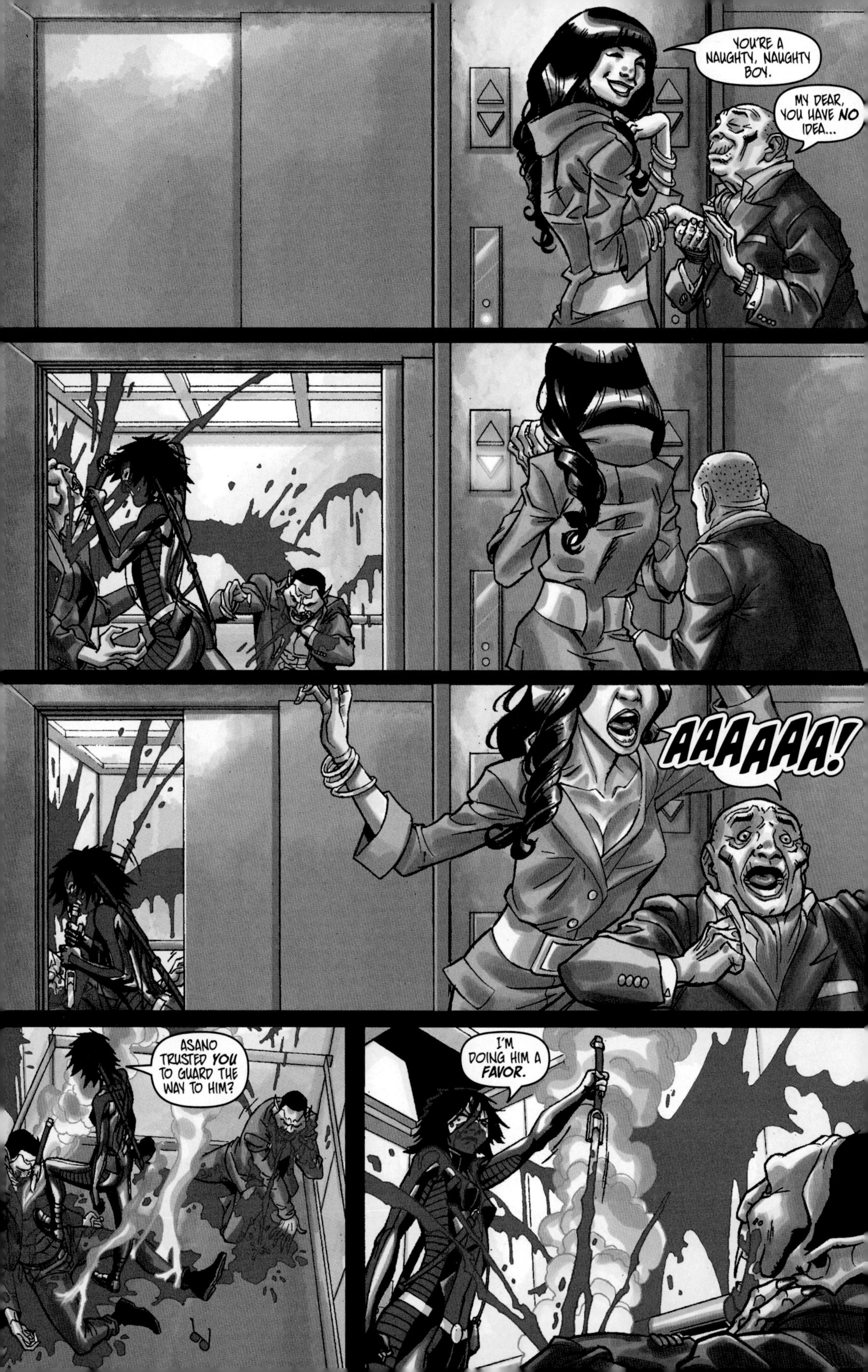

YOU'RE A NAUGHTY, NAUGHTY BOY.
MY DEAR, YOU HAVE NO IDEA...
AAAAAA!
ASANO TRUSTED YOU TO GUARD THE WAY TO HIM?
I'M DOING HIM A FAVOR.

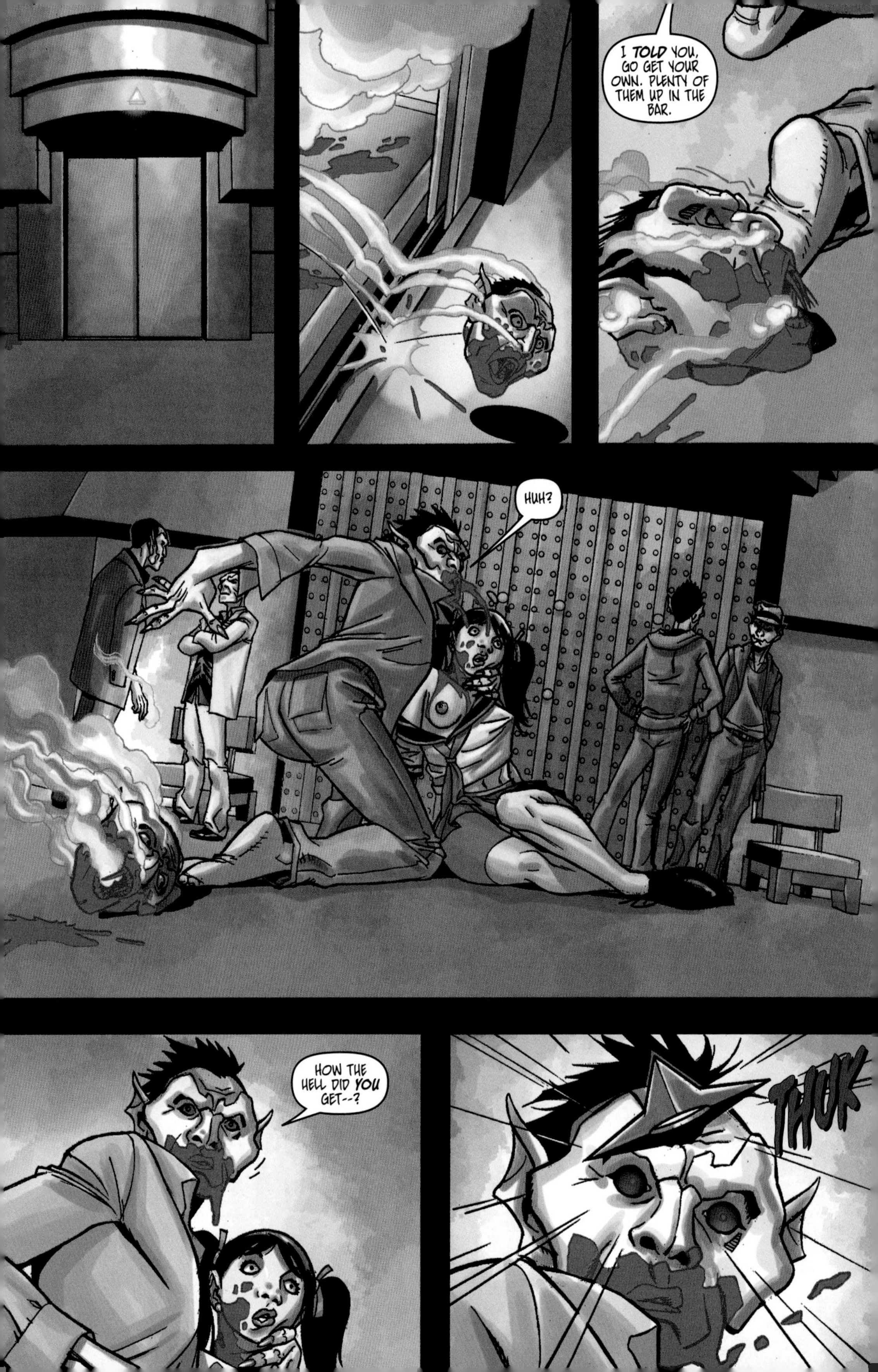
I TOLD YOU, GO GET YOUR OWN. PLENTY OF THEM UP IN THE BAR.
HUH?
HOW THE HELL DID YOU GET--?
THUK

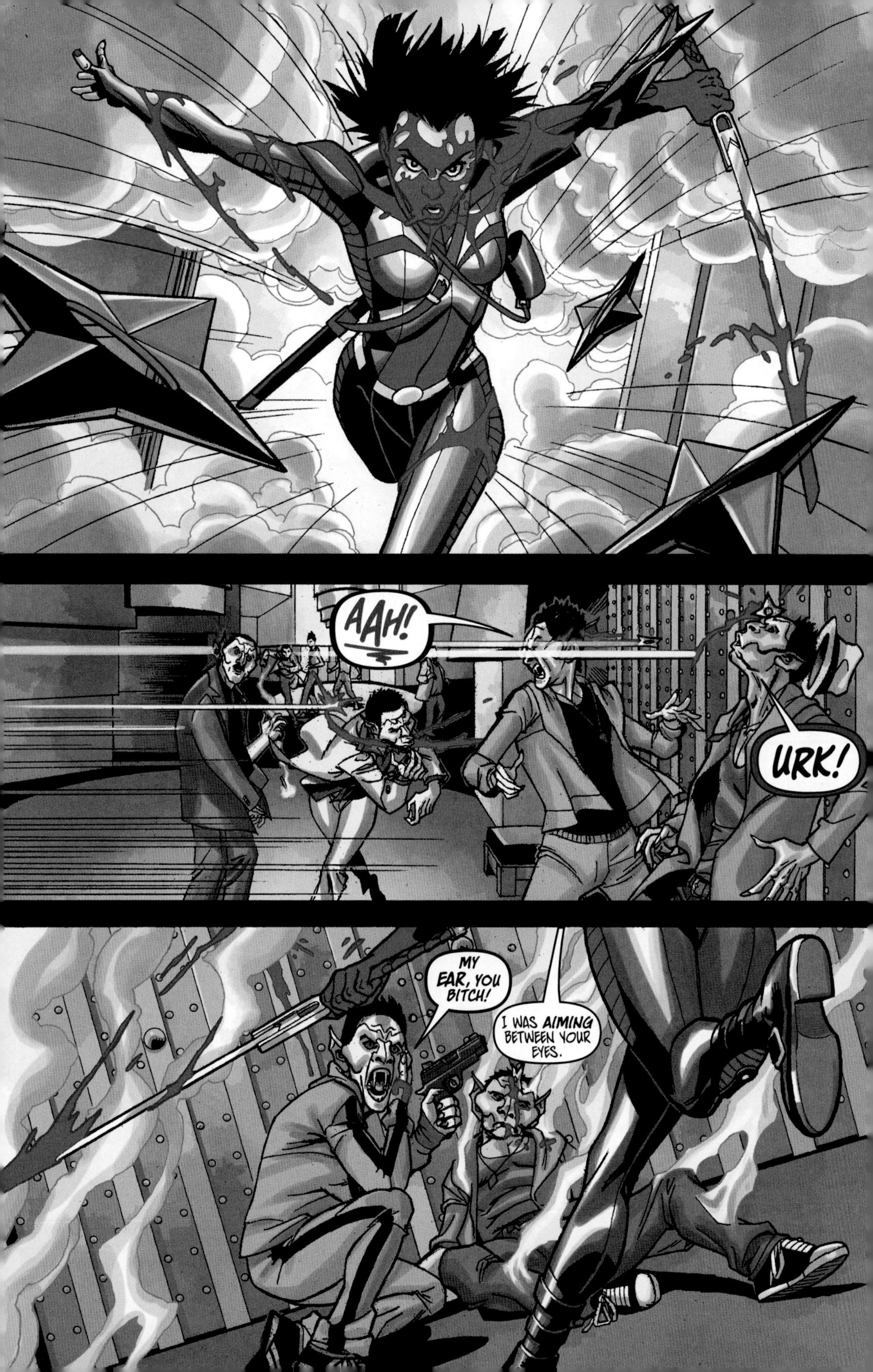
AAH!
URK!
MY EAR, YOU BITCH!
I WAS AIMING BETWEEN YOUR EYES.

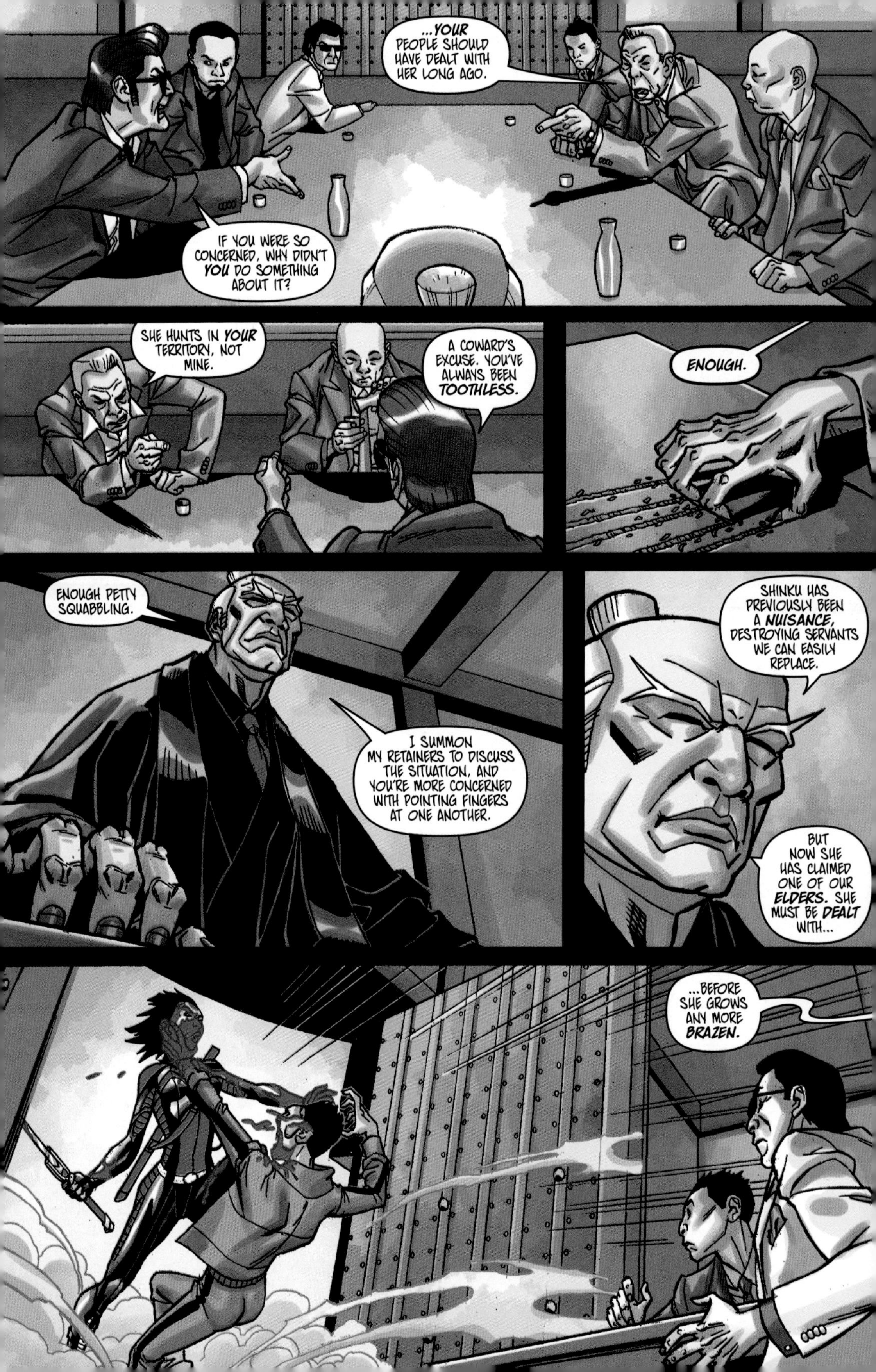
...YOUR PEOPLE SHOULD HAVE DEALT WITH HER LONG AGO.
IF YOU WERE SO CONCERNED, WHY DIDN'T YOU DO SOMETHING ABOUT IT?
SHE HUNTS IN YOUR TERRITORY, NOT MINE.
A COWARD'S EXCUSE. YOU'VE ALWAYS BEEN TOOTHLESS.
ENOUGH.
ENOUGH PETTY SQUABBLING.
I SUMMON MY RETAINERS TO DISCUSS THE SITUATION, AND YOU'RE MORE CONCERNED WITH POINTING FINGERS AT ONE ANOTHER.
SHINKU HAS PREVIOUSLY BEEN A NUISANCE, DESTROYING SERVANTS WE CAN EASILY REPLACE.
BUT NOW SHE HAS CLAIMED ONE OF OUR ELDERS. SHE MUST BE DEALT WITH...
...BEFORE SHE GROWS ANY MORE BRAZEN.

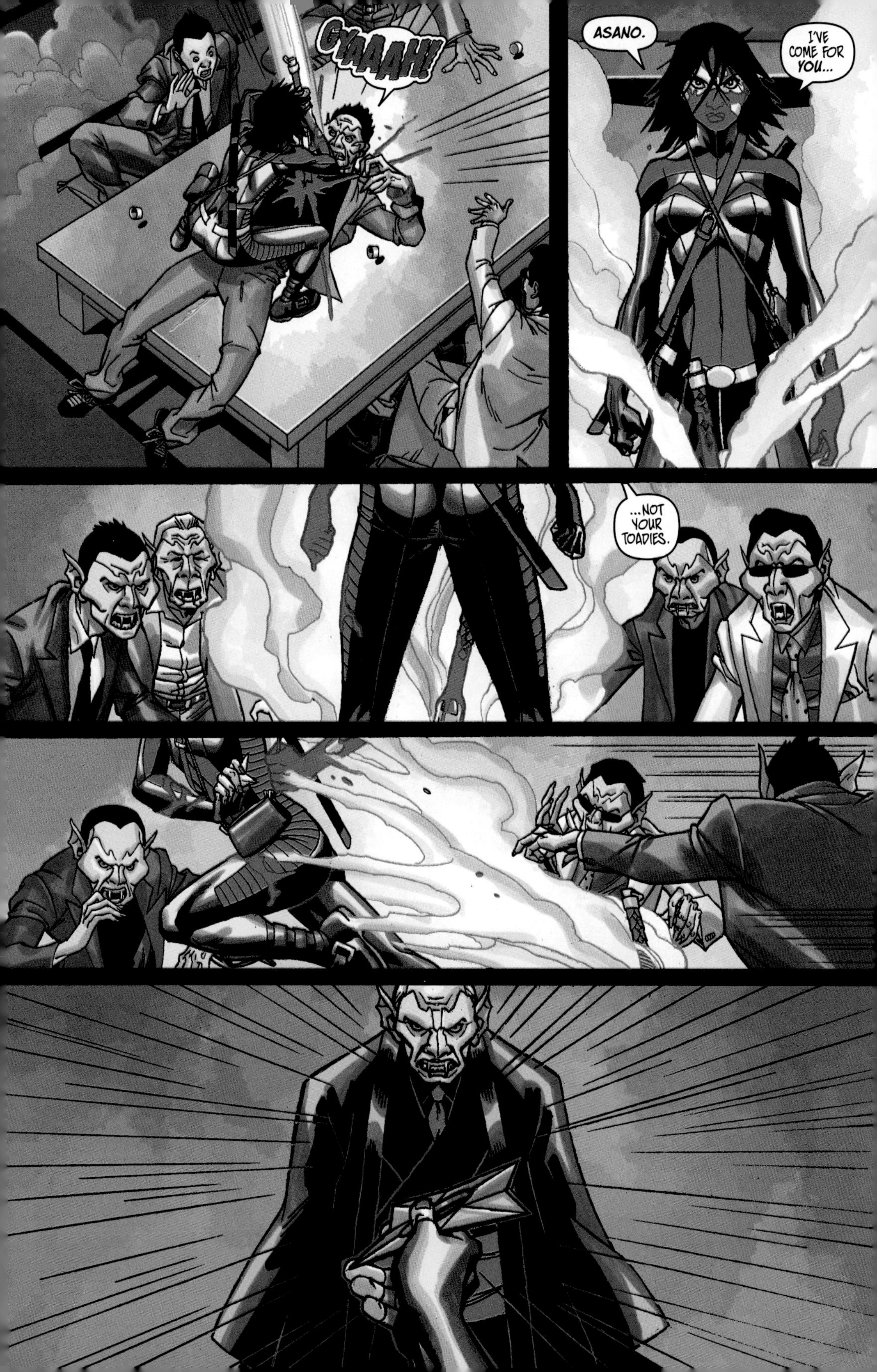
GYAAAH!
ASANO.
I'VE COME FOR YOU...
...NOT YOUR TOADIES.

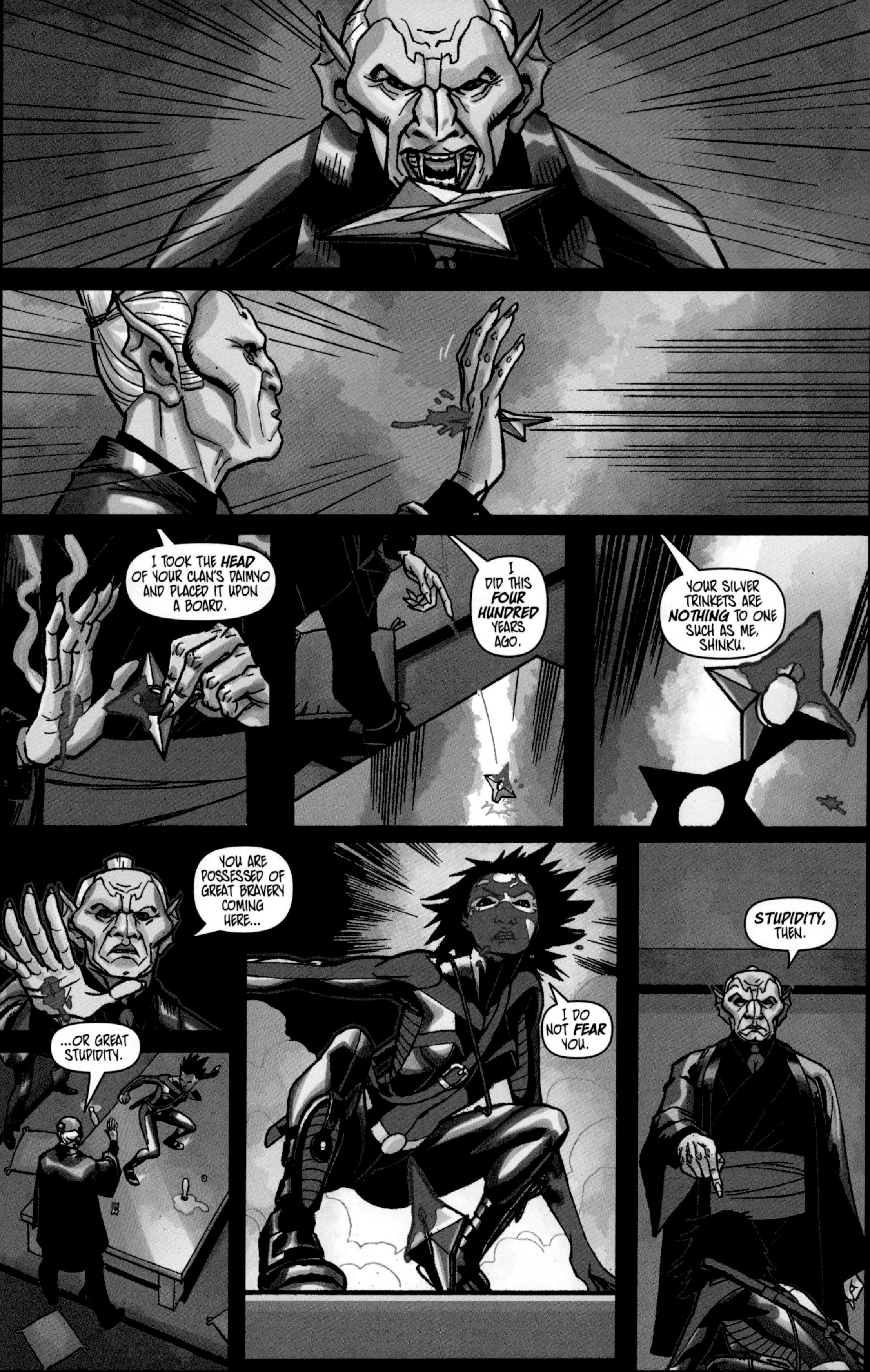
I TOOK THE HEAD OF YOUR CLAN'S DAIMYO AND PLACED IT UPON A BOARD.
I DID THIS FOUR HUNDRED YEARS AGO.
YOUR SILVER TRINKETS ARE NOTHING TO ONE SUCH AS ME, SHINKU.
YOU ARE POSSESSED OF GREAT BRAVERY COMING HERE...
...OR GREAT STUPIDITY.
I DO NOT FEAR YOU.
STUPIDITY, THEN.

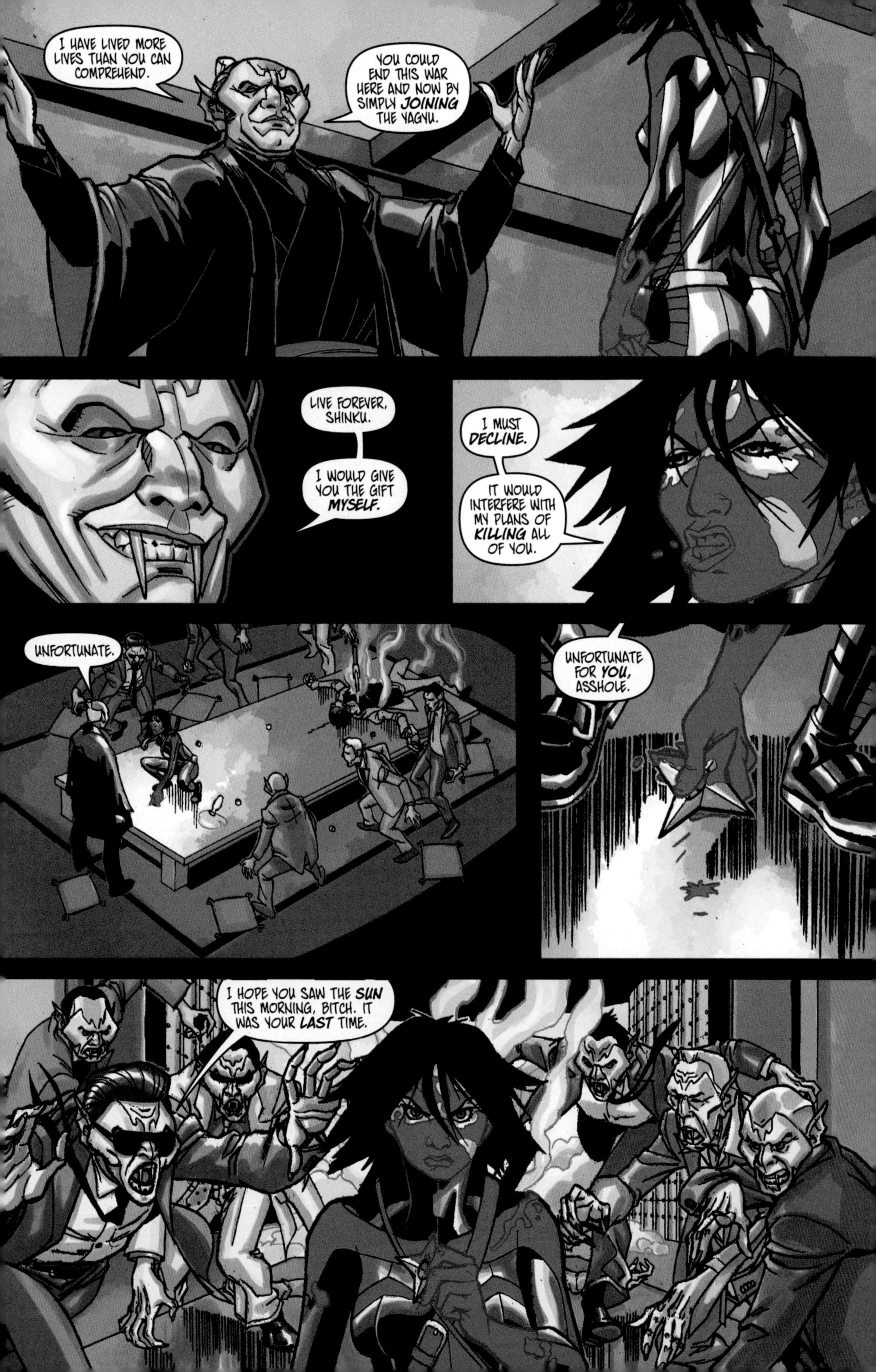
I HAVE LIVED MORE LIVES THAN YOU CAN COMPREHEND.
YOU COULD END THIS WAR HERE AND NOW BY SIMPLY JOINING THE YAGYU.
LIVE FOREVER, SHINKU.
I WOULD GIVE YOU THE GIFT MYSELF.
I MUST DECLINE.
IT WOULD INTERFERE WITH MY PLANS OF KILLING ALL OF YOU.
UNFORTUNATE.
UNFORTUNATE FOR YOU, ASSHOLE.
I HOPE YOU SAW THE SUN THIS MORNING, BITCH. IT WAS YOUR LAST TIME.

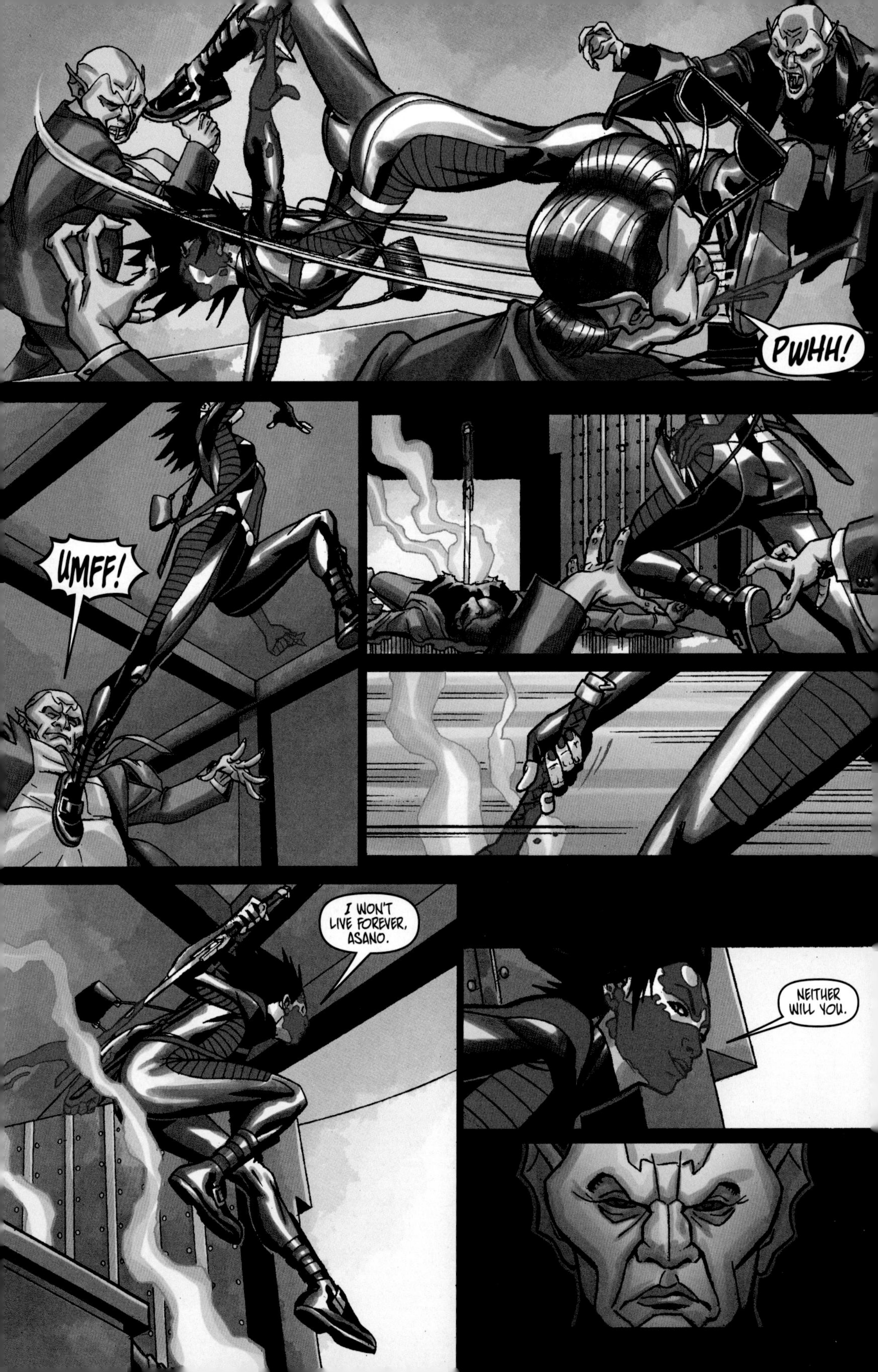
PWHH!
UMFF!
I WON'T LIVE FOREVER, ASANO.
NEITHER WILL YOU.

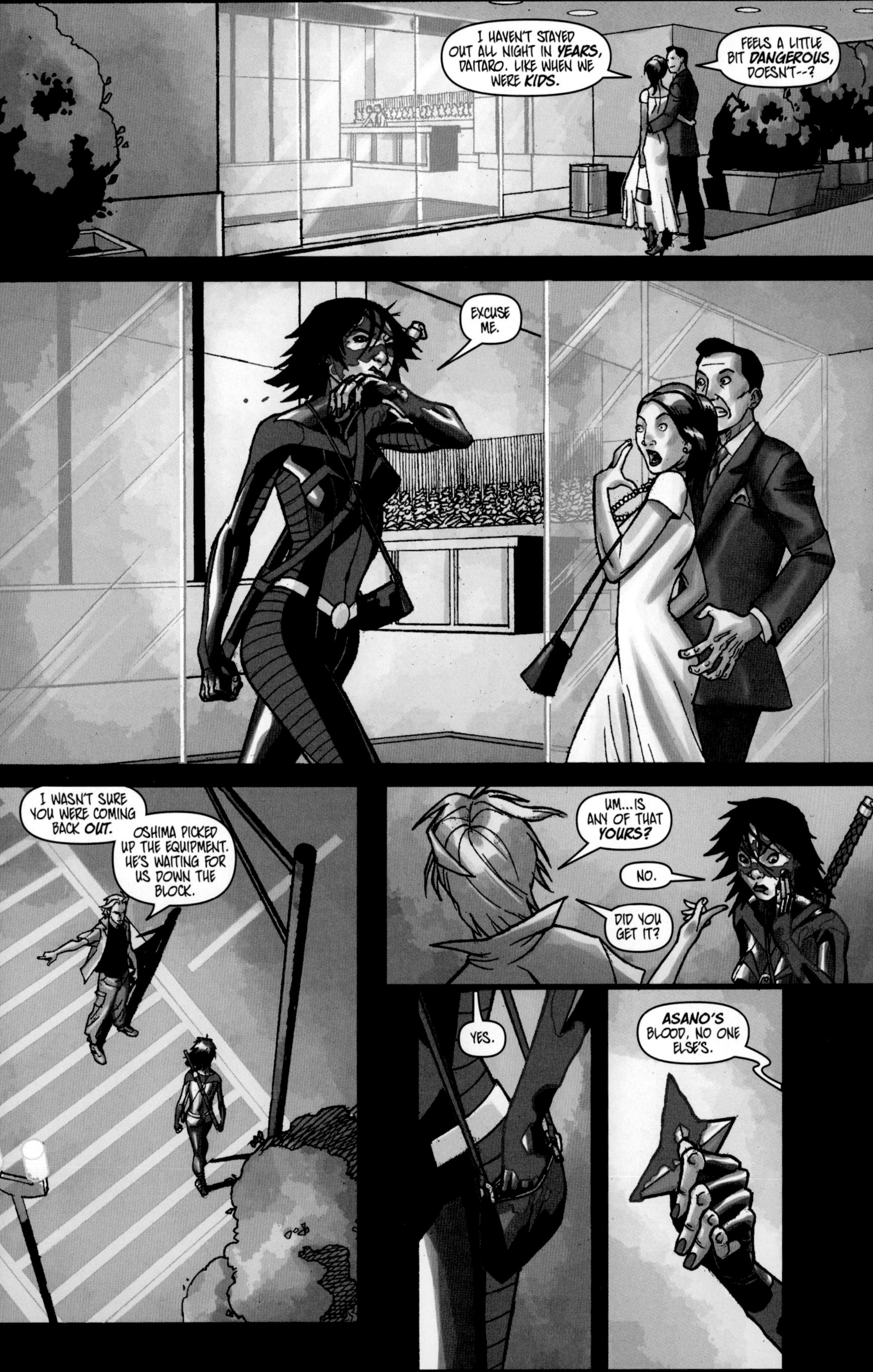
I HAVEN'T STAYED OUT ALL NIGHT IN YEARS, DAITARO. LIKE WHEN WE WERE KIDS.
FEELS A LITTLE BIT DANGEROUS, DOESN'T--?
EXCUSE ME.
I WASN'T SURE YOU WERE COMING BACK OUT.
OSHIMA PICKED UP THE EQUIPMENT. HE'S WAITING FOR US DOWN THE BLOCK.
UM...IS ANY OF THAT YOURS?
NO.
DID YOU GET IT?
YES.
ASANO'S BLOOD, NO ONE ELSE'S.

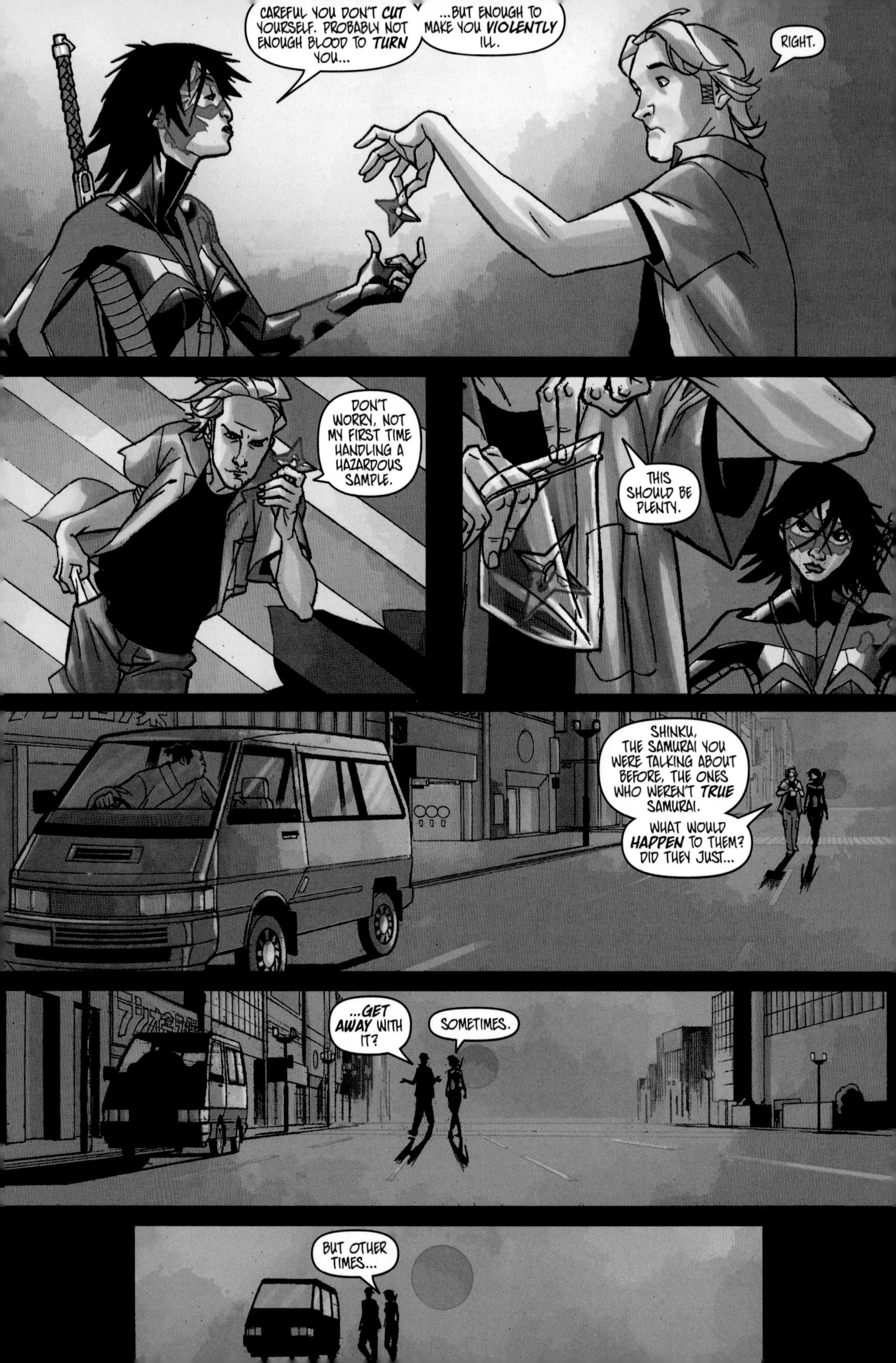
CAREFUL YOU DON'T CUT YOURSELF. PROBABLY NOT ENOUGH BLOOD TO TURN YOU...
...BUT ENOUGH TO MAKE YOU VIOLENTLY ILL.
RIGHT.
DON'T WORRY, NOT MY FIRST TIME HANDLING A HAZARDOUS SAMPLE.
THIS SHOULD BE PLENTY.
SHINKU, THE SAMURAI YOU WERE TALKING ABOUT BEFORE, THE ONES WHO WEREN'T TRUE SAMURAI.
WHAT WOULD HAPPEN TO THEM? DID THEY JUST...
...GET AWAY WITH IT?
SOMETIMES.
BUT OTHER TIMES...

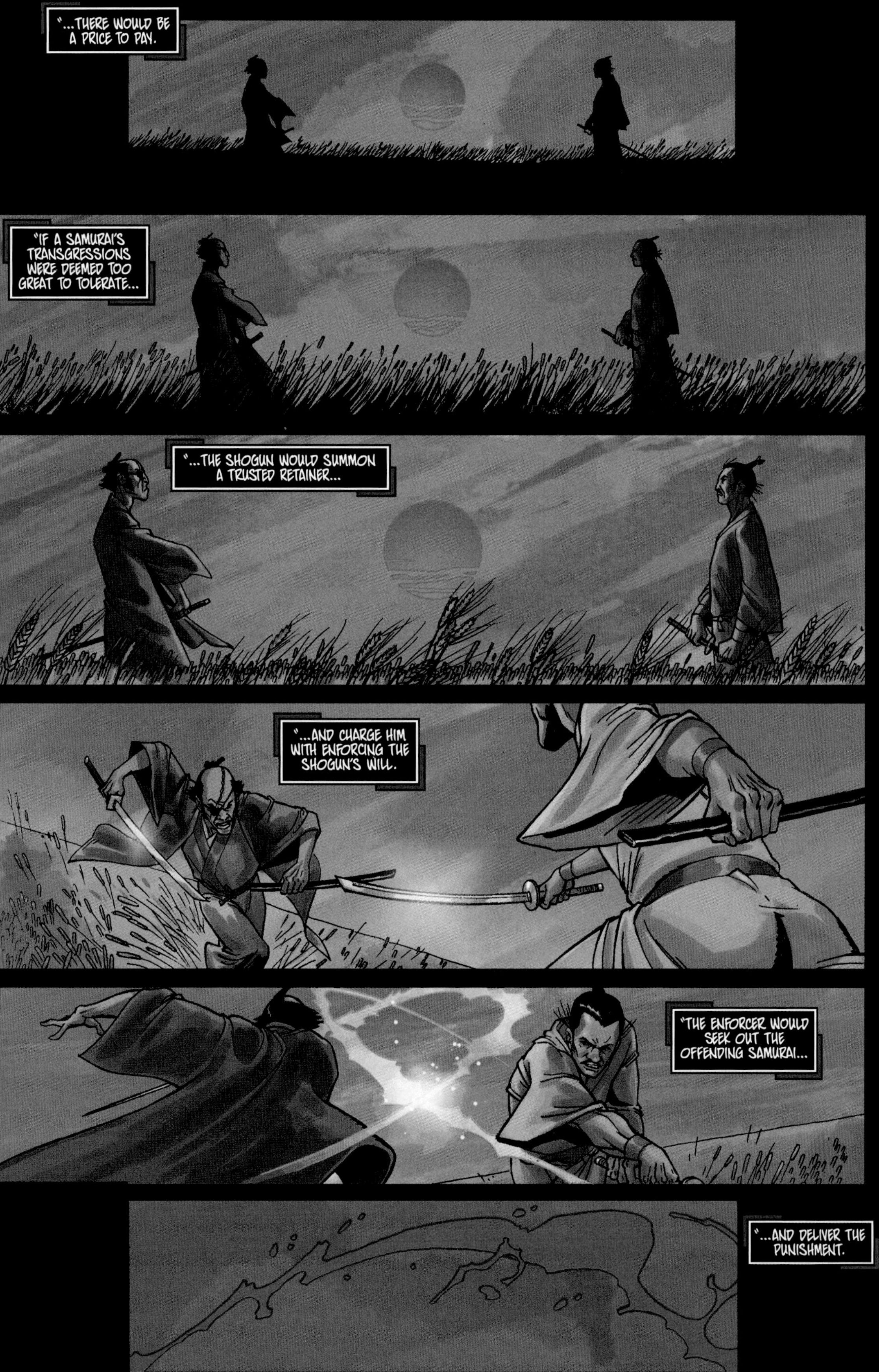
"...THERE WOULD BE A PRICE TO PAY.
"IF A SAMURAI'S TRANSGRESSIONS WERE DEEMED TOO GREAT TO TOLERATE...
"...THE SHOGUN WOULD SUMMON A TRUSTED RETAINER...
"...AND CHARGE HIM WITH ENFORCING THE SHOGUN'S WILL.
"THE ENFORCER WOULD SEEK OUT THE OFFENDING SAMURAI...
"...AND DELIVER THE PUNISHMENT.

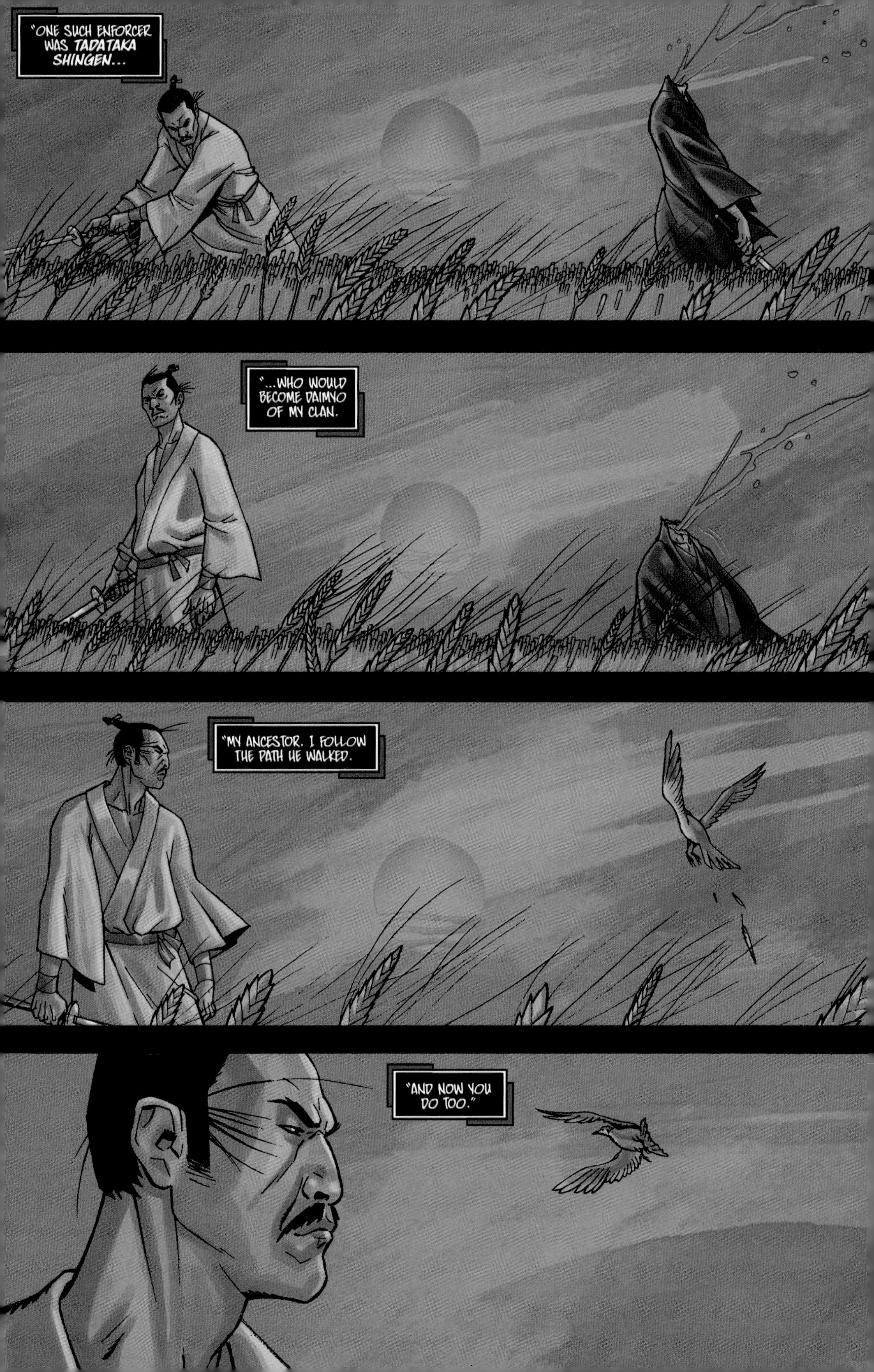
"ONE SUCH ENFORCER WAS TADATAKA SHINGEN...
"...WHO WOULD BECOME DAIMYO OF MY CLAN.
"MY ANCESTOR. I FOLLOW THE PATH HE WALKED.
"AND NOW YOU DO TOO."

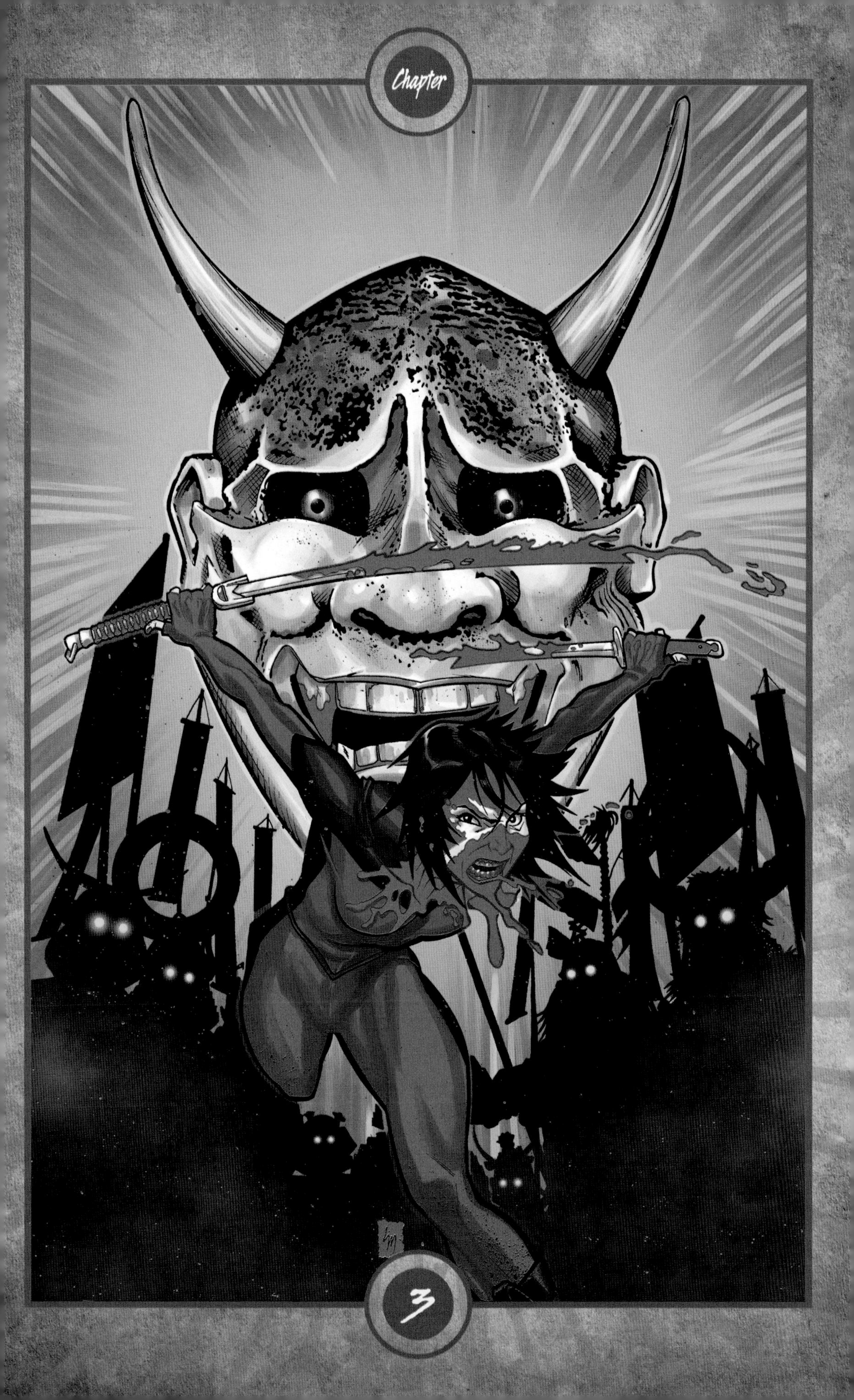
Chapter
3

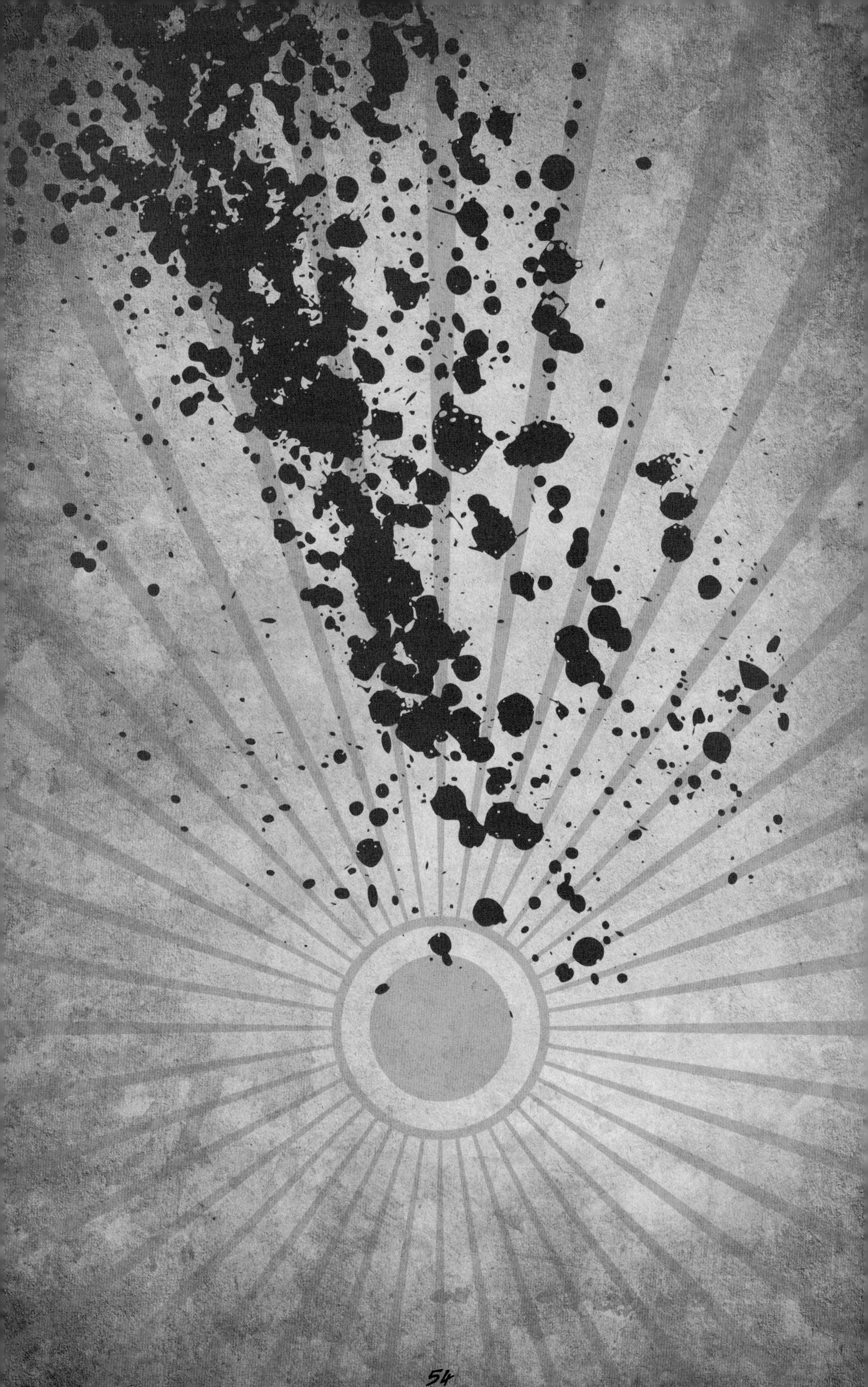

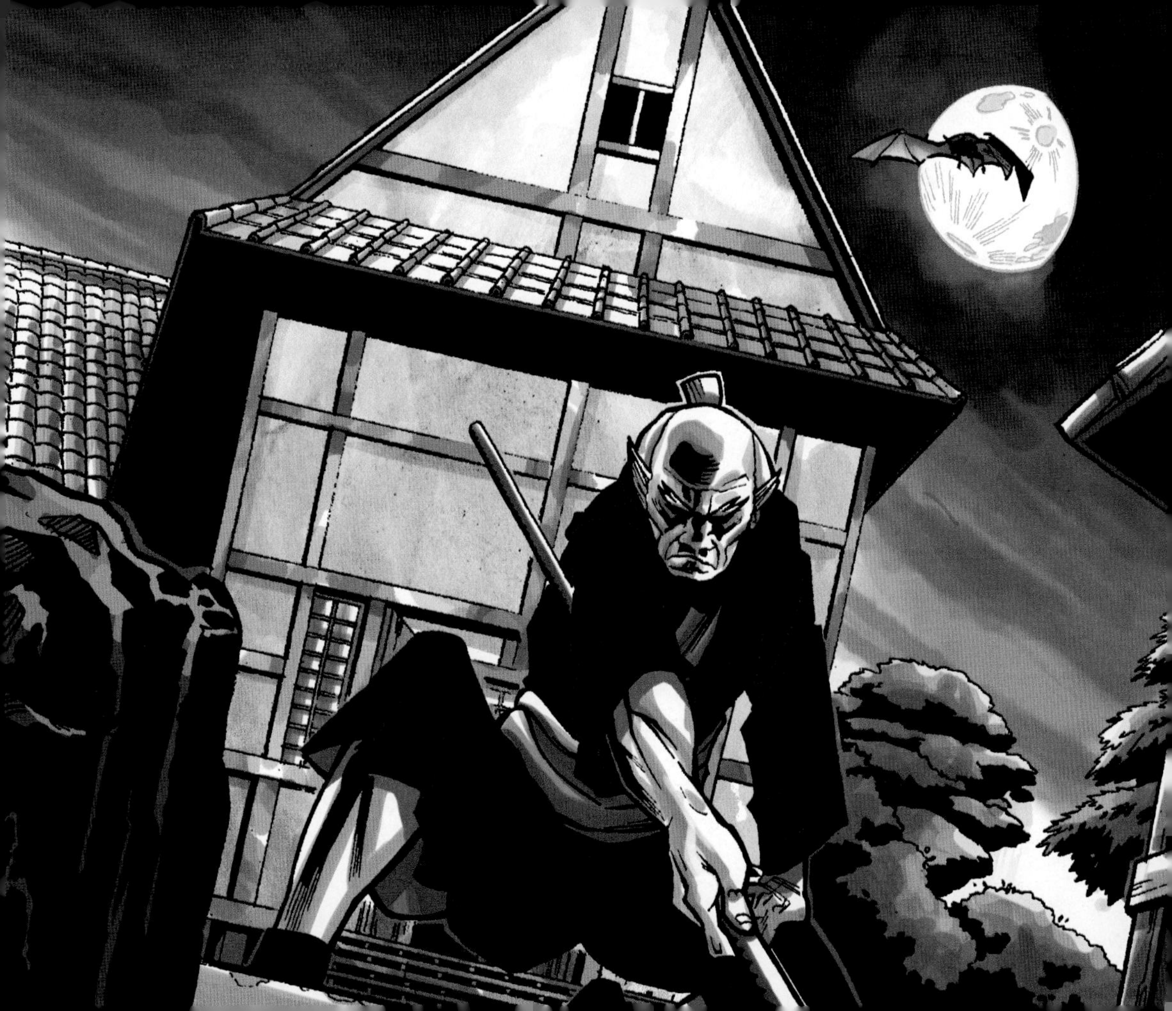

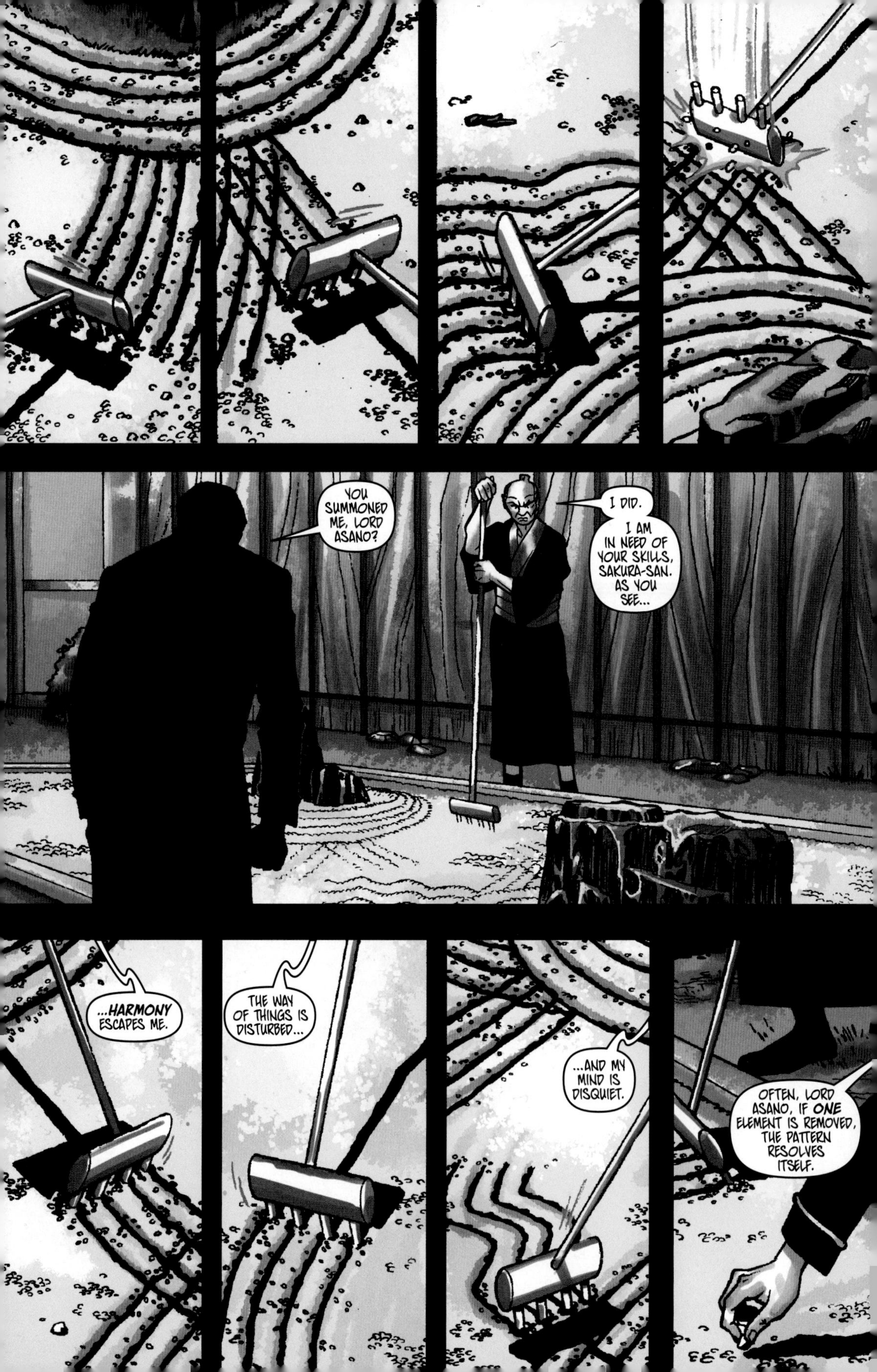
YOU SUMMONED ME, LORD ASANO?
I DID.
I AM IN NEED OF YOUR SKILLS, SAKURA-SAN. AS YOU SEE...
...HARMONY ESCAPES ME.
THE WAY OF THINGS IS DISTURBED...
...AND MY MIND IS DISQUIET.
OFTEN, LORD ASANO, IF ONE ELEMENT IS REMOVED, THE PATTERN RESOLVES ITSELF.

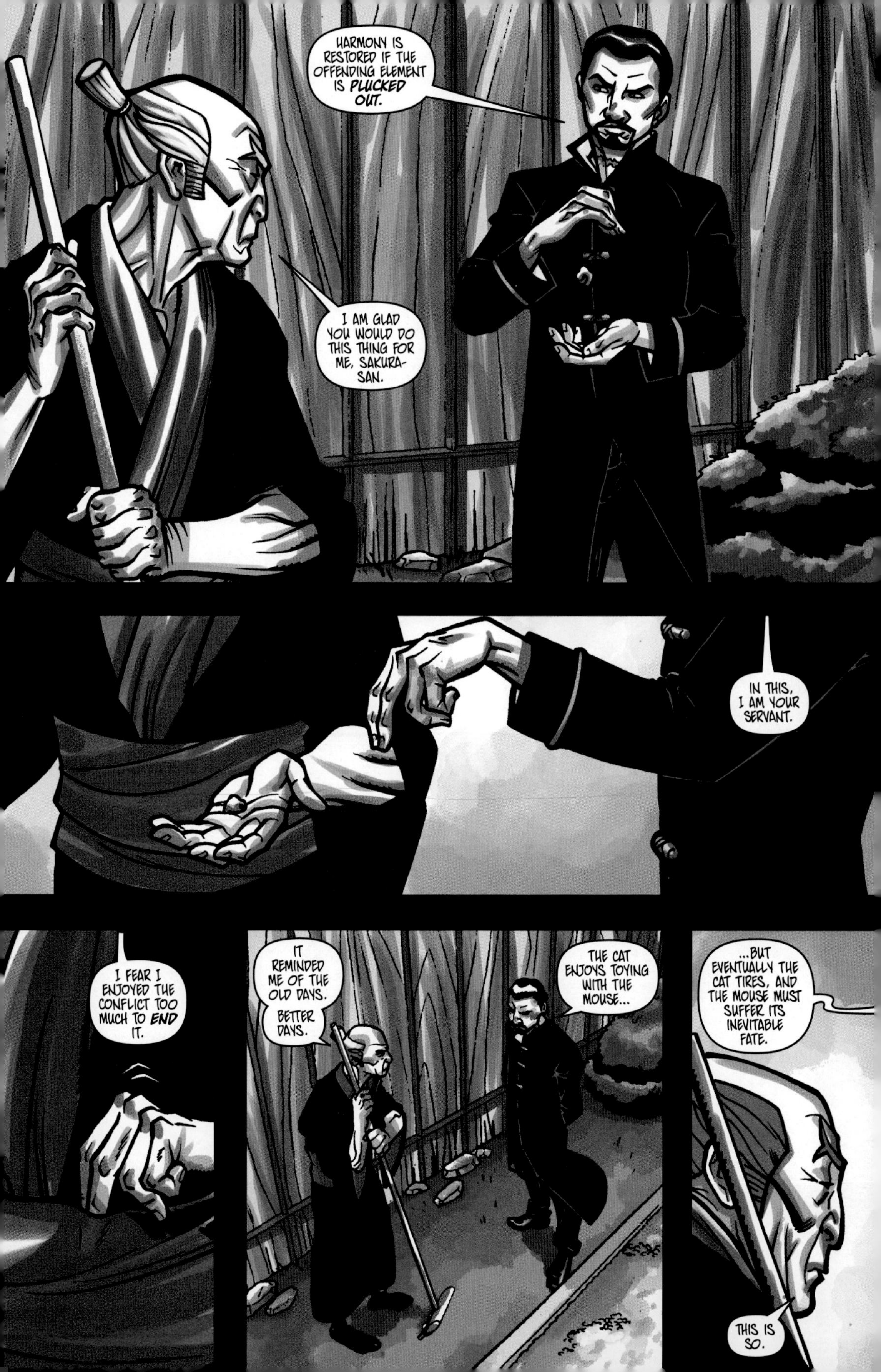
HARMONY IS RESTORED IF THE OFFENDING ELEMENT IS PLUCKED OUT.
I AM GLAD YOU WOULD DO THIS THING FOR ME, SAKURA-SAN.
IN THIS, I AM YOUR SERVANT.
I FEAR I ENJOYED THE CONFLICT TOO MUCH TO END IT.
IT REMINDED ME OF THE OLD DAYS.
BETTER DAYS.
THE CAT ENJOYS TOYING WITH THE MOUSE...
...BUT EVENTUALLY THE CAT TIRES, AND THE MOUSE MUST SUFFER ITS INEVITABLE FATE.
THIS IS SO.

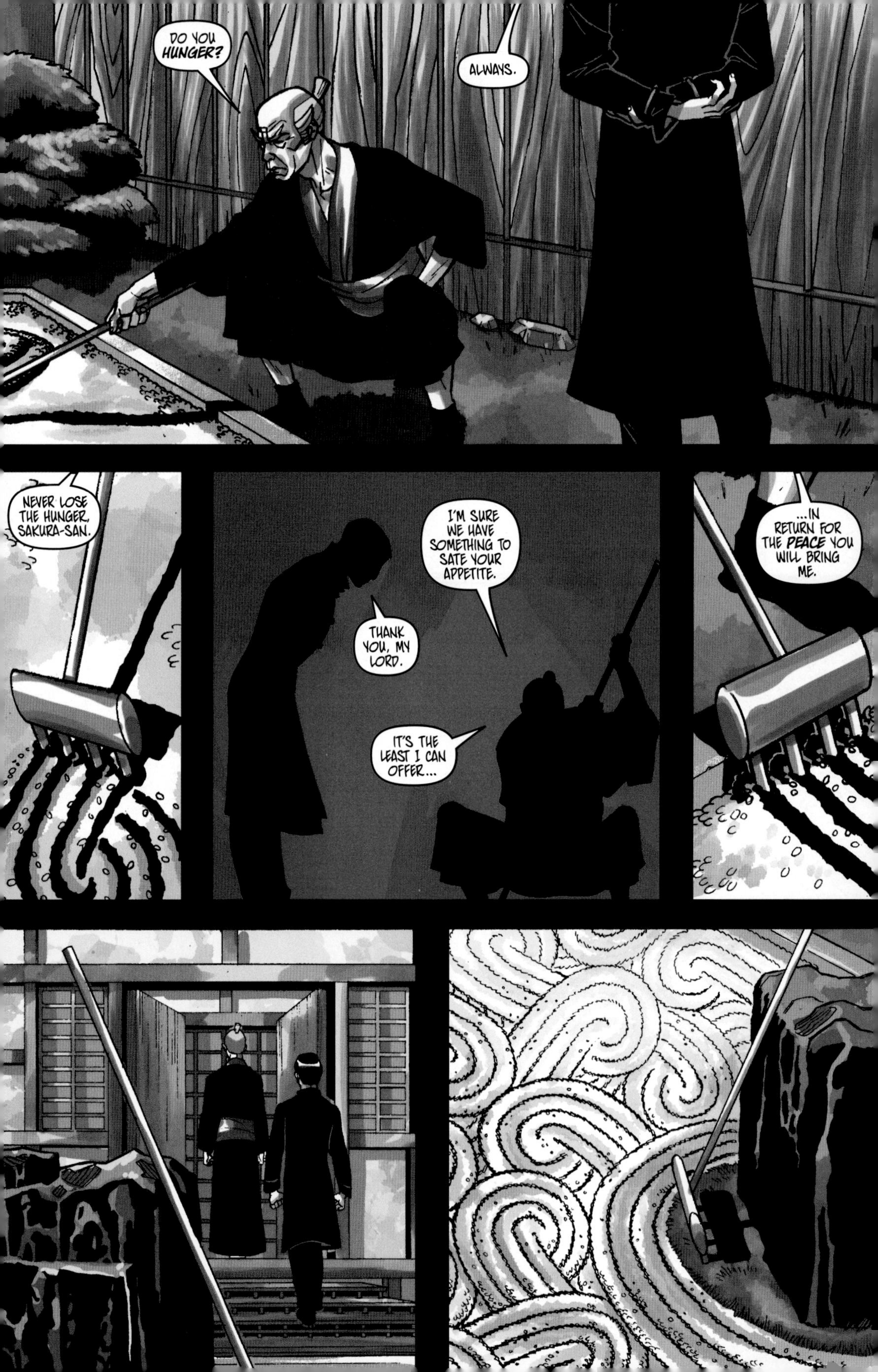
DO YOU HUNGER?
ALWAYS.
NEVER LOSE THE HUNGER, SAKURA-SAN.
I'M SURE WE HAVE SOMETHING TO SATE YOUR APPETITE.
THANK YOU, MY LORD.
IT'S THE LEAST I CAN OFFER...
...IN RETURN FOR THE PEACE YOU WILL BRING ME.

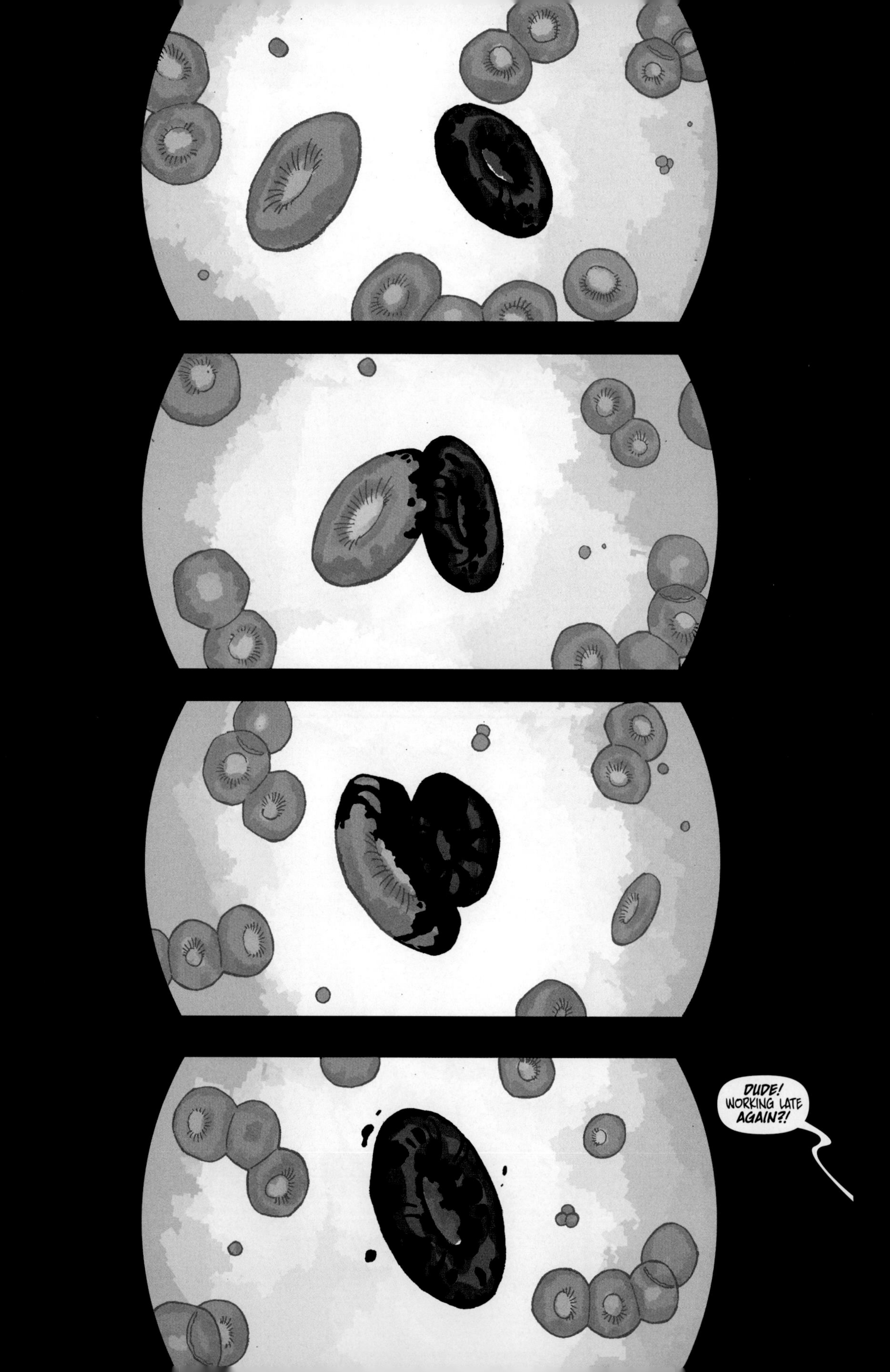
DUDE! WORKING LATE AGAIN?!

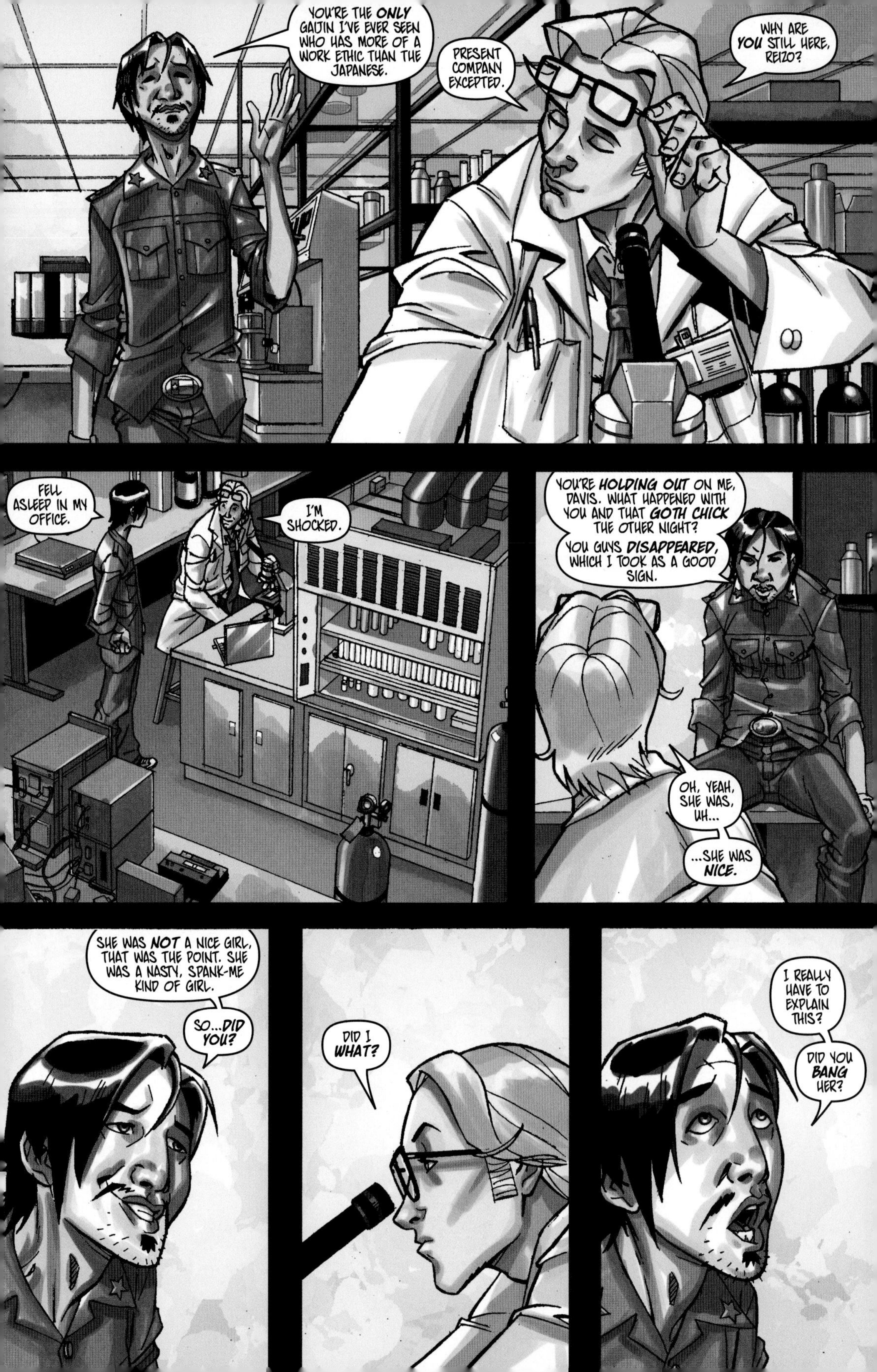
YOU'RE THE ONLY GAIJIN I'VE EVER SEEN WHO HAS MORE OF A WORK ETHIC THAN THE JAPANESE.
PRESENT COMPANY EXCEPTED.
WHY ARE YOU STILL HERE, REIZO?
FELL ASLEEP IN MY OFFICE.
I'M SHOCKED.
YOU'RE HOLDING OUT ON ME, DAVIS. WHAT HAPPENED WITH YOU AND THAT GOTH CHICK THE OTHER NIGHT?
YOU GUYS DISAPPEARED, WHICH I TOOK AS A GOOD SIGN.
OH, YEAH, SHE WAS, UH...
...SHE WAS NICE.
SHE WAS NOT A NICE GIRL, THAT WAS THE POINT. SHE WAS A NASTY, SPANK-ME KIND OF GIRL.
SO...DID YOU?
DID I WHAT?
I REALLY HAVE TO EXPLAIN THIS?
DID YOU BANG HER?

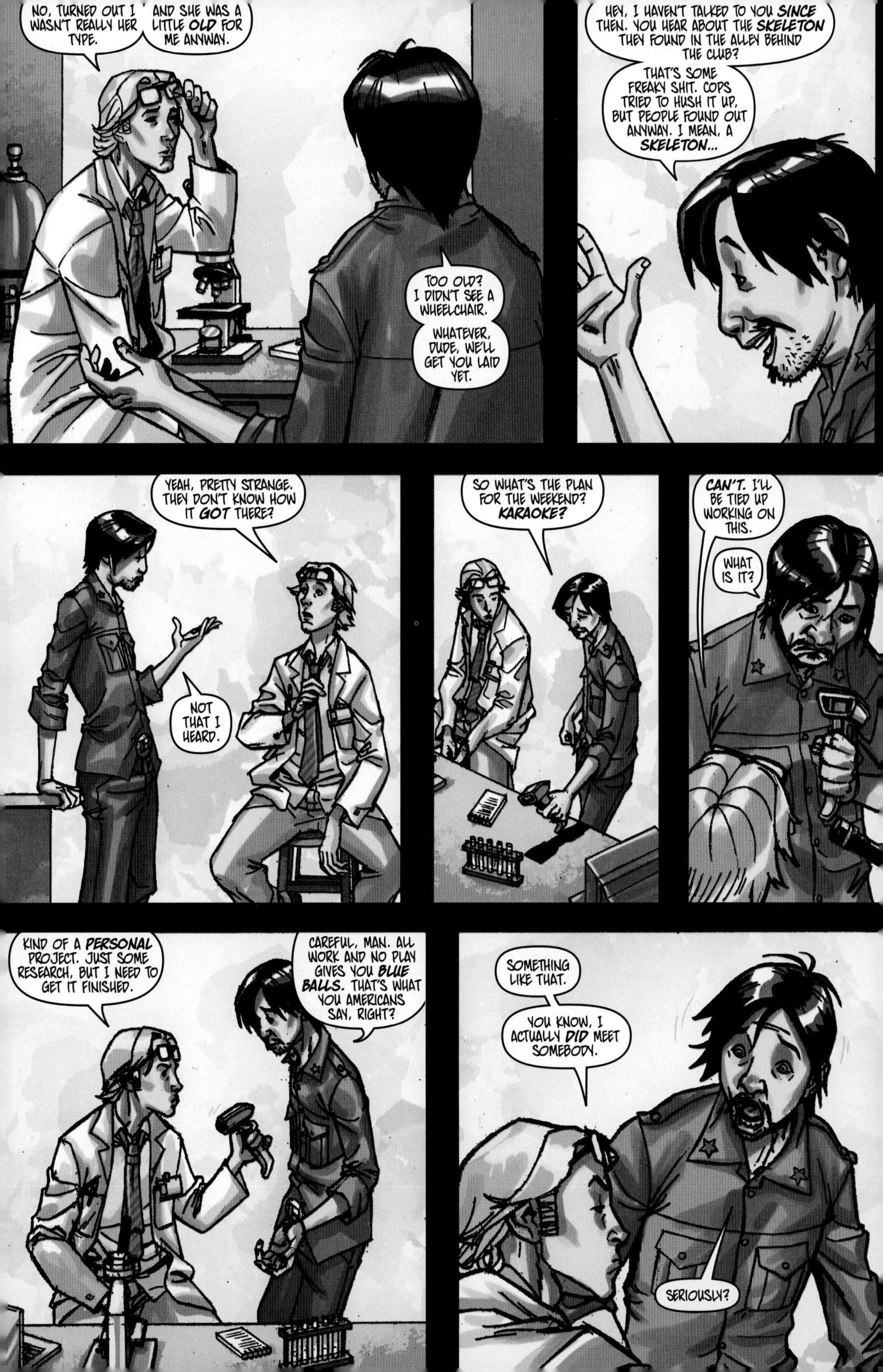
NO, TURNED OUT I WASN'T REALLY HER TYPE.
AND SHE WAS A LITTLE OLD FOR ME ANYWAY.
TOO OLD? I DIDN'T SEE A WHEELCHAIR.
WHATEVER, DUDE, WE'LL GET YOU LAID YET.
HEY, I HAVEN'T TALKED TO YOU SINCE THEN. YOU HEAR ABOUT THE SKELETON THEY FOUND IN THE ALLEY BEHIND THE CLUB?
THAT'S SOME FREAKY SHIT. COPS TRIED TO HUSH IT UP, BUT PEOPLE FOUND OUT ANYWAY. I MEAN, A SKELETON...
YEAH, PRETTY STRANGE. THEY DON'T KNOW HOW IT GOT THERE?
NOT THAT I HEARD.
SO WHAT'S THE PLAN FOR THE WEEKEND? KARAOKE?
CAN'T. I'LL BE TIED UP WORKING ON THIS.
WHAT IS IT?
KIND OF A PERSONAL PROJECT. JUST SOME RESEARCH, BUT I NEED TO GET IT FINISHED.
CAREFUL, MAN. ALL WORK AND NO PLAY GIVES YOU BLUE BALLS. THAT'S WHAT YOU AMERICANS SAY, RIGHT?
SOMETHING LIKE THAT.
YOU KNOW, I ACTUALLY DID MEET SOMEBODY.
SERIOUSLY?

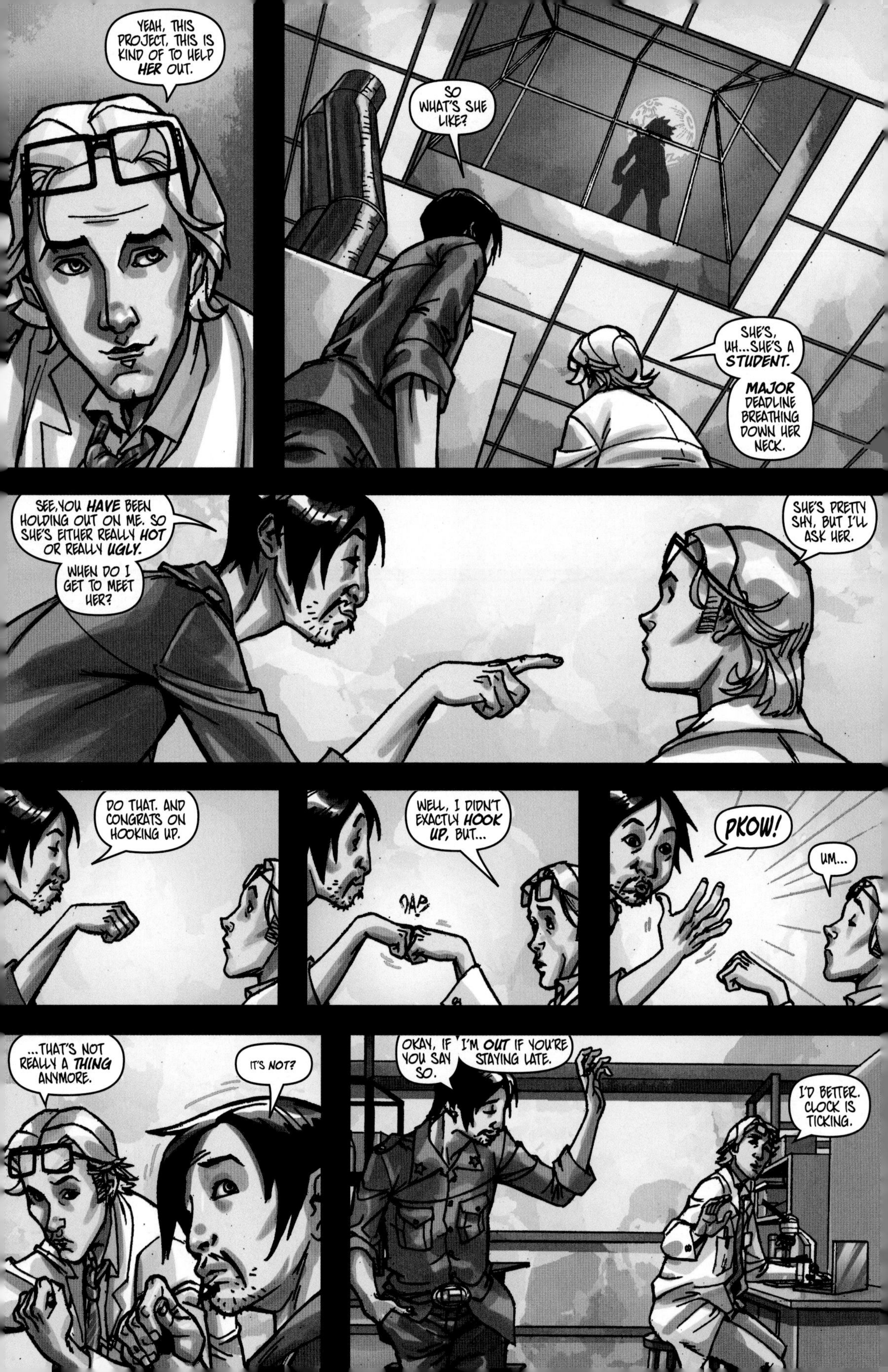
YEAH, THIS PROJECT, THIS IS KIND OF TO HELP HER OUT.
SO WHAT'S SHE LIKE?
SHE'S, UH...SHE'S A STUDENT.
MAJOR DEADLINE BREATHING DOWN HER NECK.
SEE, YOU HAVE BEEN HOLDING OUT ON ME. SO SHE'S EITHER REALLY HOT OR REALLY UGLY.
WHEN DO I GET TO MEET HER?
SHE'S PRETTY SHY, BUT I'LL ASK HER.
DO THAT. AND CONGRATS ON HOOKING UP.
WELL, I DIDN'T EXACTLY HOOK UP, BUT...
DAP
PKOW!
UM...
...THAT'S NOT REALLY A THING ANYMORE.
IT'S NOT?
OKAY, IF YOU SAY SO.
I'M OUT IF YOU'RE STAYING LATE.
I'D BETTER. CLOCK IS TICKING.

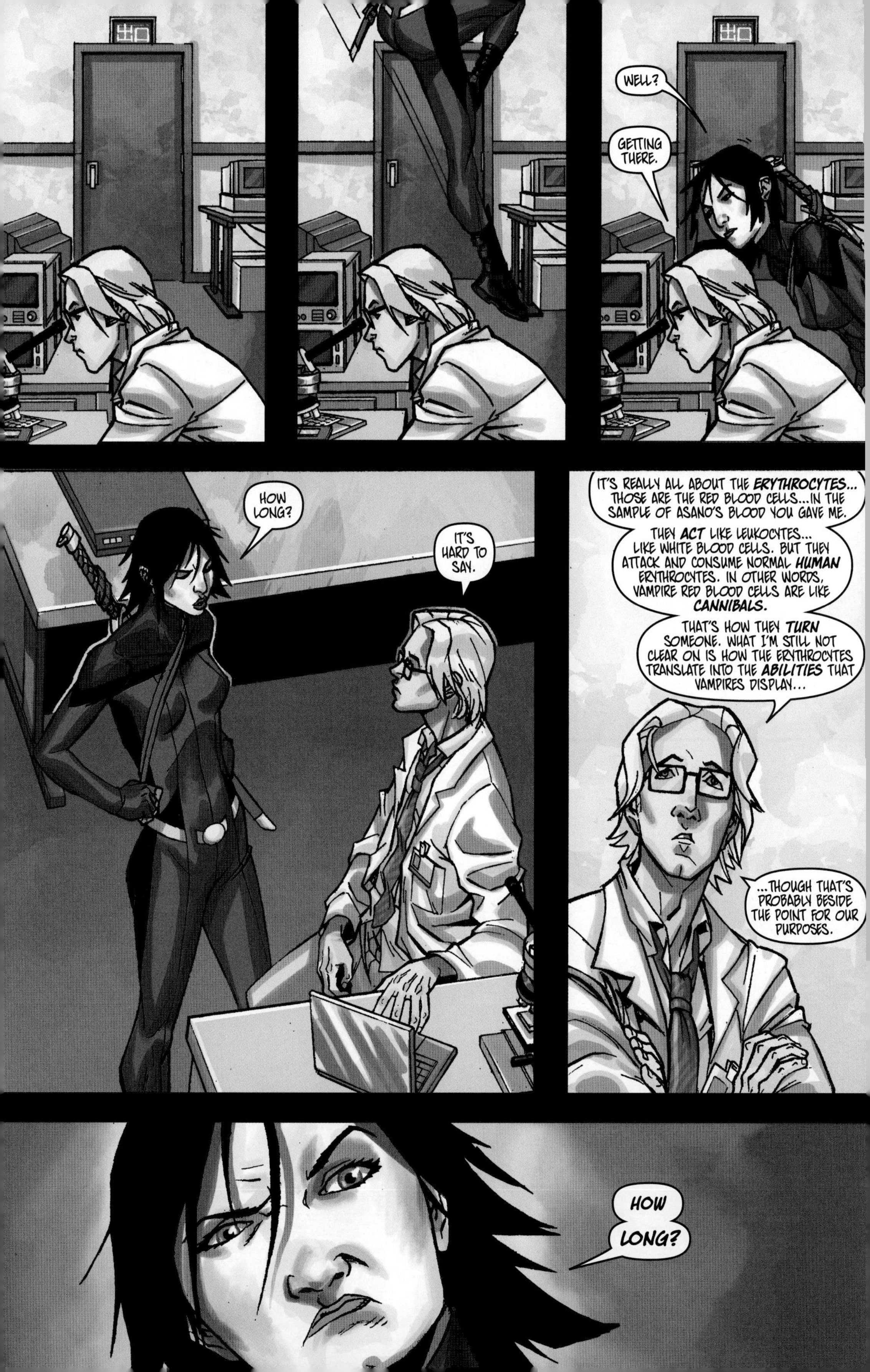
WELL?
GETTING THERE.
HOW LONG?
IT'S HARD TO SAY.
IT'S REALLY ALL ABOUT THE ERYTHROCYTES... THOSE ARE THE RED BLOOD CELLS...IN THE SAMPLE OF ASANO'S BLOOD YOU GAVE ME.
THEY ACT LIKE LEUKOCYTES... LIKE WHITE BLOOD CELLS. BUT THEY ATTACK AND CONSUME NORMAL HUMAN ERYTHROCYTES. IN OTHER WORDS, VAMPIRE RED BLOOD CELLS ARE LIKE CANNIBALS.
THAT'S HOW THEY TURN SOMEONE. WHAT I'M STILL NOT CLEAR ON IS HOW THE ERYTHROCYTES TRANSLATE INTO THE ABILITIES THAT VAMPIRES DISPLAY...
...THOUGH THAT'S PROBABLY BESIDE THE POINT FOR OUR PURPOSES.
HOW LONG?

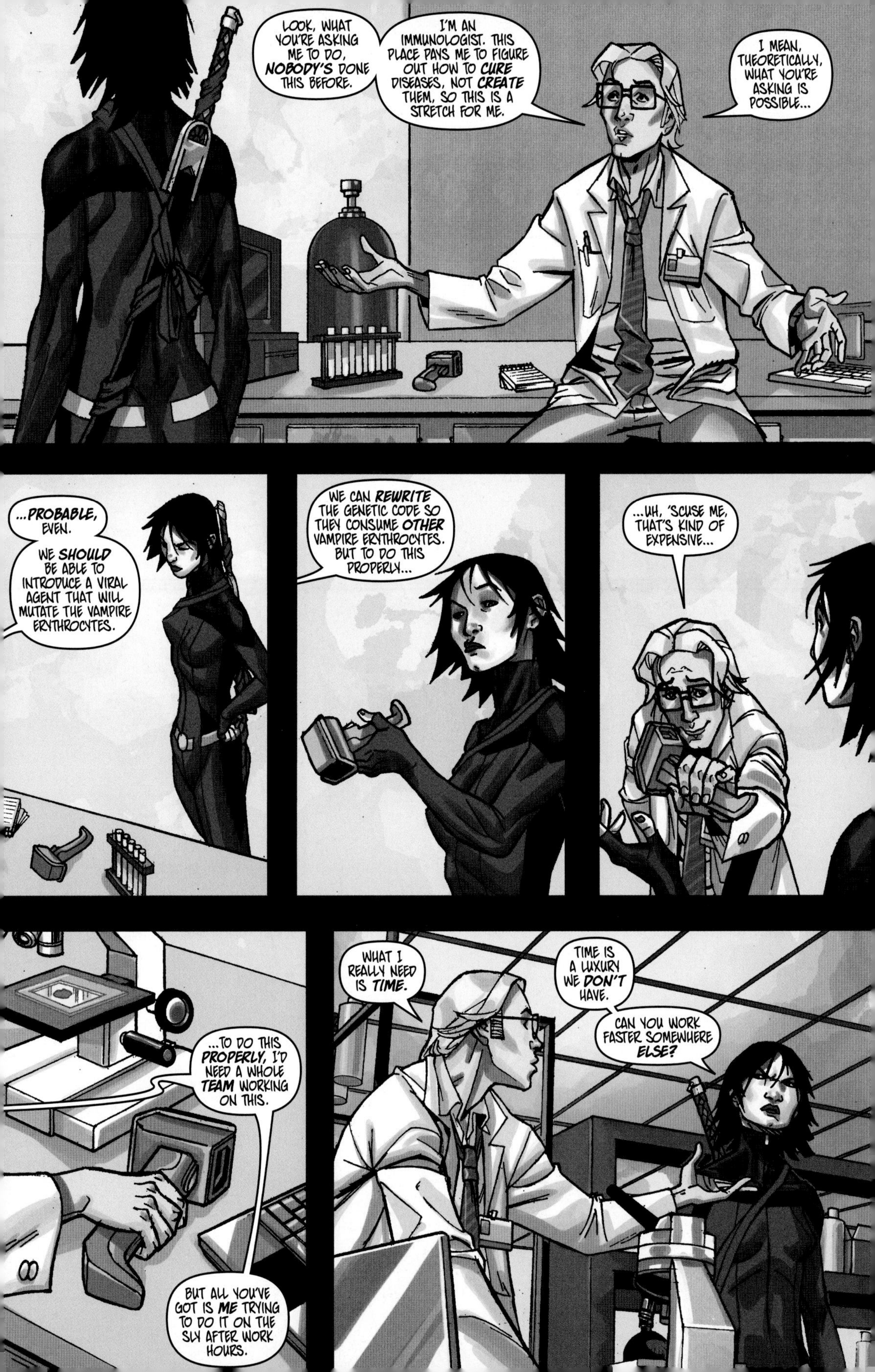
LOOK, WHAT YOU'RE ASKING ME TO DO, NOBODY'S DONE THIS BEFORE.
I'M AN IMMUNOLOGIST. THIS PLACE PAYS ME TO FIGURE OUT HOW TO CURE DISEASES, NOT CREATE THEM, SO THIS IS A STRETCH FOR ME.
I MEAN, THEORETICALLY, WHAT YOU'RE ASKING IS POSSIBLE...
...PROBABLE, EVEN.
WE SHOULD BE ABLE TO INTRODUCE A VIRAL AGENT THAT WILL MUTATE THE VAMPIRE ERYTHROCYTES.
WE CAN REWRITE THE GENETIC CODE SO THEY CONSUME OTHER VAMPIRE ERYTHROCYTES. BUT TO DO THIS PROPERLY...
...UH, 'SCUSE ME, THAT'S KIND OF EXPENSIVE...
...TO DO THIS PROPERLY, I'D NEED A WHOLE TEAM WORKING ON THIS.
BUT ALL YOU'VE GOT IS ME TRYING TO DO IT ON THE SLY AFTER WORK HOURS.
WHAT I REALLY NEED IS TIME.
TIME IS A LUXURY WE DON'T HAVE.
CAN YOU WORK FASTER SOMEWHERE ELSE?

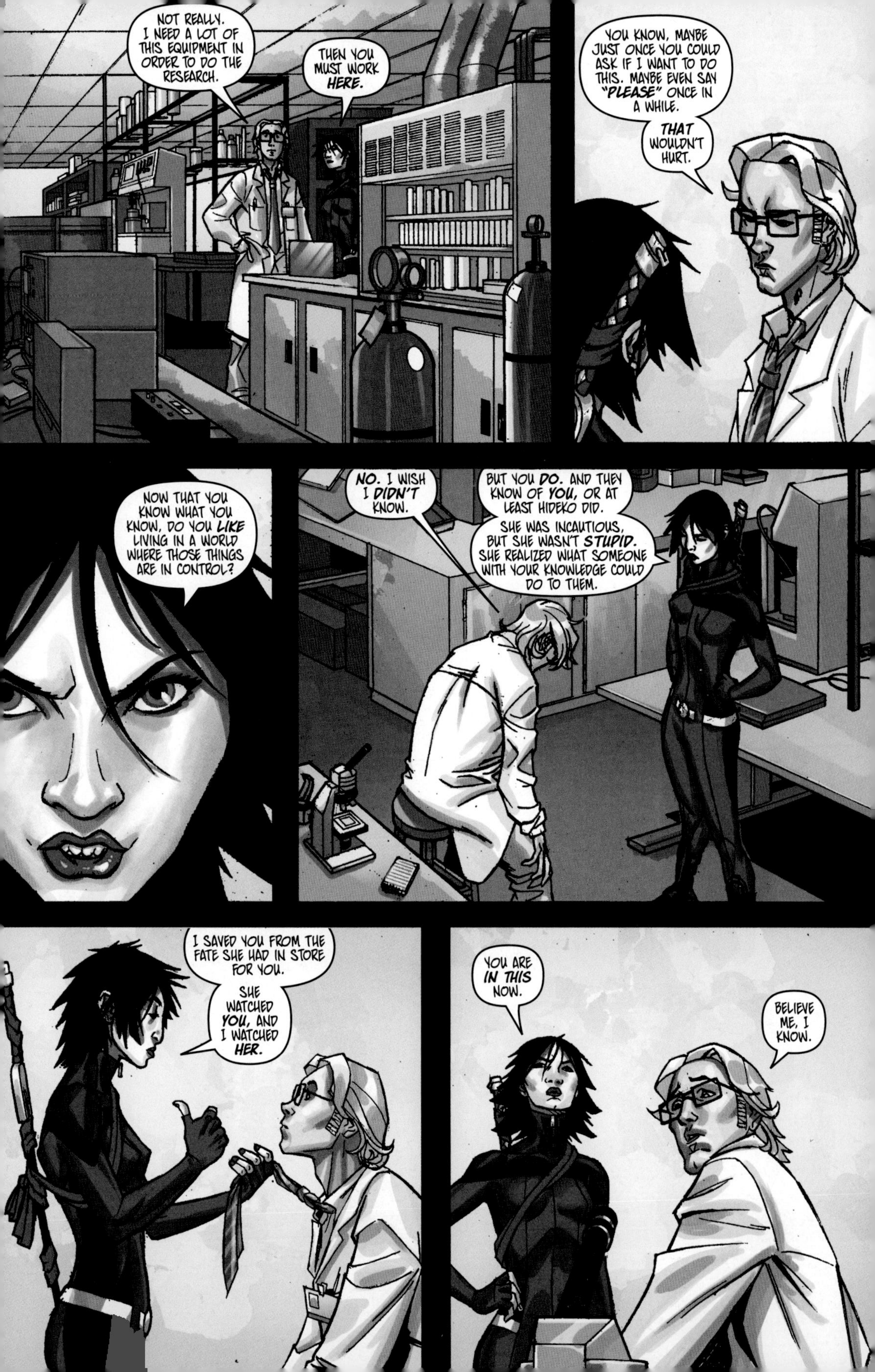
NOT REALLY. I NEED A LOT OF THIS EQUIPMENT IN ORDER TO DO THE RESEARCH.
THEN YOU MUST WORK HERE.
YOU KNOW, MAYBE JUST ONCE YOU COULD ASK IF I WANT TO DO THIS. MAYBE EVEN SAY "PLEASE" ONCE IN A WHILE.
THAT WOULDN'T HURT.
NOW THAT YOU KNOW WHAT YOU KNOW, DO YOU LIKE LIVING IN A WORLD WHERE THOSE THINGS ARE IN CONTROL?
NO. I WISH I DIDN'T KNOW.
BUT YOU DO. AND THEY KNOW OF YOU, OR AT LEAST HIDEKO DID.
SHE WAS INCAUTIOUS, BUT SHE WASN'T STUPID. SHE REALIZED WHAT SOMEONE WITH YOUR KNOWLEDGE COULD DO TO THEM.
I SAVED YOU FROM THE FATE SHE HAD IN STORE FOR YOU.
SHE WATCHED YOU, AND I WATCHED HER.
YOU ARE IN THIS NOW.
BELIEVE ME, I KNOW.

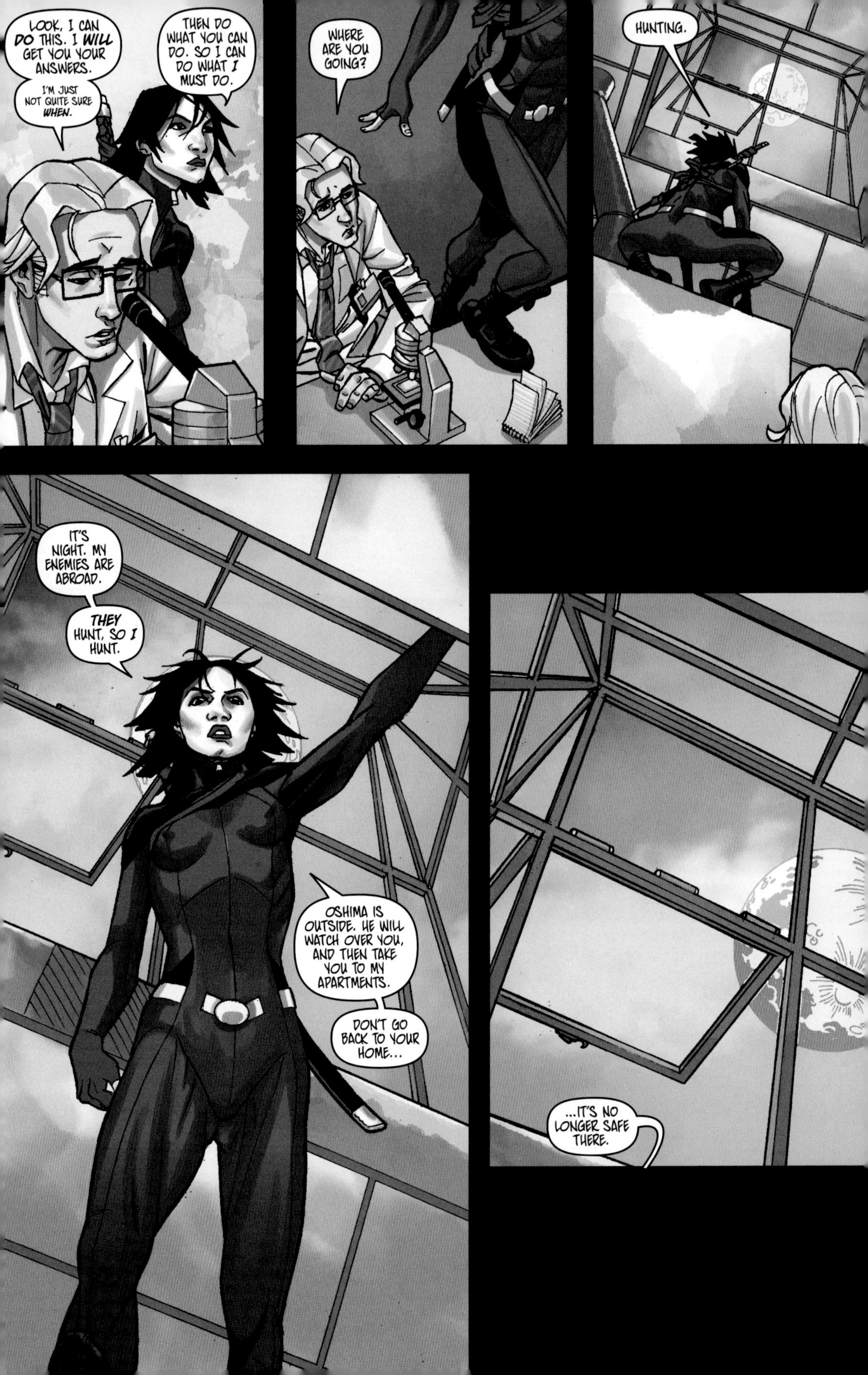

LOOK, I CAN **DO** THIS. I **WILL** GET YOU YOUR ANSWERS.
I'M JUST NOT QUITE SURE ***WHEN***.
THEN DO WHAT YOU CAN DO. SO I CAN DO WHAT ***I*** MUST DO.
WHERE ARE YOU GOING?
HUNTING.
IT'S NIGHT. MY ENEMIES ARE ABROAD.
THEY HUNT, SO ***I*** HUNT.
OSHIMA IS OUTSIDE. HE WILL WATCH OVER YOU, AND THEN TAKE YOU TO MY APARTMENTS.
DON'T GO BACK TO YOUR HOME...
...IT'S NO LONGER SAFE THERE.

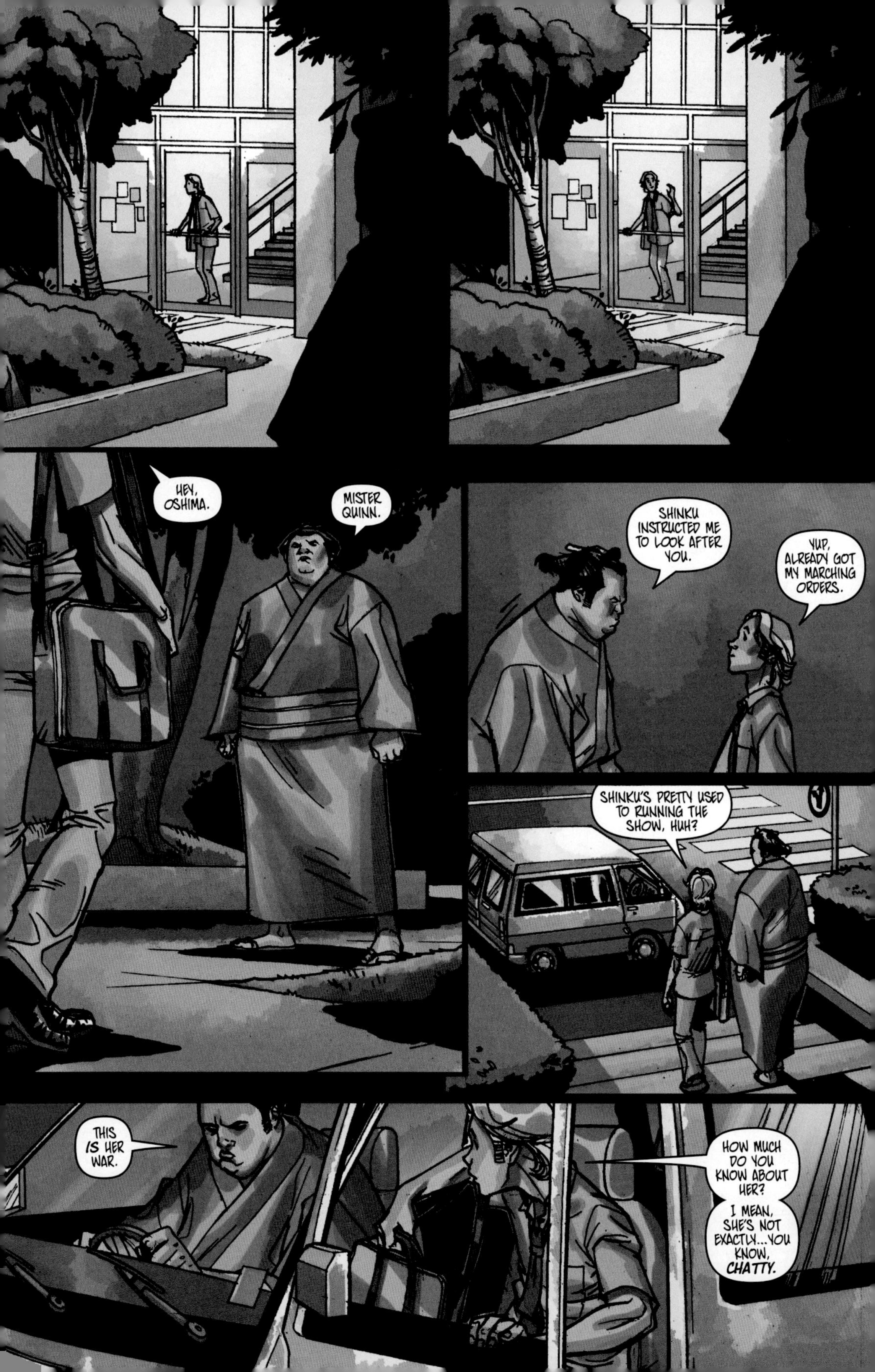
HEY, OSHIMA.
MISTER QUINN.
SHINKU INSTRUCTED ME TO LOOK AFTER YOU.
YUP, ALREADY GOT MY MARCHING ORDERS.
SHINKU'S PRETTY USED TO RUNNING THE SHOW, HUH?
THIS *IS* HER WAR.
HOW MUCH DO YOU KNOW ABOUT HER?
I MEAN, SHE'S NOT EXACTLY...YOU KNOW, ***CHATTY***.

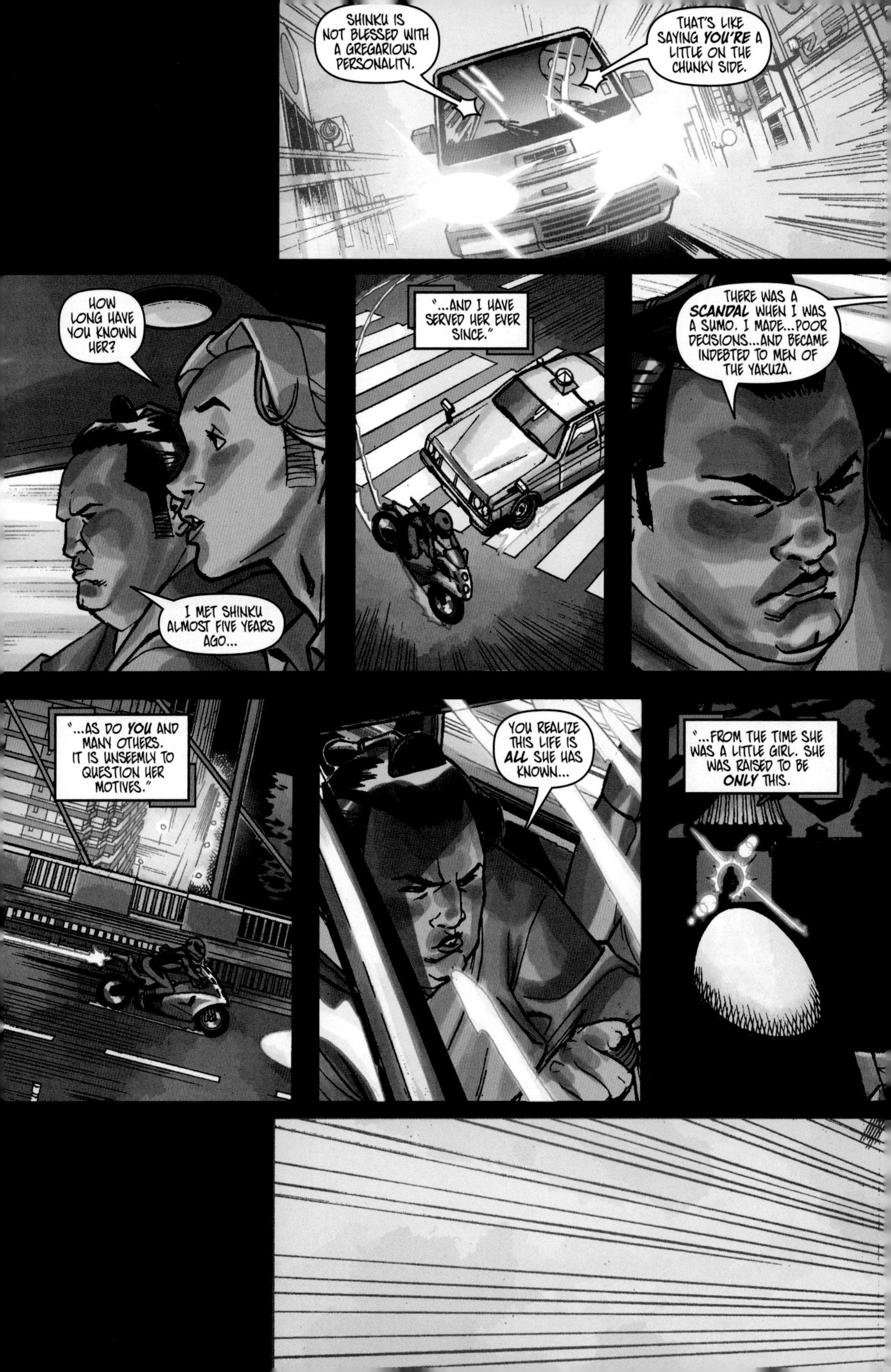
SHINKU IS NOT BLESSED WITH A GREGARIOUS PERSONALITY.
THAT'S LIKE SAYING YOU'RE A LITTLE ON THE CHUNKY SIDE.
HOW LONG HAVE YOU KNOWN HER?
I MET SHINKU ALMOST FIVE YEARS AGO...
"...AND I HAVE SERVED HER EVER SINCE."
THERE WAS A SCANDAL WHEN I WAS A SUMO. I MADE...POOR DECISIONS...AND BECAME INDEBTED TO MEN OF THE YAKUZA.
"...AS DO YOU AND MANY OTHERS. IT IS UNSEEMLY TO QUESTION HER MOTIVES."
YOU REALIZE THIS LIFE IS ALL SHE HAS KNOWN...
"...FROM THE TIME SHE WAS A LITTLE GIRL. SHE WAS RAISED TO BE ONLY THIS.

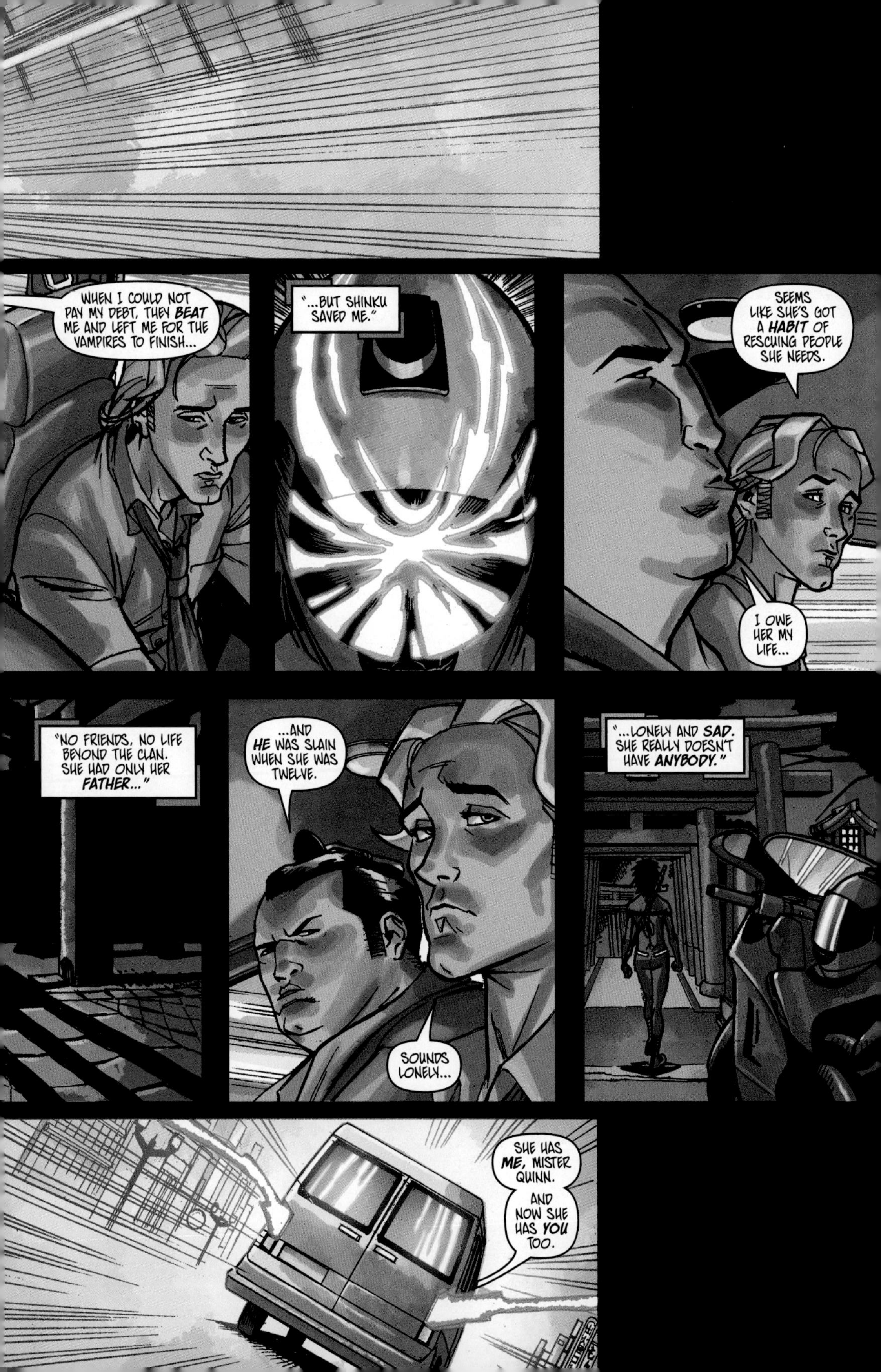
WHEN I COULD NOT PAY MY DEBT, THEY BEAT ME AND LEFT ME FOR THE VAMPIRES TO FINISH...
"...BUT SHINKU SAVED ME."
SEEMS LIKE SHE'S GOT A HABIT OF RESCUING PEOPLE SHE NEEDS.
I OWE HER MY LIFE...
"NO FRIENDS, NO LIFE BEYOND THE CLAN. SHE HAD ONLY HER FATHER..."
...AND HE WAS SLAIN WHEN SHE WAS TWELVE.
SOUNDS LONELY...
"...LONELY AND SAD. SHE REALLY DOESN'T HAVE ANYBODY."
SHE HAS ME, MISTER QUINN.
AND NOW SHE HAS YOU TOO.

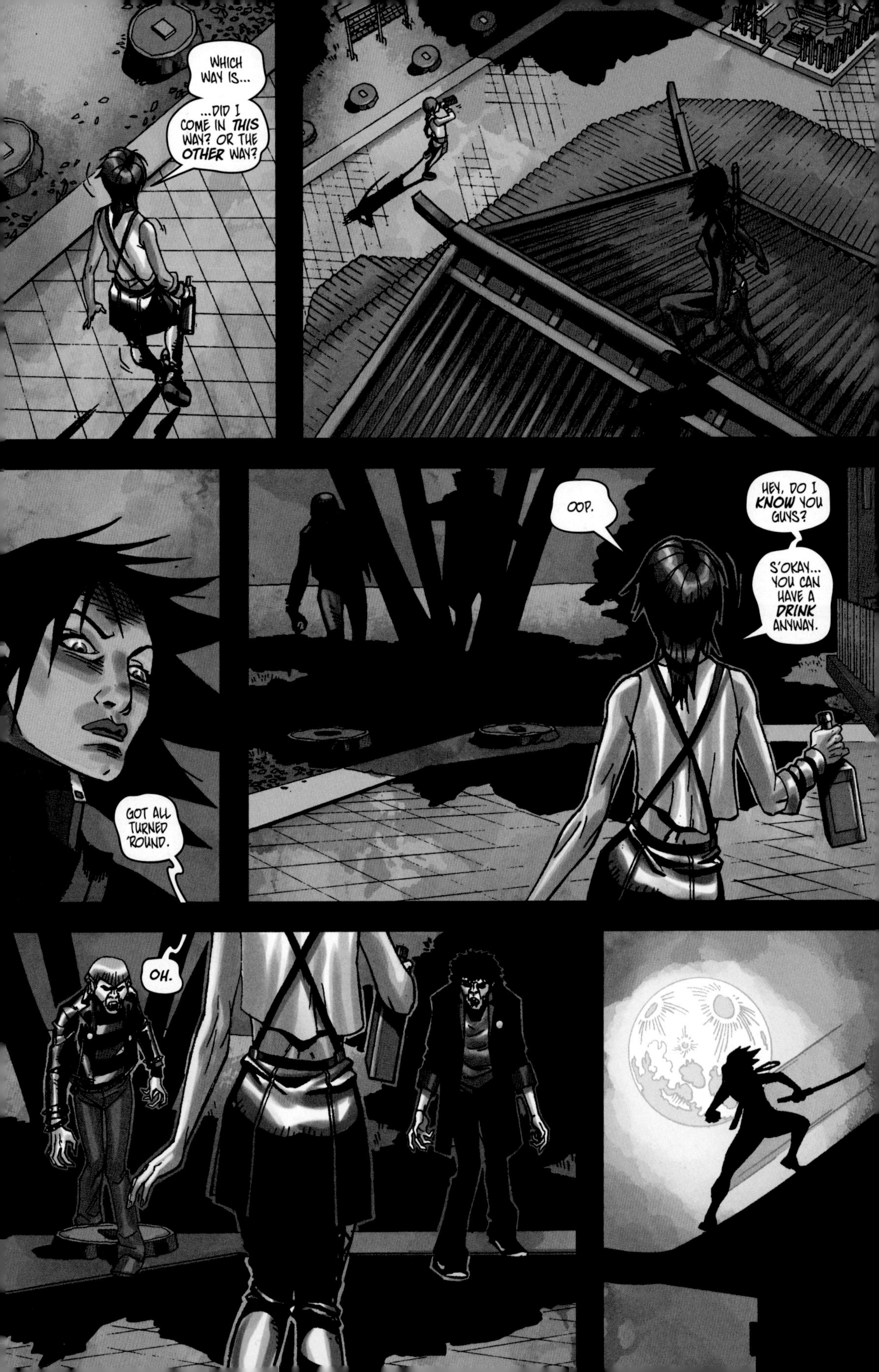
WHICH WAY IS...
...DID I COME IN THIS WAY? OR THE OTHER WAY?
GOT ALL TURNED 'ROUND.
OOP.
HEY, DO I KNOW YOU GUYS?
S'OKAY... YOU CAN HAVE A DRINK ANYWAY.
OH.

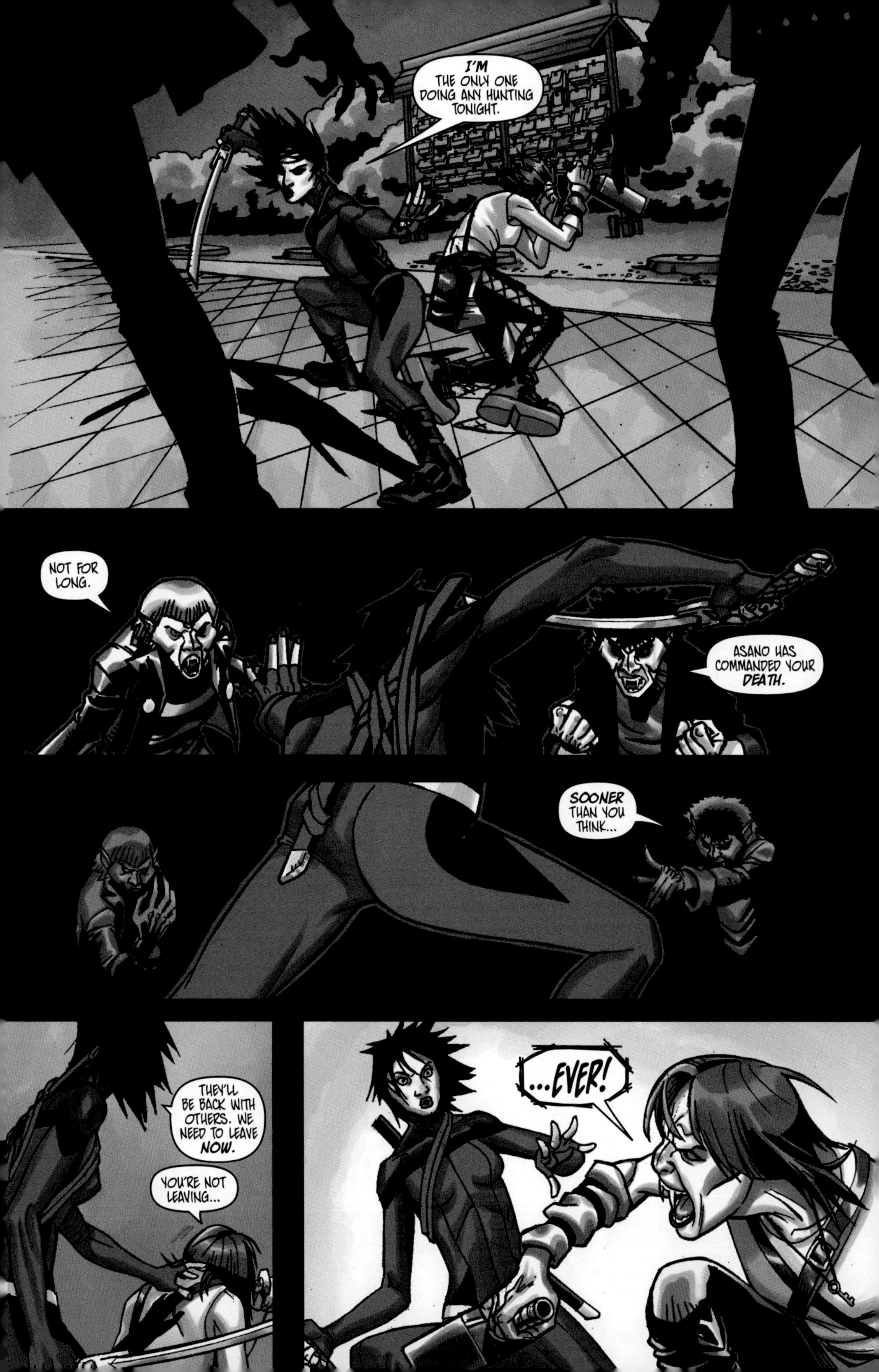
I'M THE ONLY ONE DOING ANY HUNTING TONIGHT.
NOT FOR LONG.
ASANO HAS COMMANDED YOUR DEATH.
SOONER THAN YOU THINK...
THEY'LL BE BACK WITH OTHERS. WE NEED TO LEAVE NOW.
YOU'RE NOT LEAVING...
...EVER!

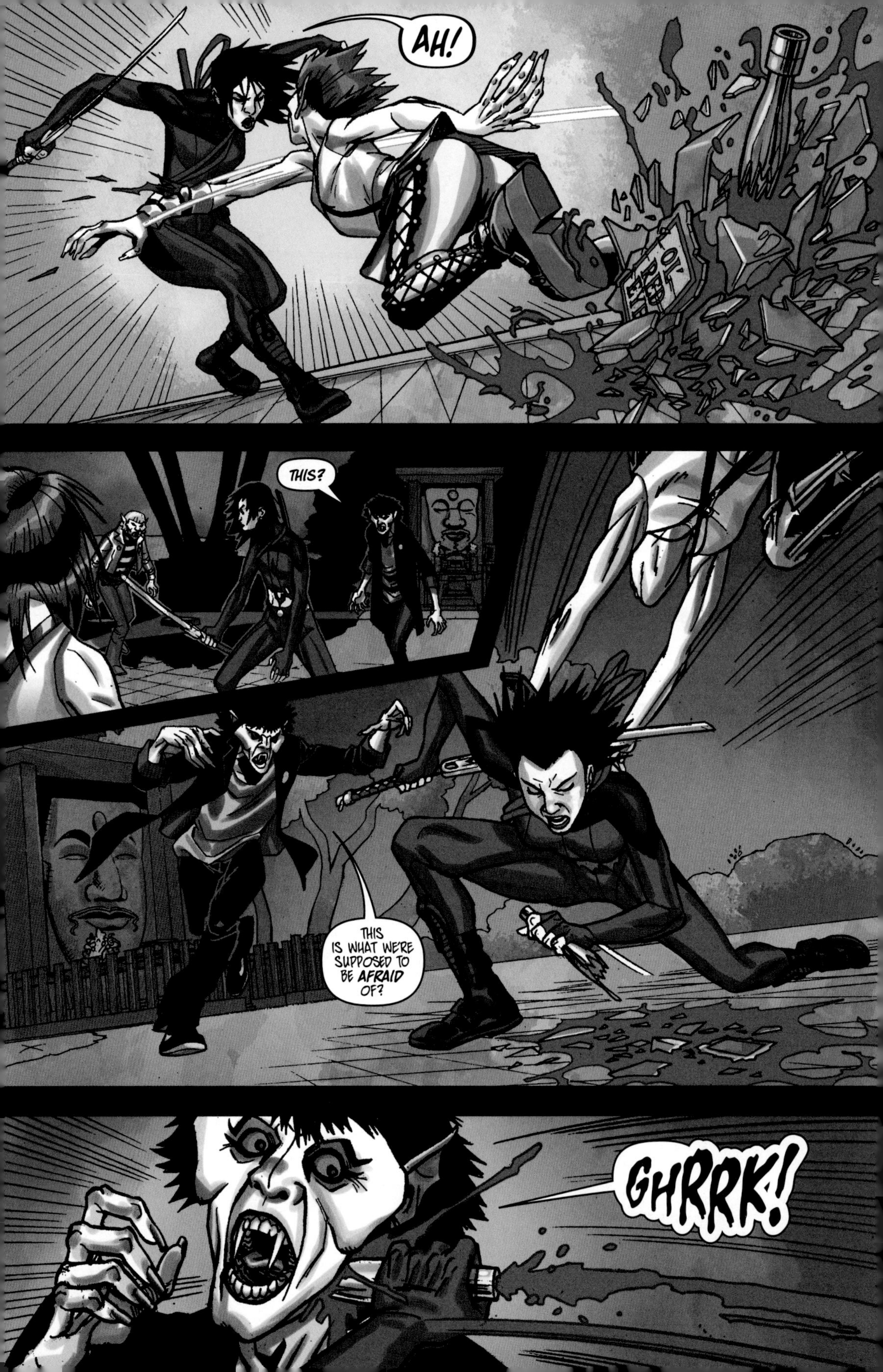
AH!
THIS?
THIS IS WHAT WE'RE SUPPOSED TO BE AFRAID OF?
GHRRK!

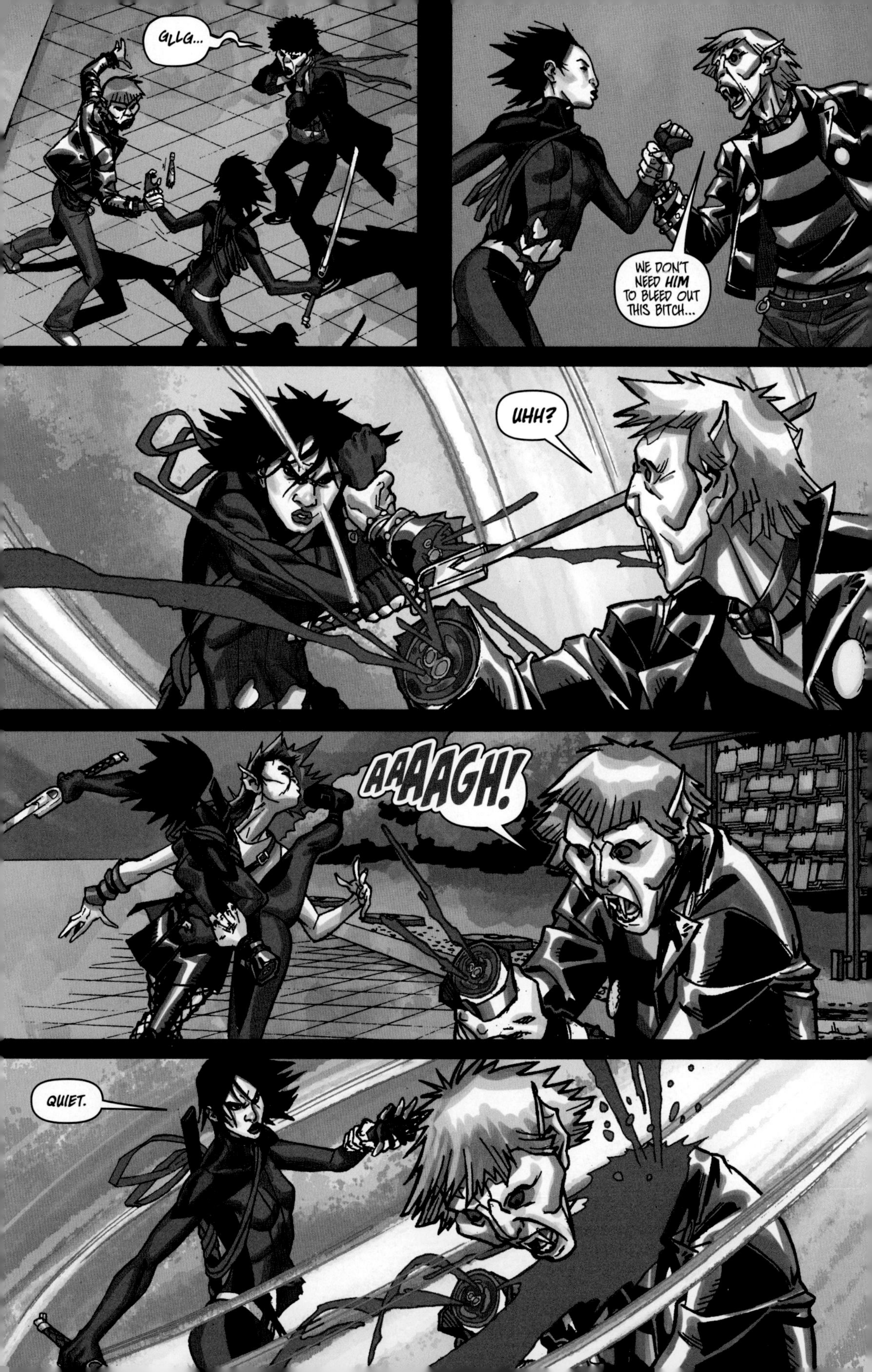
GLLG...
WE DON'T NEED HIM TO BLEED OUT THIS BITCH...
UHH?
AAAAGH!
QUIET.

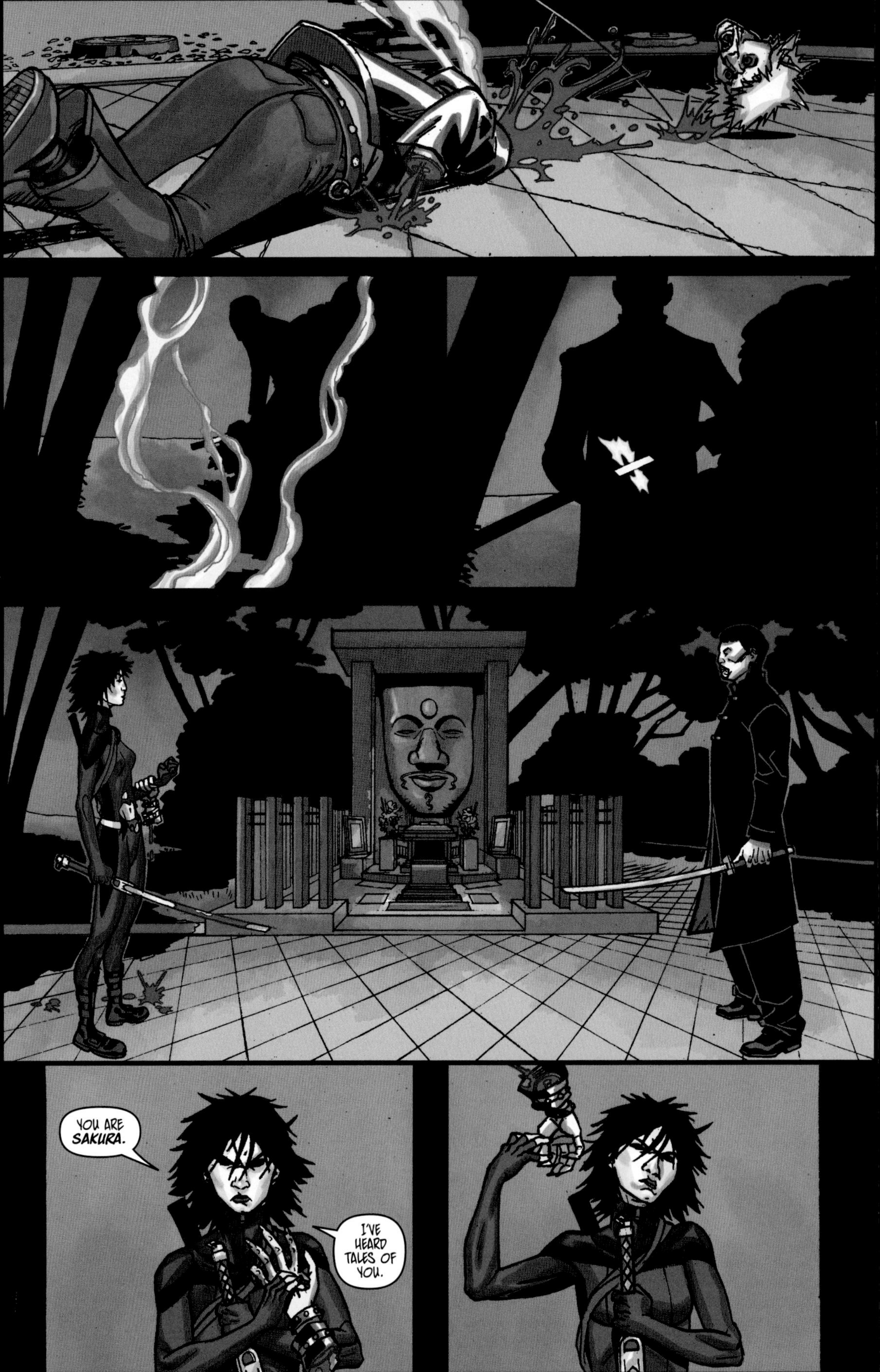
YOU ARE **SAKURA**.
I'VE HEARD TALES OF YOU.

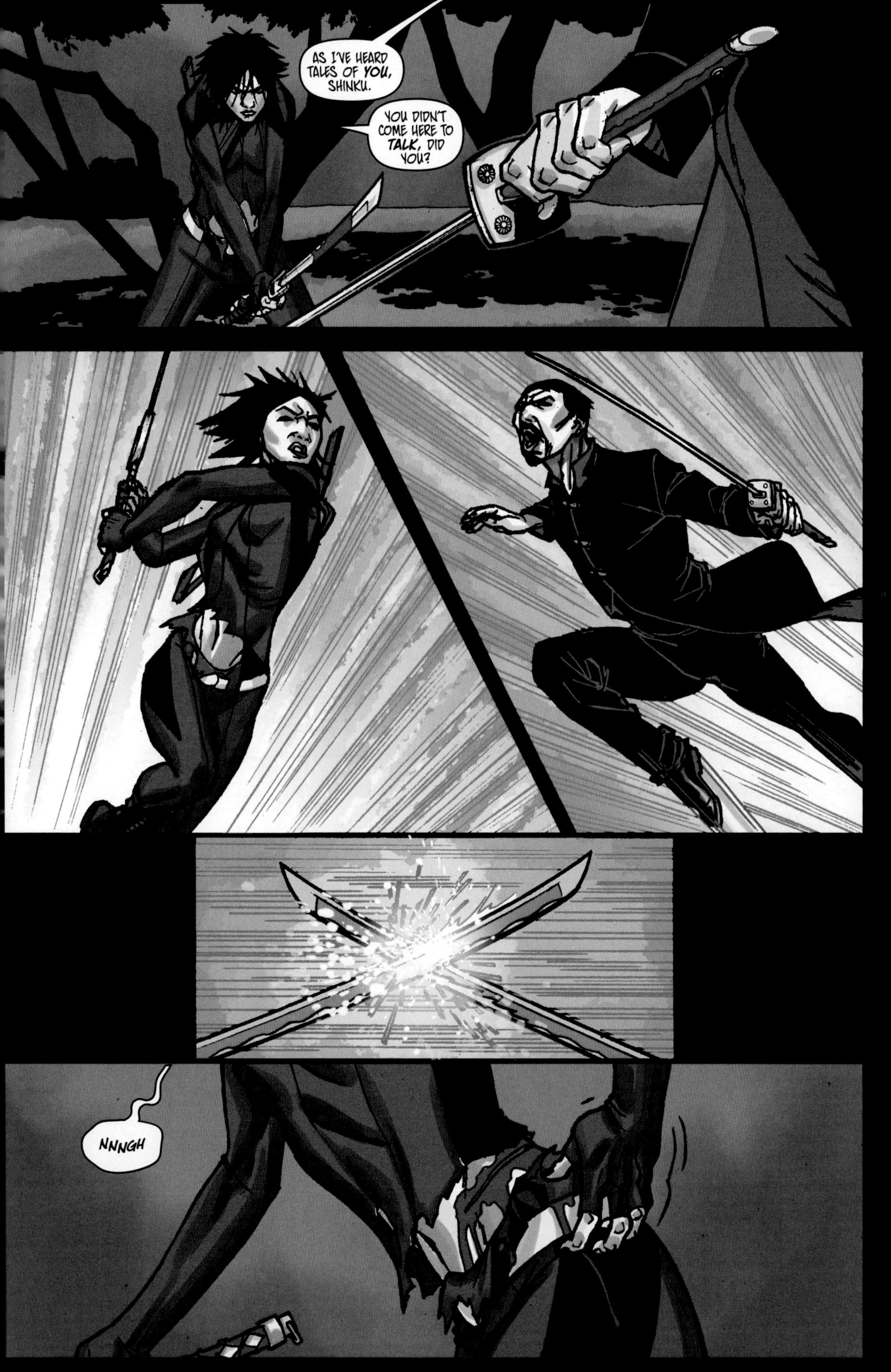
AS I'VE HEARD TALES OF YOU, SHINKU.
YOU DIDN'T COME HERE TO TALK, DID YOU?
NNNGH

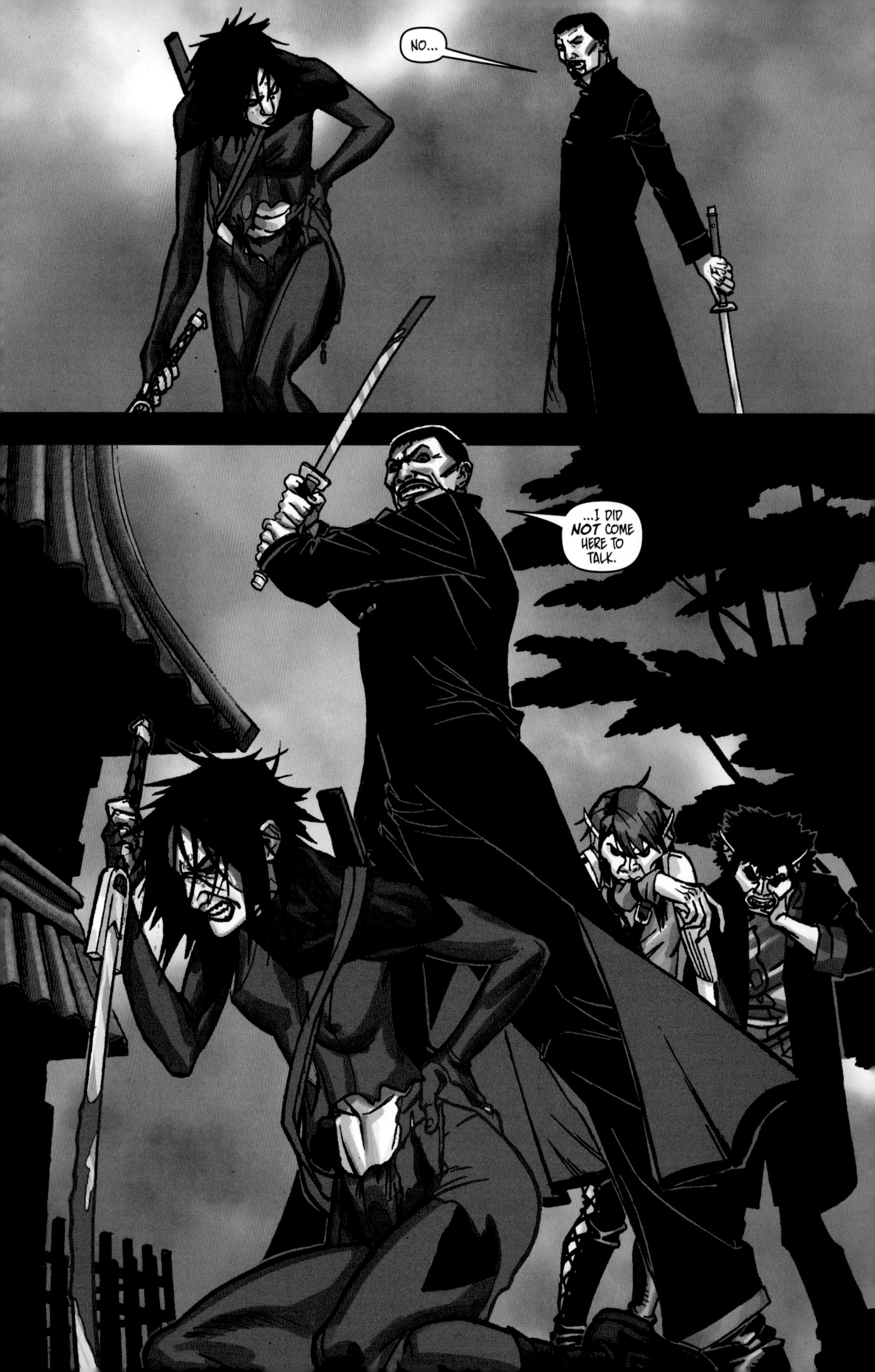
NO...
...I DID NOT COME HERE TO TALK.

Chapter 4

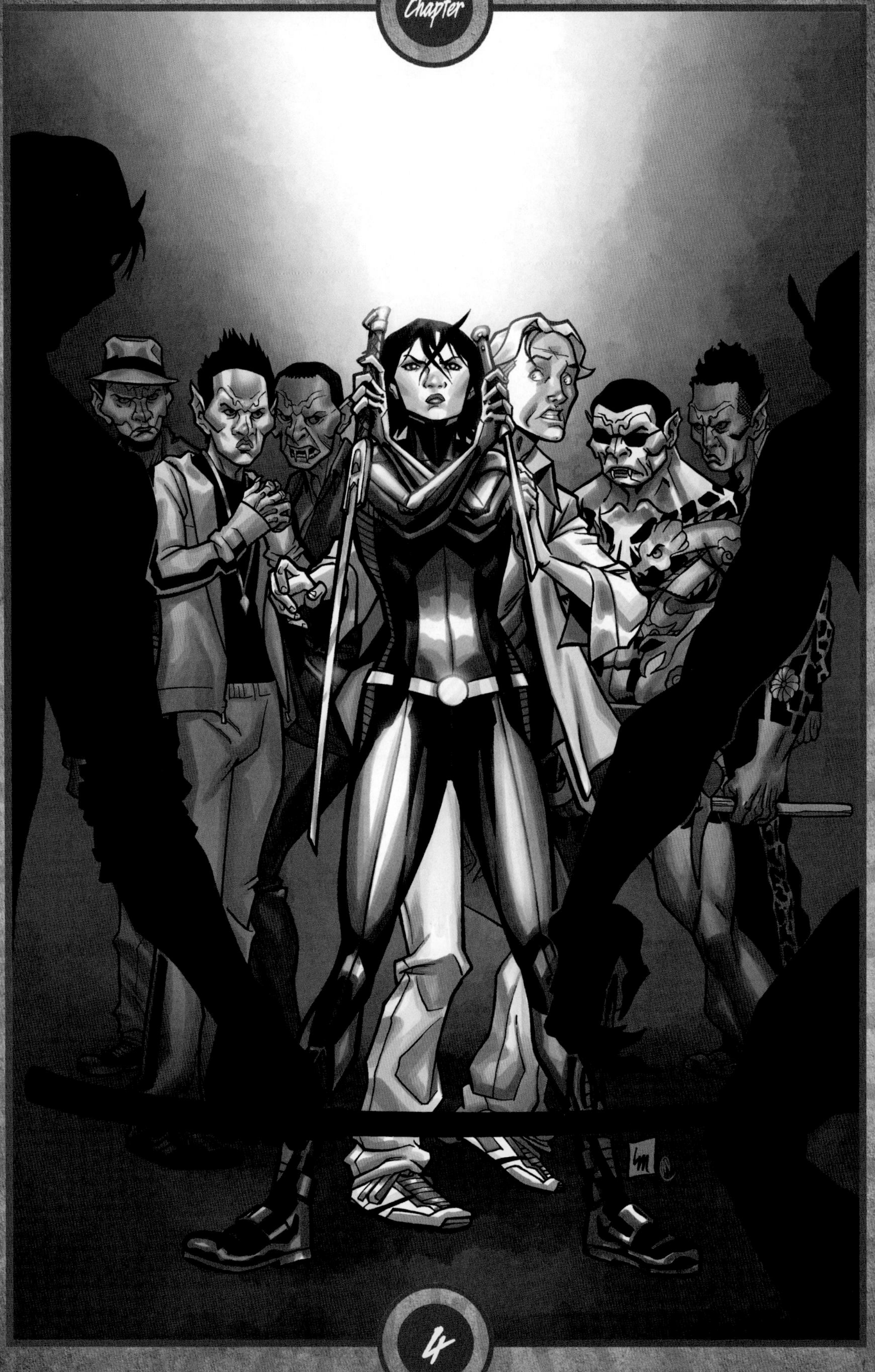

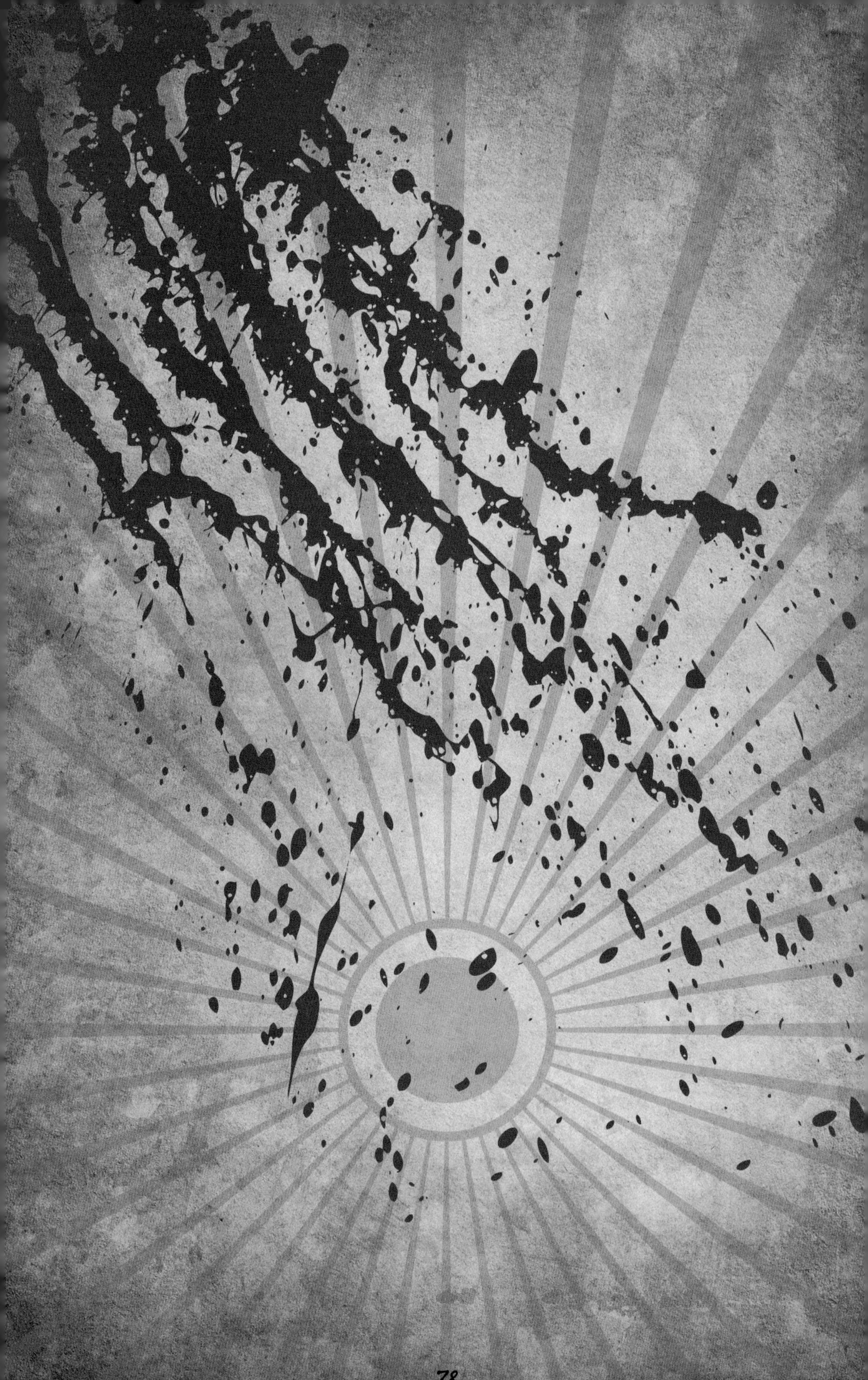

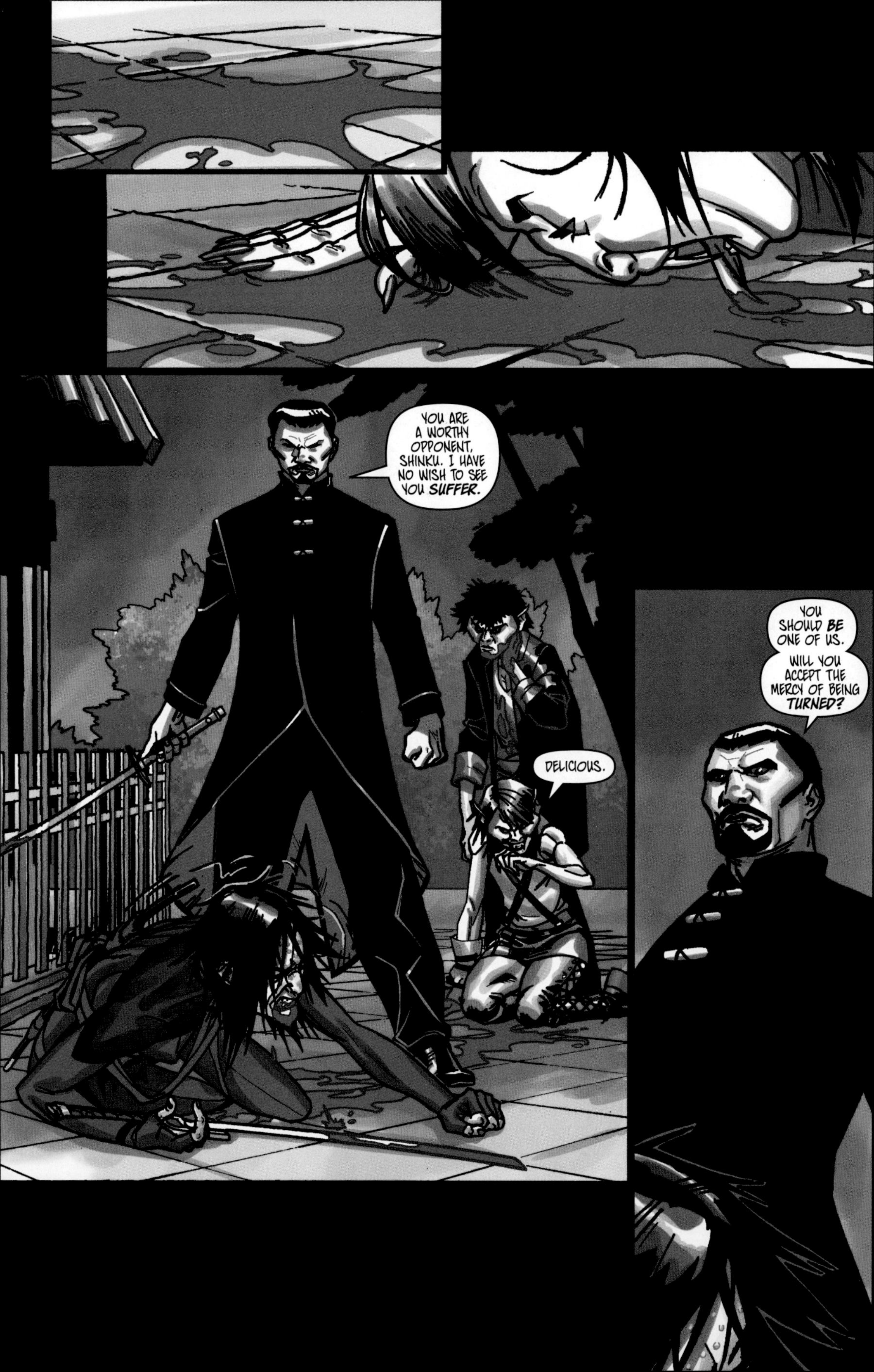
YOU ARE A WORTHY OPPONENT, SHINKU. I HAVE NO WISH TO SEE YOU SUFFER.
DELICIOUS.
YOU SHOULD BE ONE OF US.
WILL YOU ACCEPT THE MERCY OF BEING TURNED?

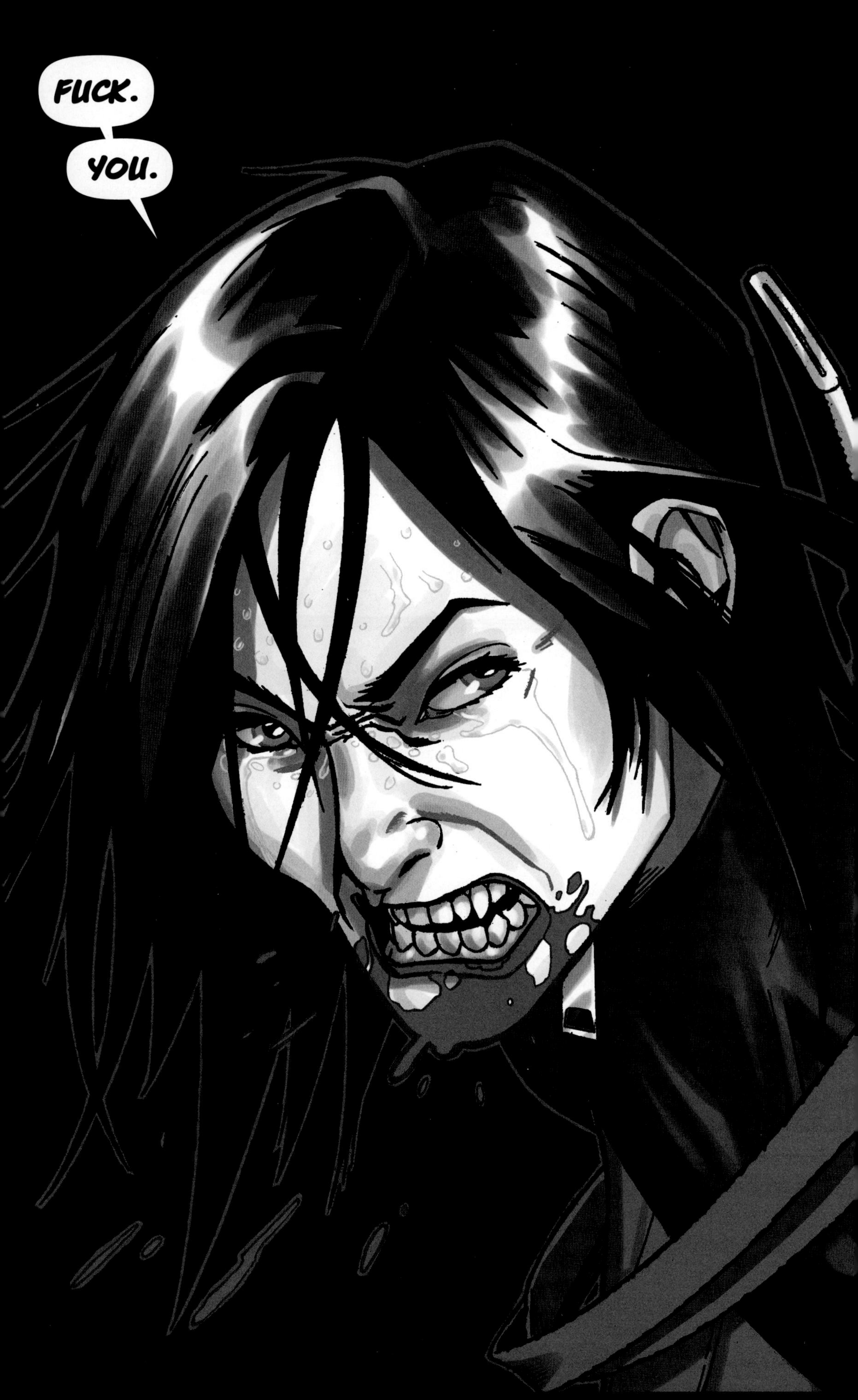
FUCK.
YOU.

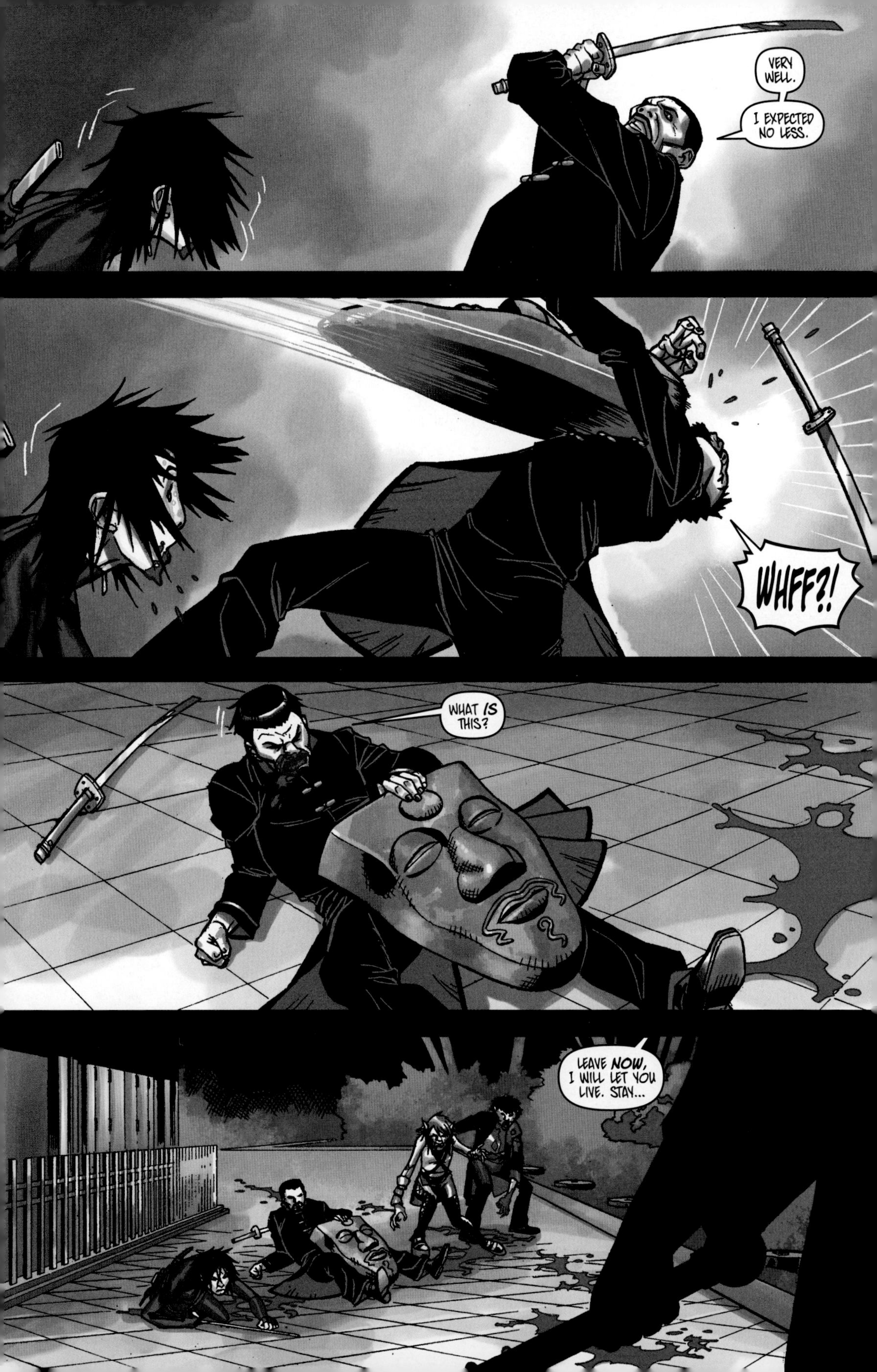

VERY WELL.
I EXPECTED NO LESS.
WHFF?!
WHAT IS THIS?
LEAVE NOW, I WILL LET YOU LIVE. STAY...

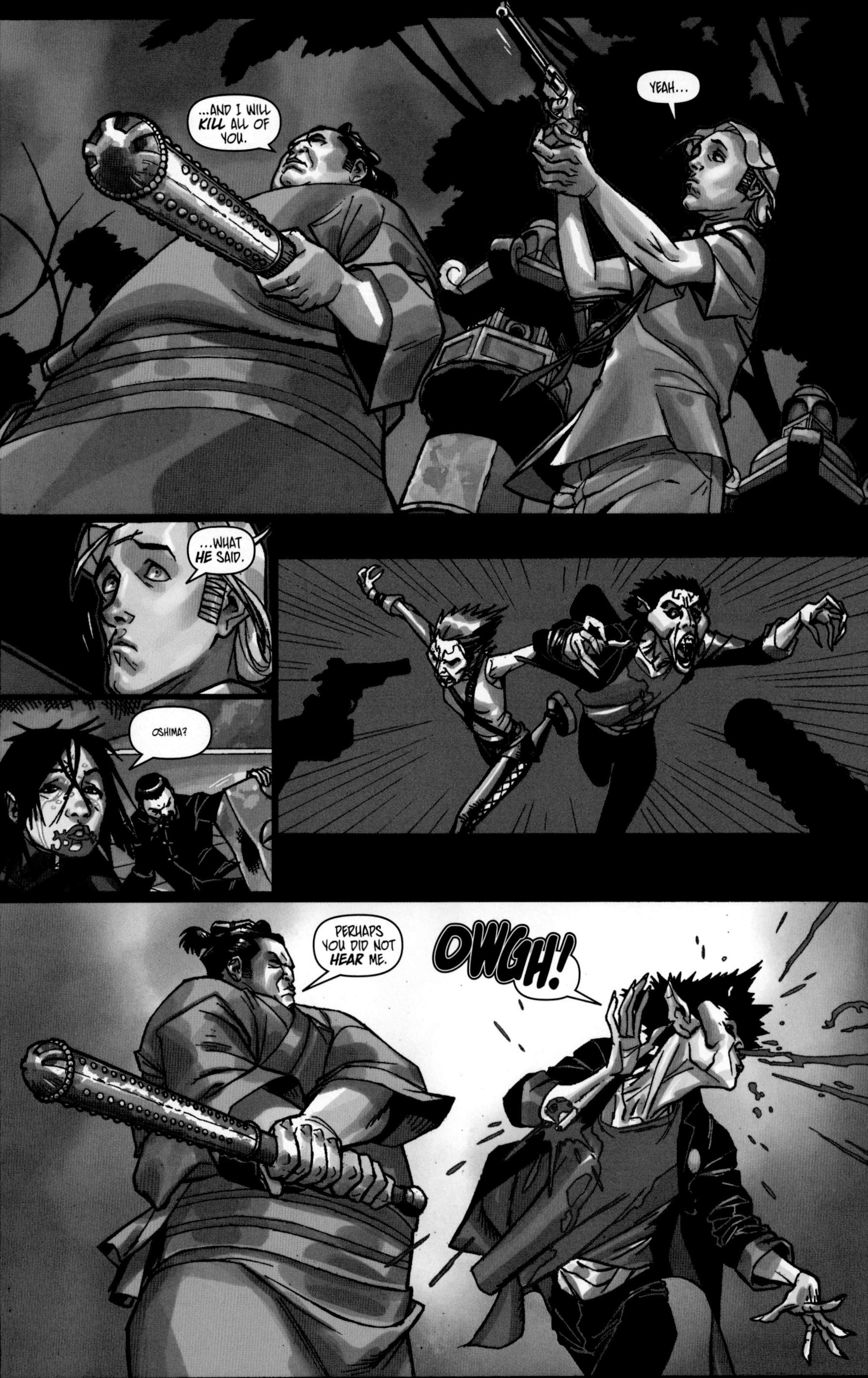
...AND I WILL KILL ALL OF YOU.
YEAH...
...WHAT HE SAID.
OSHIMA?
PERHAPS YOU DID NOT HEAR ME.
OWGH!

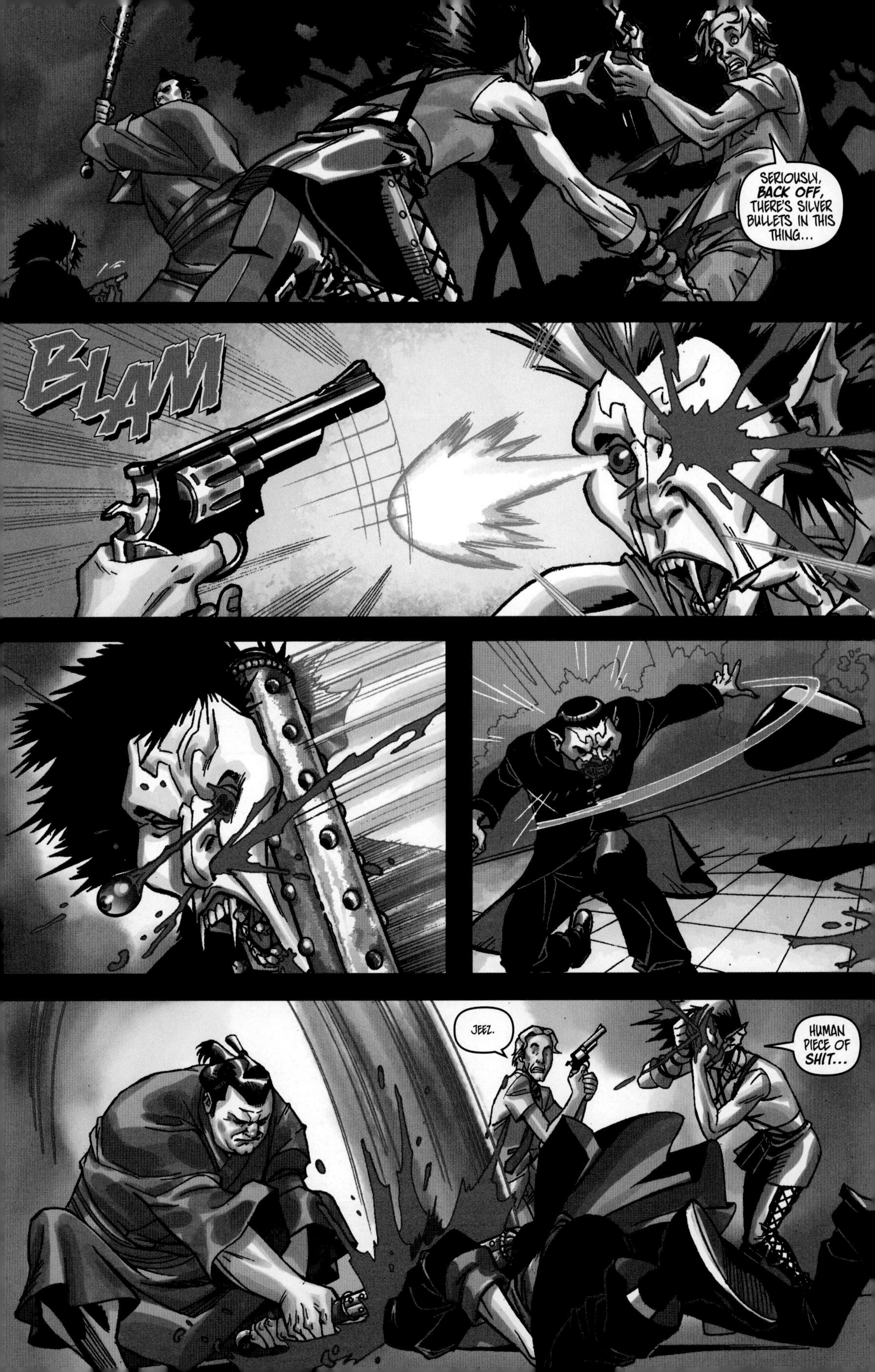
SERIOUSLY, BACK OFF, THERE'S SILVER BULLETS IN THIS THING...
BLAM
JEEZ.
HUMAN PIECE OF SHIT...

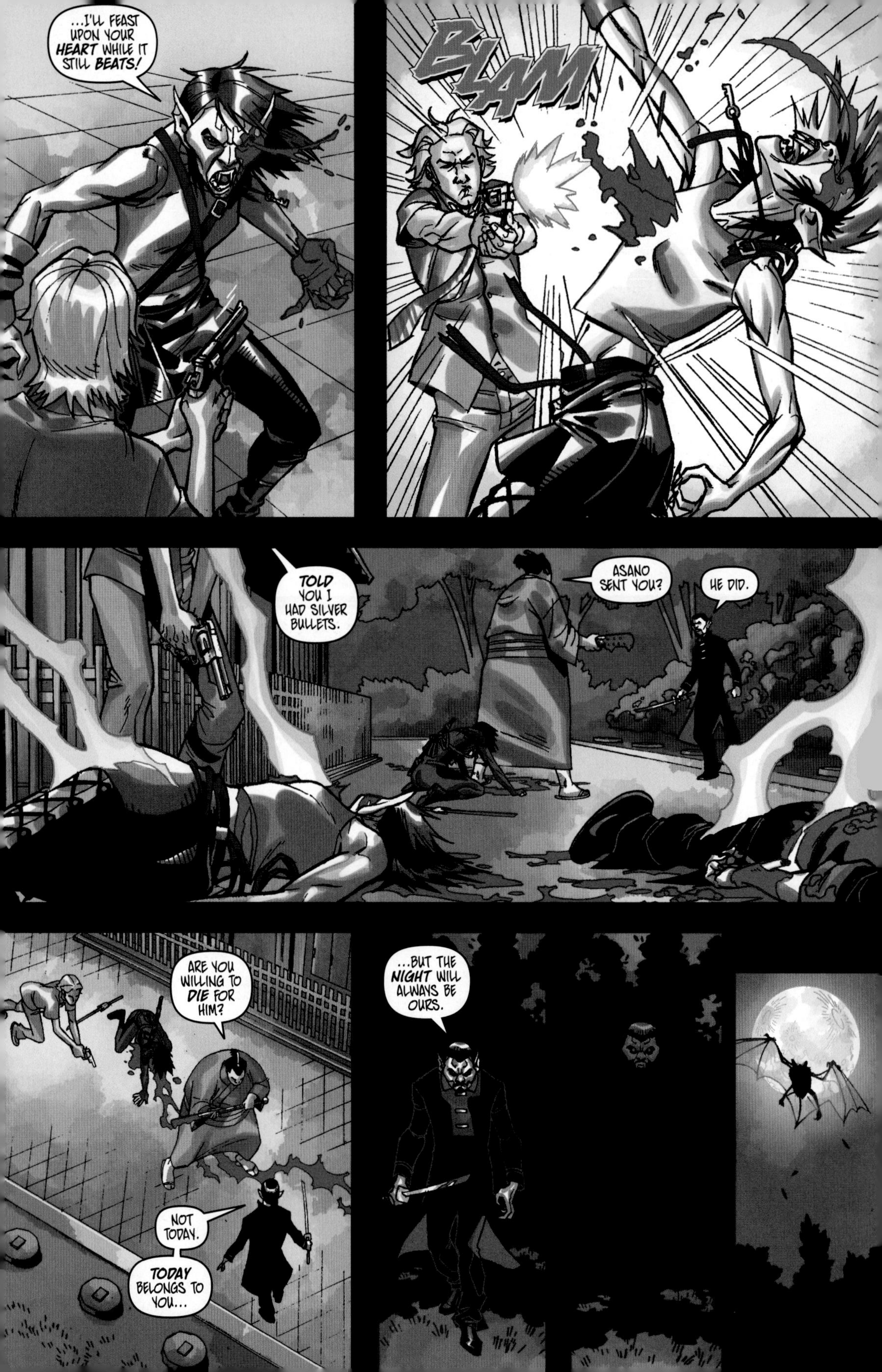
...I'LL FEAST UPON YOUR HEART WHILE IT STILL BEATS!
BLAM
TOLD YOU I HAD SILVER BULLETS.
ASANO SENT YOU?
HE DID.
ARE YOU WILLING TO DIE FOR HIM?
NOT TODAY.
TODAY BELONGS TO YOU...
...BUT THE NIGHT WILL ALWAYS BE OURS.

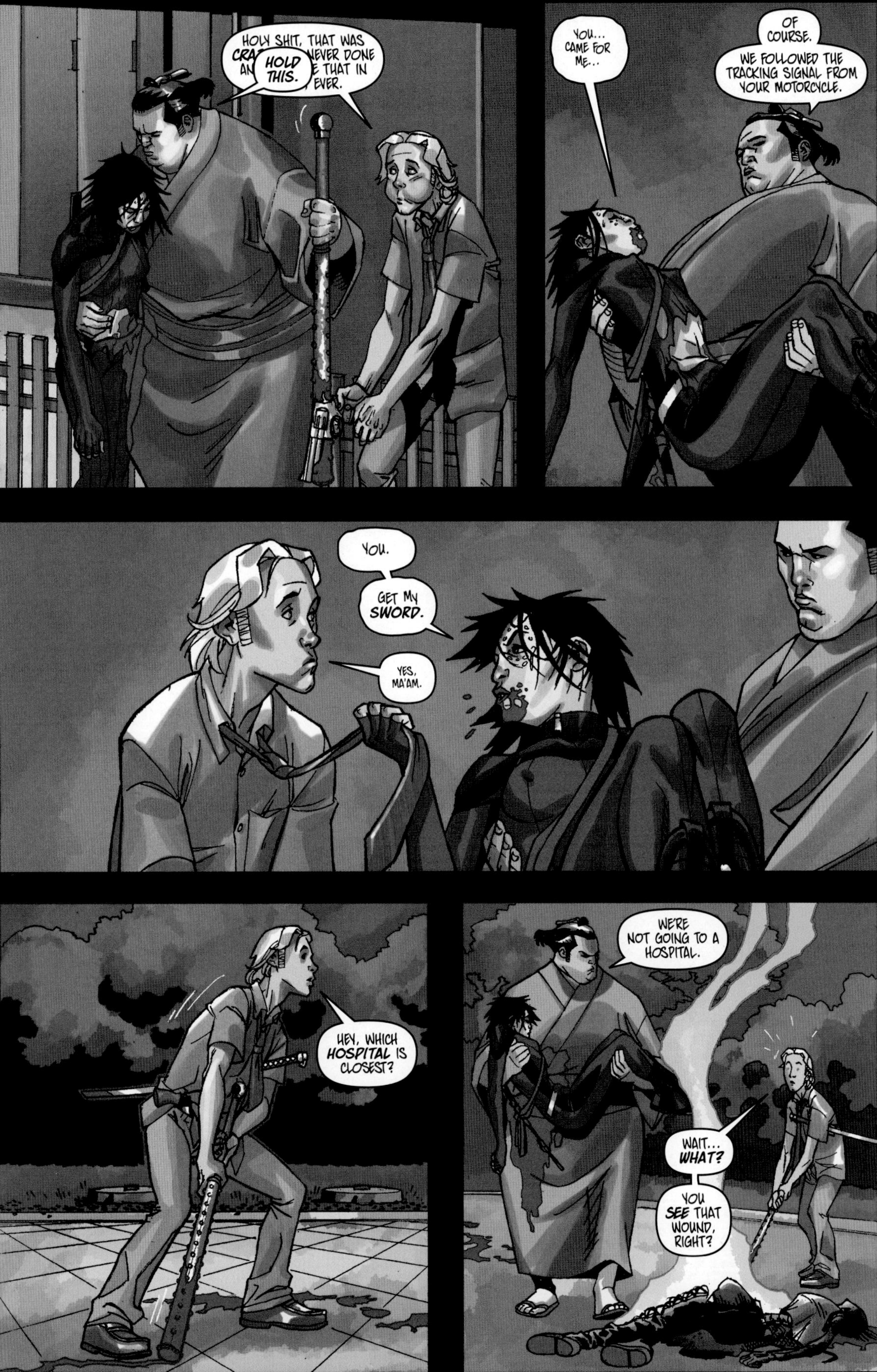

HOLY SHIT, THAT WAS CRA... NEVER DONE AN... E THAT IN ... EVER.
HOLD THIS.
YOU... CAME FOR ME...
OF COURSE.
WE FOLLOWED THE TRACKING SIGNAL FROM YOUR MOTORCYCLE.
YOU.
GET MY SWORD.
YES, MA'AM.
HEY, WHICH HOSPITAL IS CLOSEST?
WE'RE NOT GOING TO A HOSPITAL.
WAIT... WHAT?
YOU SEE THAT WOUND, RIGHT?

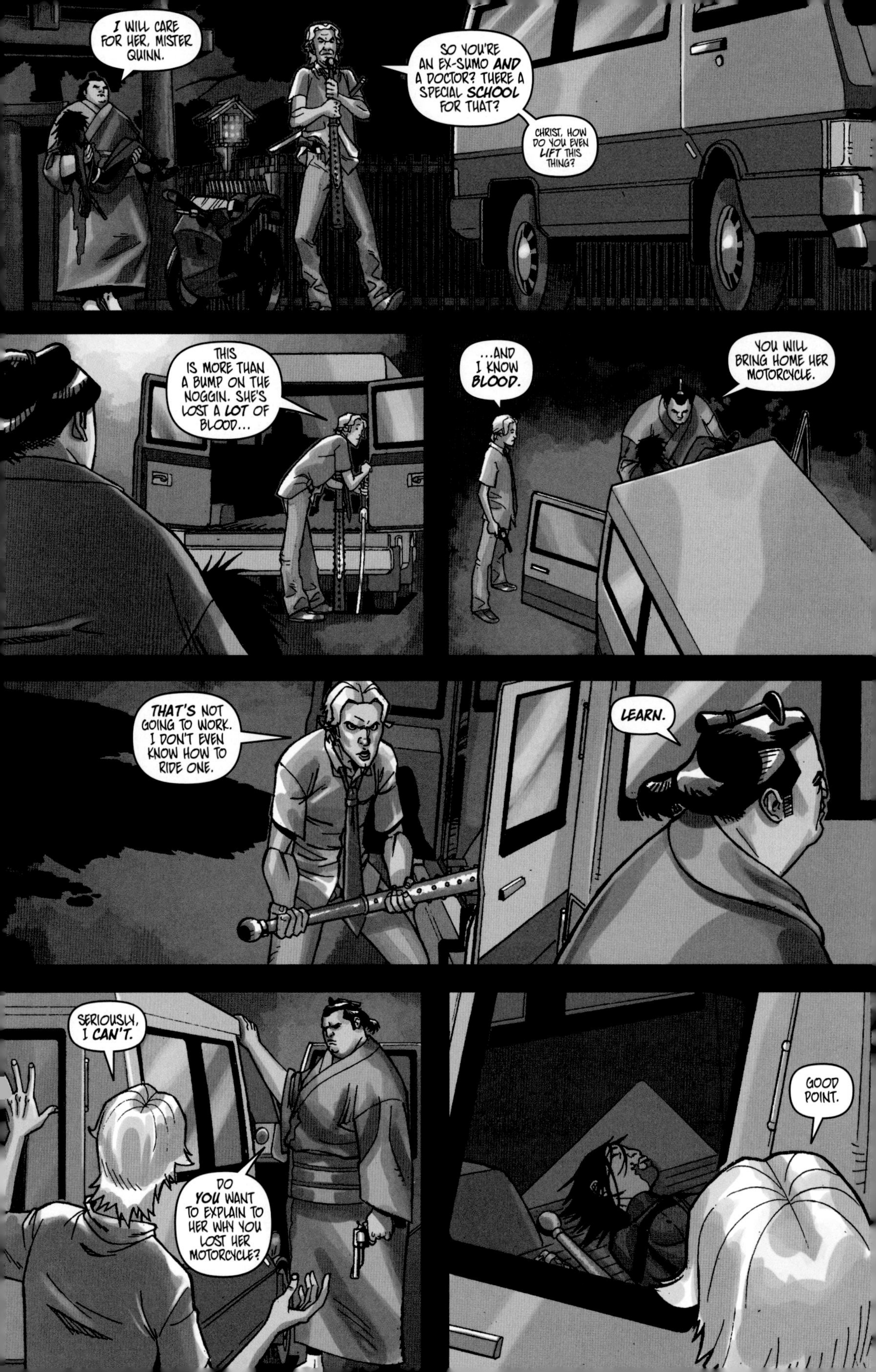
I WILL CARE FOR HER, MISTER QUINN.
SO YOU'RE AN EX-SUMO AND A DOCTOR? THERE A SPECIAL SCHOOL FOR THAT?
CHRIST, HOW DO YOU EVEN LIFT THIS THING?
THIS IS MORE THAN A BUMP ON THE NOGGIN. SHE'S LOST A LOT OF BLOOD...
...AND I KNOW BLOOD.
YOU WILL BRING HOME HER MOTORCYCLE.
THAT'S NOT GOING TO WORK. I DON'T EVEN KNOW HOW TO RIDE ONE.
LEARN.
SERIOUSLY, I CAN'T.
DO YOU WANT TO EXPLAIN TO HER WHY YOU LOST HER MOTORCYCLE?
GOOD POINT.

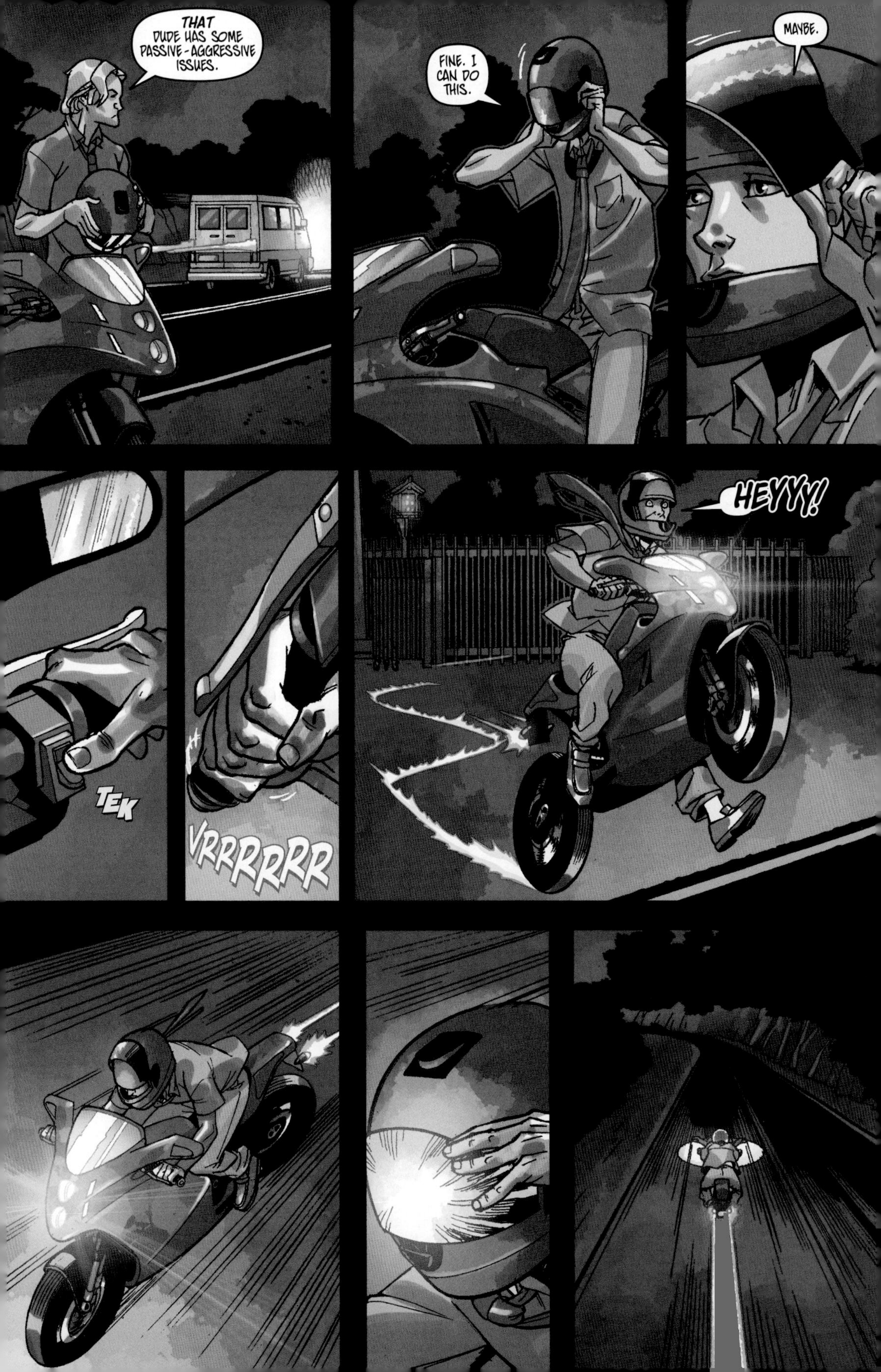
THAT DUDE HAS SOME PASSIVE-AGGRESSIVE ISSUES.
FINE. I CAN DO THIS.
MAYBE.
TEK
VRRRRRR
HEYYY!

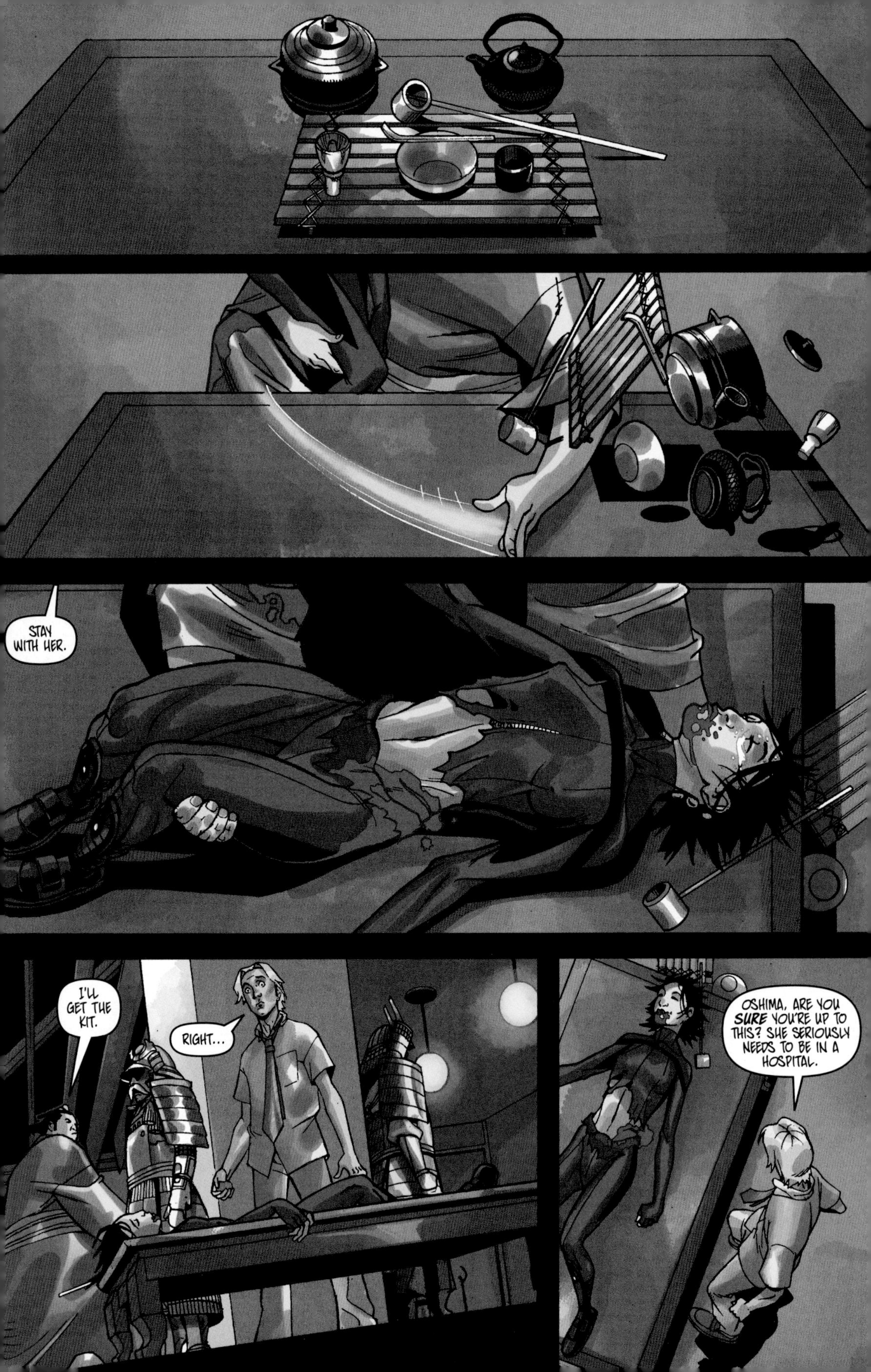
STAY WITH HER.
I'LL GET THE KIT.
RIGHT...
OSHIMA, ARE YOU SURE YOU'RE UP TO THIS? SHE SERIOUSLY NEEDS TO BE IN A HOSPITAL.

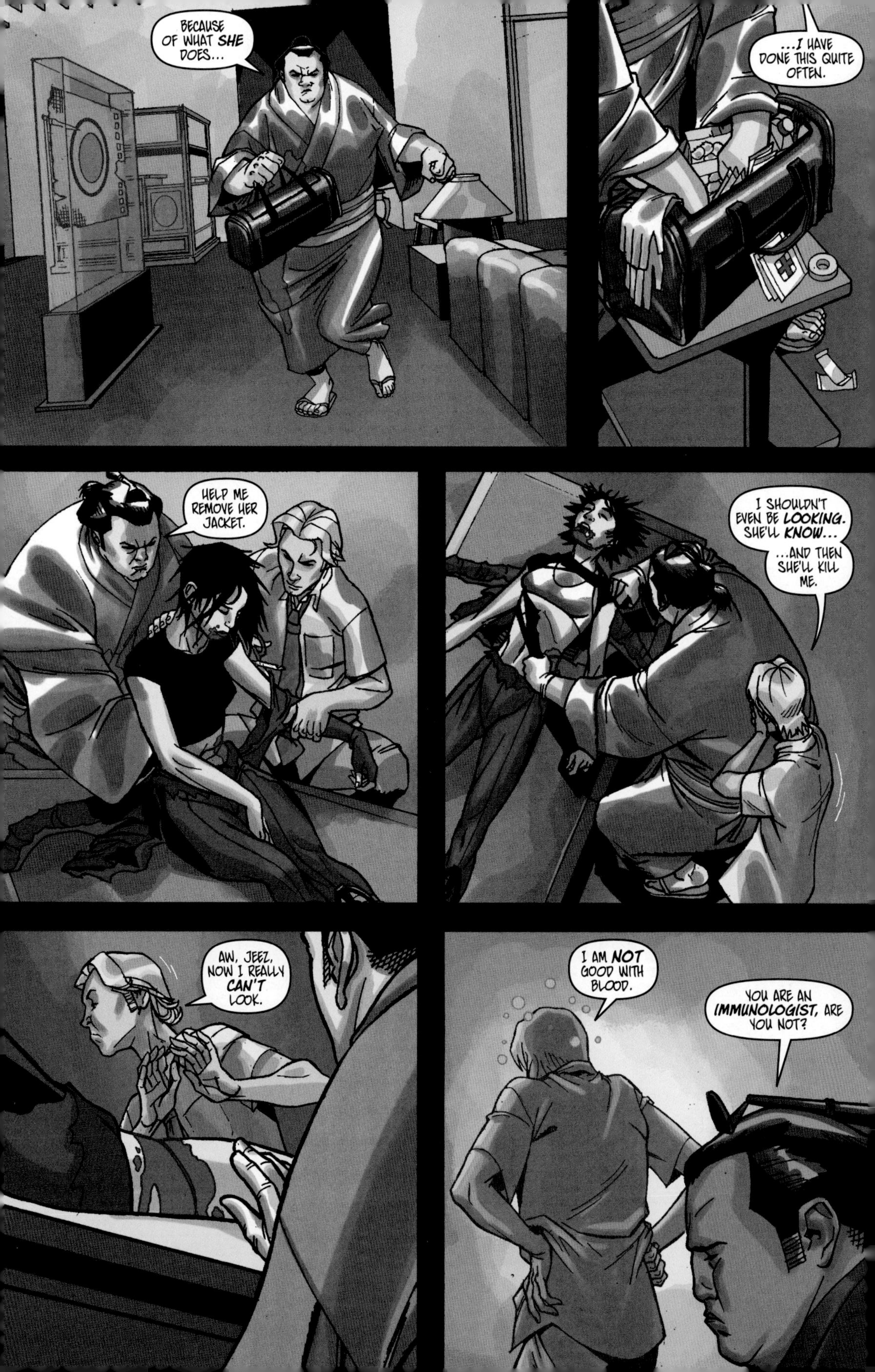
BECAUSE OF WHAT **SHE** DOES...
...*I* HAVE DONE THIS QUITE OFTEN.
HELP ME REMOVE HER JACKET.
I SHOULDN'T EVEN BE **LOOKING**. SHE'LL **KNOW**...
...AND THEN SHE'LL KILL ME.
AW, JEEZ, NOW I REALLY **CAN'T** LOOK.
I AM **NOT** GOOD WITH BLOOD.
YOU ARE AN ***IMMUNOLOGIST,*** ARE YOU NOT?

I'M OKAY WITH IT WHEN IT'S IN A TEST TUBE OR UNDER A MICROSCOPE, NOT...

...YOU KNOW, SPILLING OUT OF SOMEBODY.

HER WOUND ITSELF IS NOT LIFE-THREATENING, BUT AS YOU SAID, SHE HAS LOST A GREAT DEAL OF BLOOD.

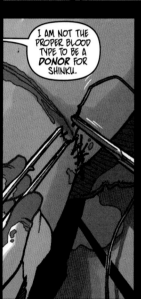

I AM NOT THE PROPER BLOOD TYPE TO BE A DONOR FOR SHINKU.

I'M O-NEG. UNIVERSAL DONOR.

SO YOU WANT ME TO...

GIVE HER A TRANSFUSION, YES.

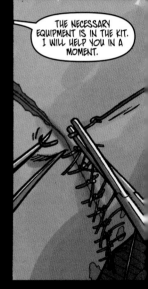

THE NECESSARY EQUIPMENT IS IN THE KIT. I WILL HELP YOU IN A MOMENT.

NO, I KNOW HOW TO DO IT, IT JUST...GROSSES ME OUT.

WHY DON'T YOU STORE HER BLOOD?

WE DO.

BUT ALL OF IT WAS USED PREVIOUSLY, AND SHINKU HAS IGNORED MY REQUESTS TO COLLECT MORE.

SO WE'LL MAKE DUE.

BUT DO ME A FAVOR. IF I PASS OUT...

...CATCH ME BEFORE I SPLIT MY HEAD OPEN ON THE TABLE.

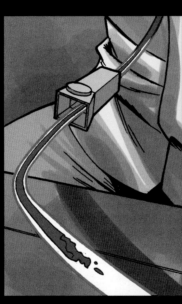

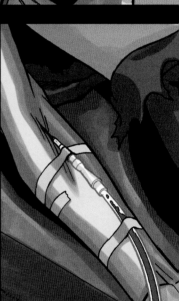

I WILL GO CLEAN UP.

THANK YOU, MISTER QUINN. WE ARE IN YOUR DEBT.

LIKE YOU SAID, I OWE HER MY LIFE.

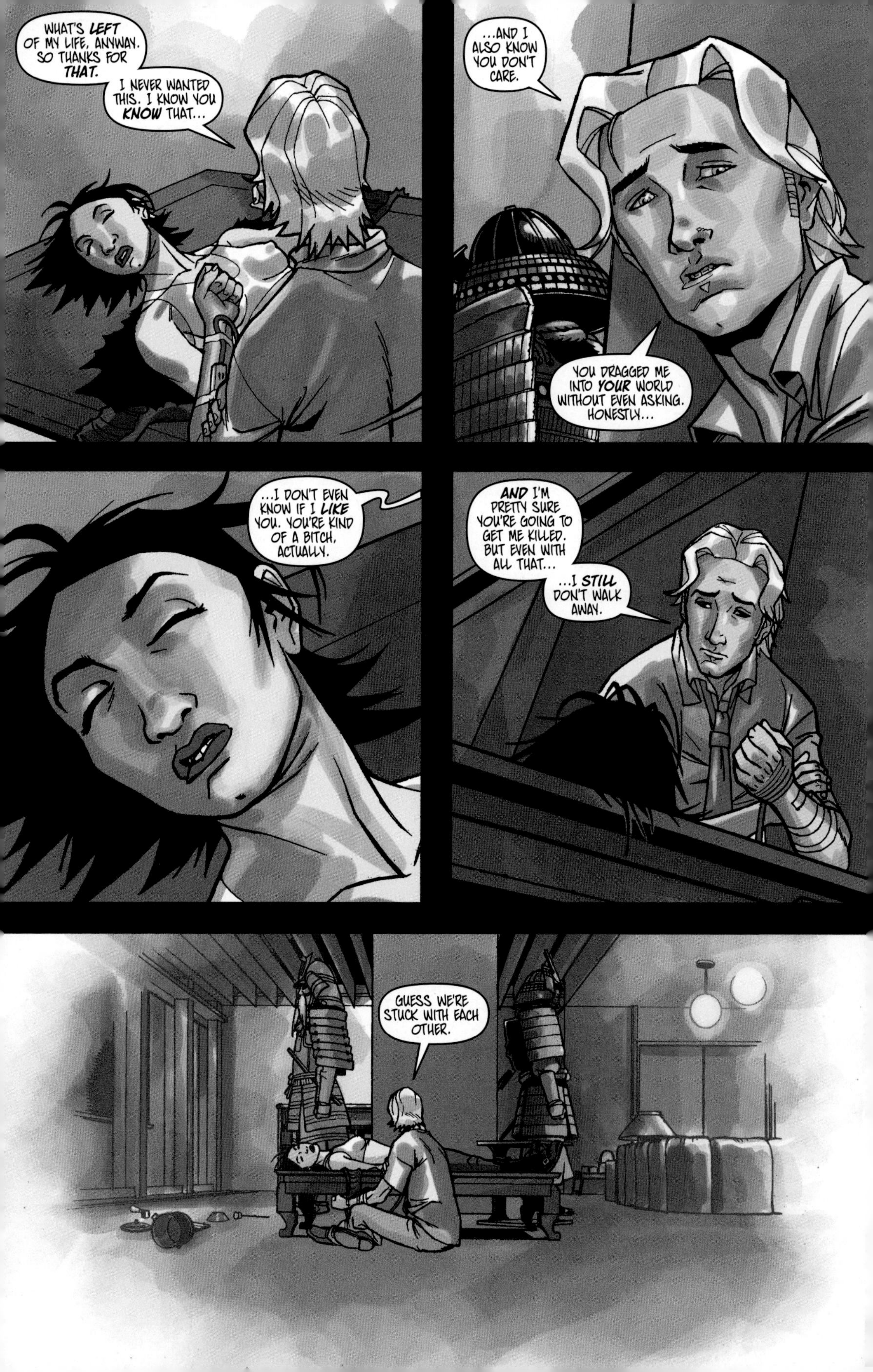
WHAT'S **LEFT** OF MY LIFE, ANYWAY. SO THANKS FOR **THAT.**
I NEVER WANTED THIS. I KNOW YOU **KNOW** THAT...
...AND I ALSO KNOW YOU DON'T CARE.
YOU DRAGGED ME INTO **YOUR** WORLD WITHOUT EVEN ASKING. HONESTLY...
...I DON'T EVEN KNOW IF I **LIKE** YOU. YOU'RE KIND OF A BITCH, ACTUALLY.
AND I'M PRETTY SURE YOU'RE GOING TO GET ME KILLED. BUT EVEN WITH ALL THAT...
...I **STILL** DON'T WALK AWAY.
GUESS WE'RE STUCK WITH EACH OTHER.

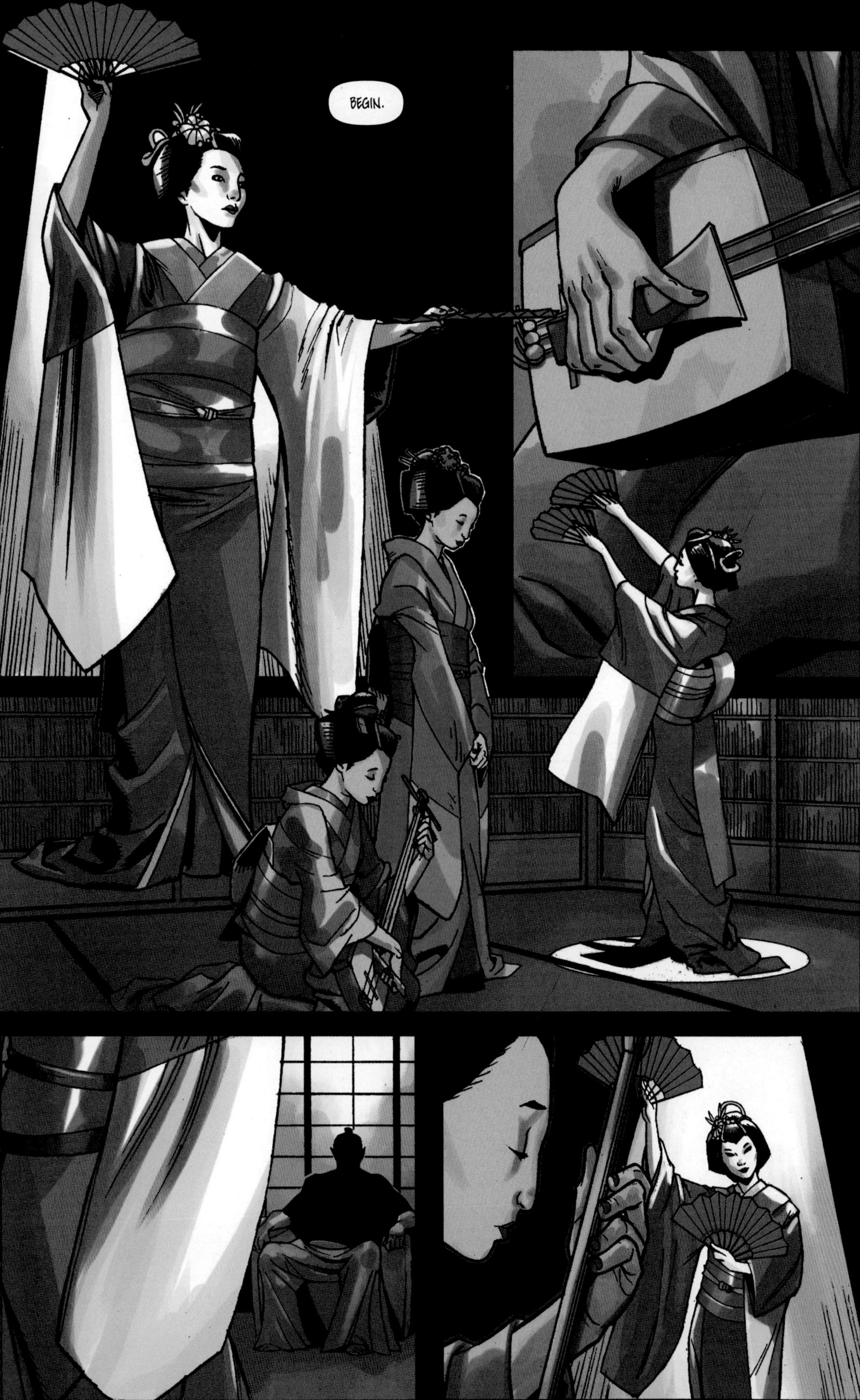
BEGIN.

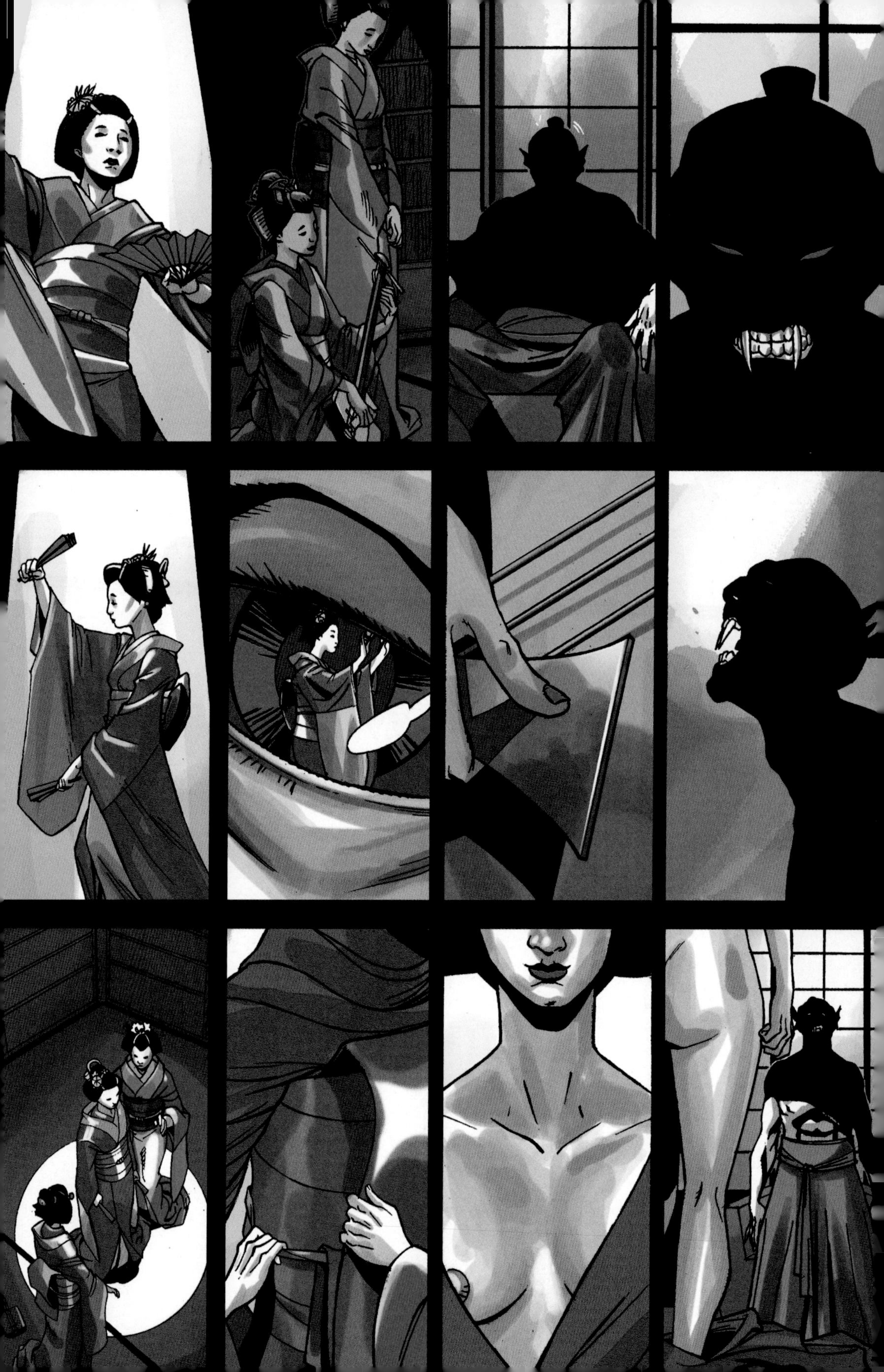

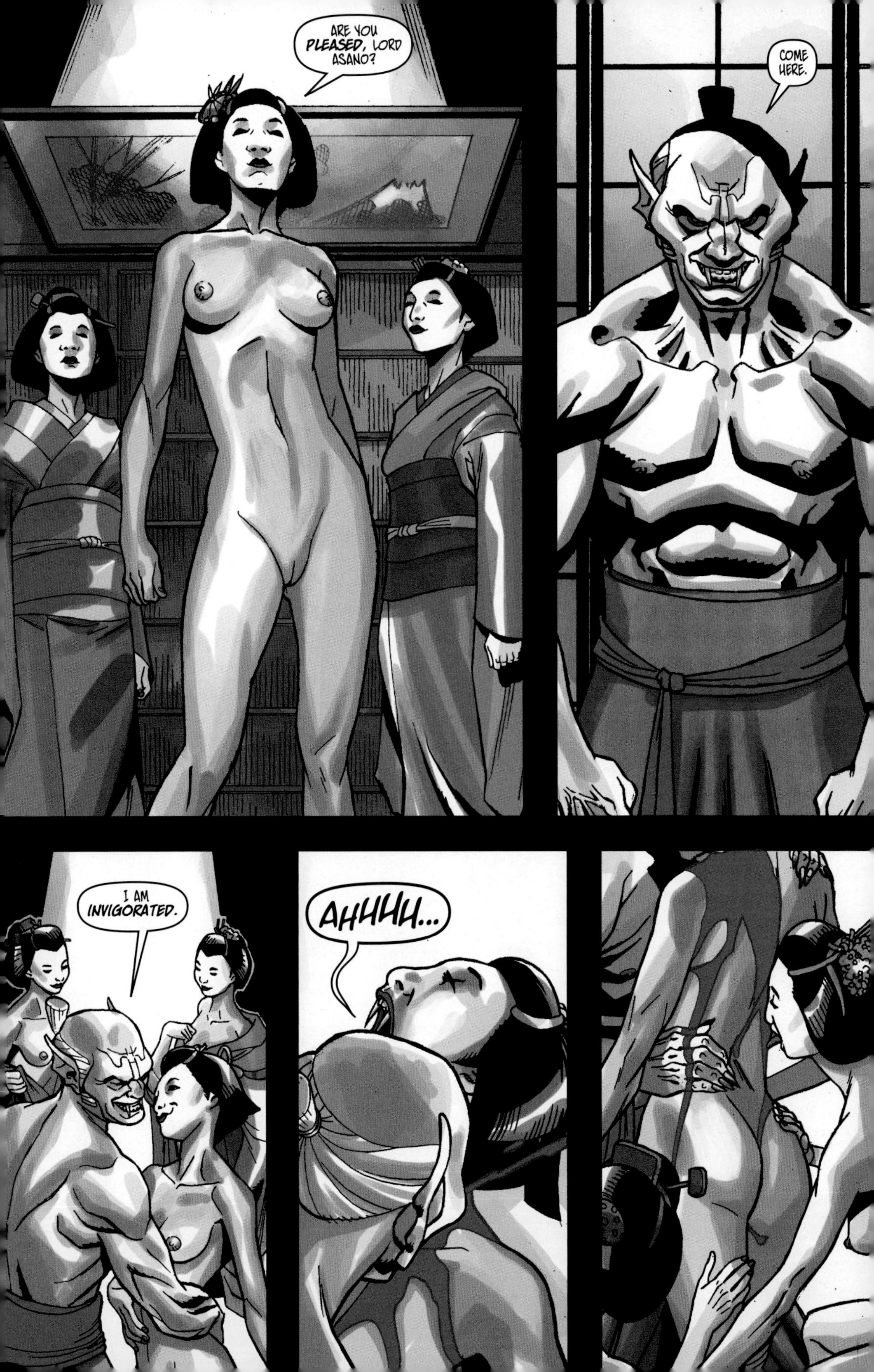
ARE YOU PLEASED, LORD ASANO?
COME HERE.
I AM INVIGORATED.
AHHHH...

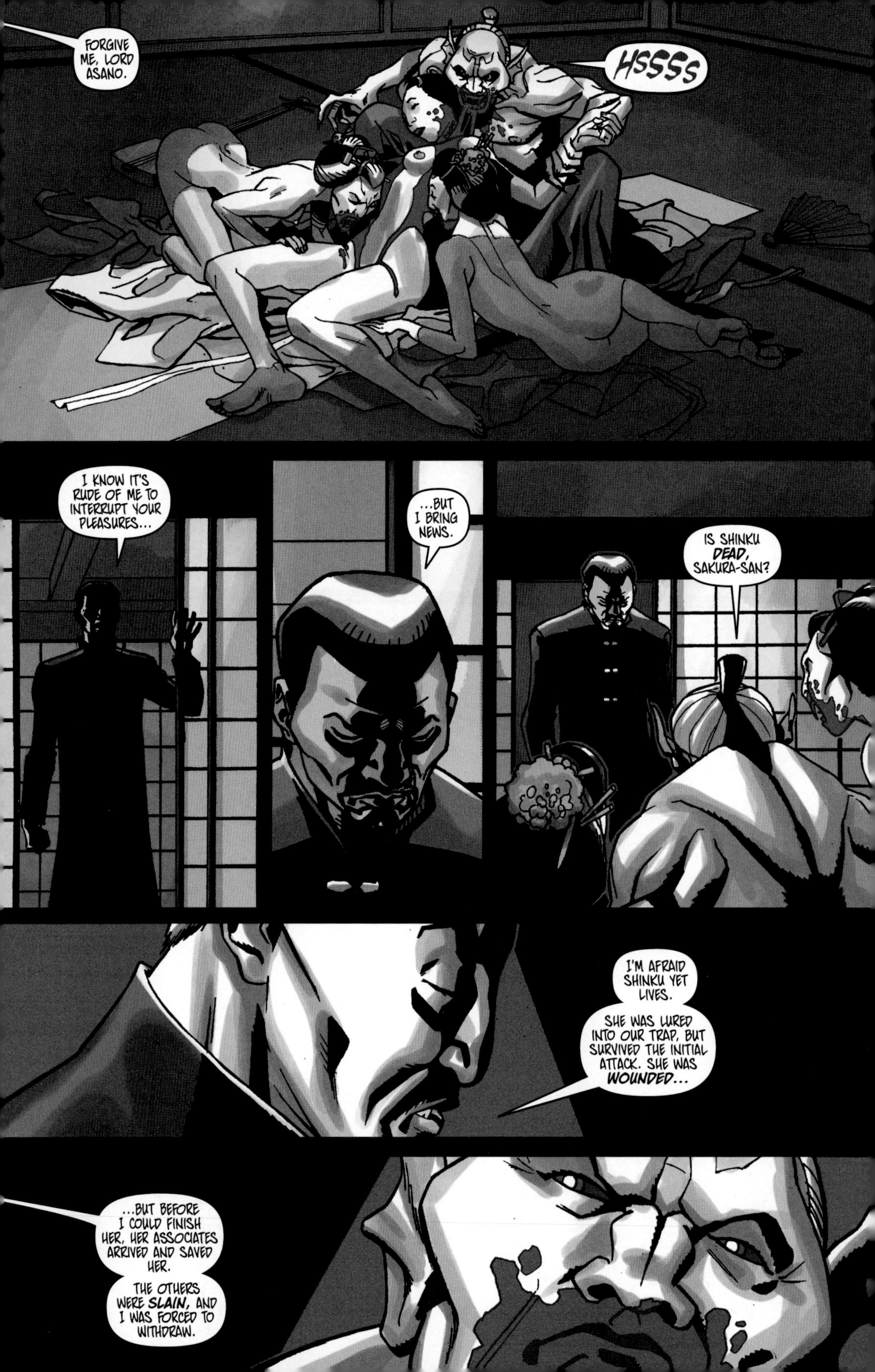
FORGIVE ME, LORD ASANO.
HSSSS
I KNOW IT'S RUDE OF ME TO INTERRUPT YOUR PLEASURES...
...BUT I BRING NEWS.
IS SHINKU **DEAD**, SAKURA-SAN?
I'M AFRAID SHINKU YET LIVES.
SHE WAS LURED INTO OUR TRAP, BUT SURVIVED THE INITIAL ATTACK. SHE WAS **WOUNDED**...
...BUT BEFORE I COULD FINISH HER, HER ASSOCIATES ARRIVED AND SAVED HER.
THE OTHERS WERE **SLAIN**, AND I WAS FORCED TO WITHDRAW.

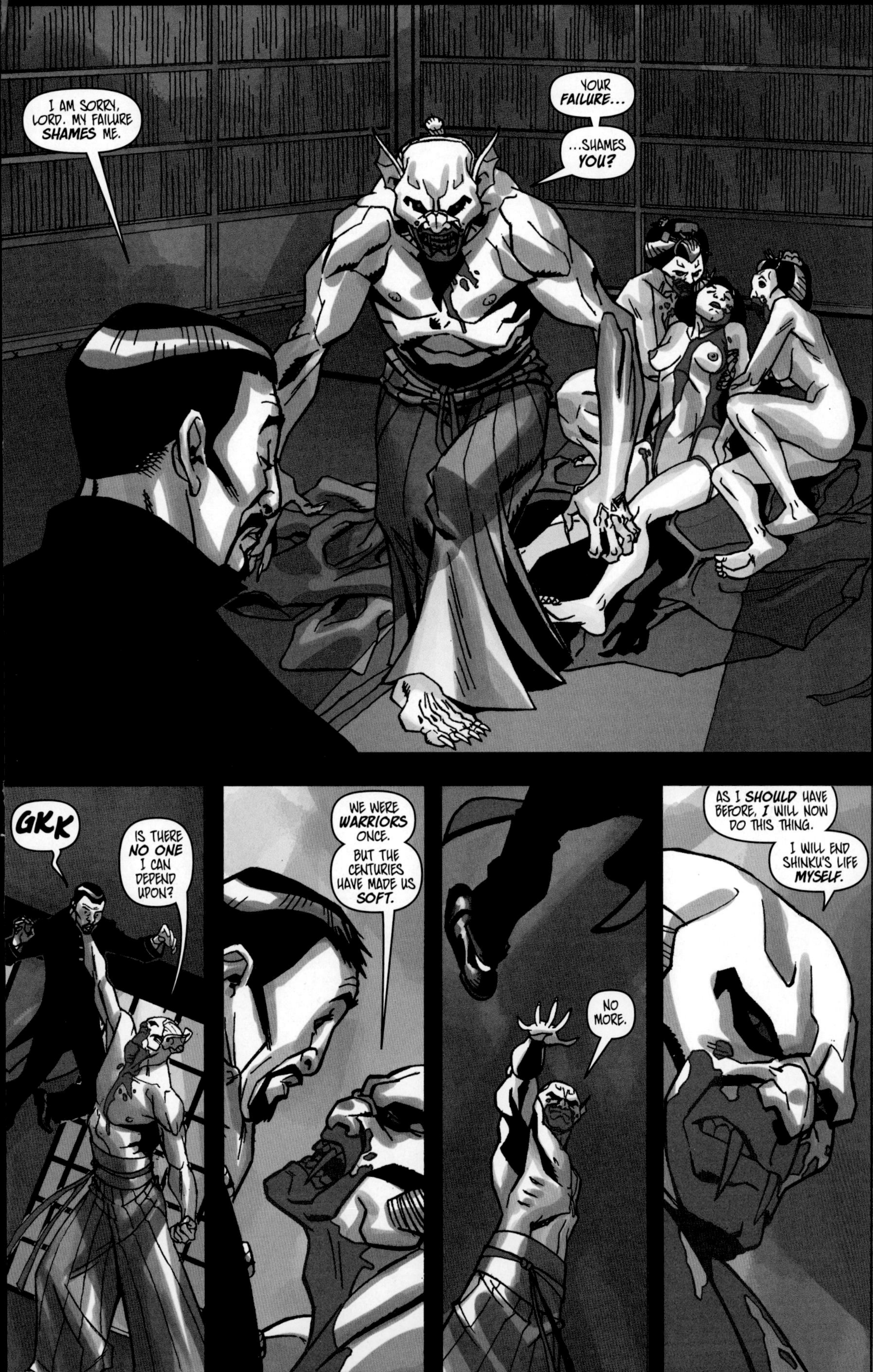
I AM SORRY, LORD. MY FAILURE SHAMES ME.
YOUR FAILURE...
...SHAMES YOU?
GKK
IS THERE NO ONE I CAN DEPEND UPON?
WE WERE WARRIORS ONCE.
BUT THE CENTURIES HAVE MADE US SOFT.
NO MORE.
AS I SHOULD HAVE BEFORE, I WILL NOW DO THIS THING.
I WILL END SHINKU'S LIFE MYSELF.

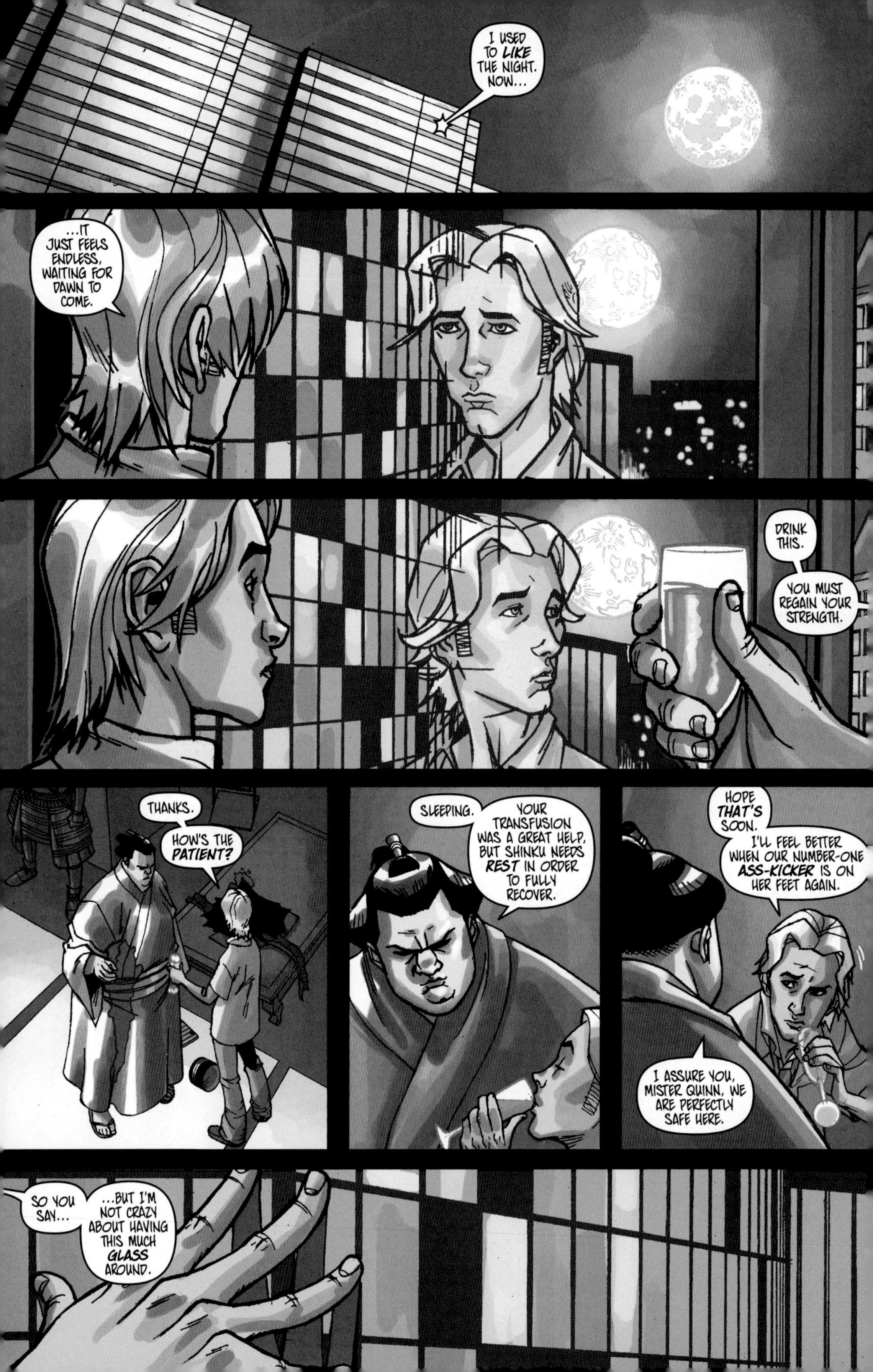
I USED TO **LIKE** THE NIGHT. NOW...
...IT JUST FEELS ENDLESS, WAITING FOR DAWN TO COME.
DRINK THIS.
YOU MUST REGAIN YOUR STRENGTH.
THANKS.
HOW'S THE **PATIENT?**
SLEEPING.
YOUR TRANSFUSION WAS A GREAT HELP, BUT SHINKU NEEDS **REST** IN ORDER TO FULLY RECOVER.
HOPE **THAT'S** SOON.
I'LL FEEL BETTER WHEN OUR NUMBER-ONE **ASS-KICKER** IS ON HER FEET AGAIN.
I ASSURE YOU, MISTER QUINN, WE ARE PERFECTLY SAFE HERE.
SO YOU SAY...
...BUT I'M NOT CRAZY ABOUT HAVING THIS MUCH **GLASS** AROUND.

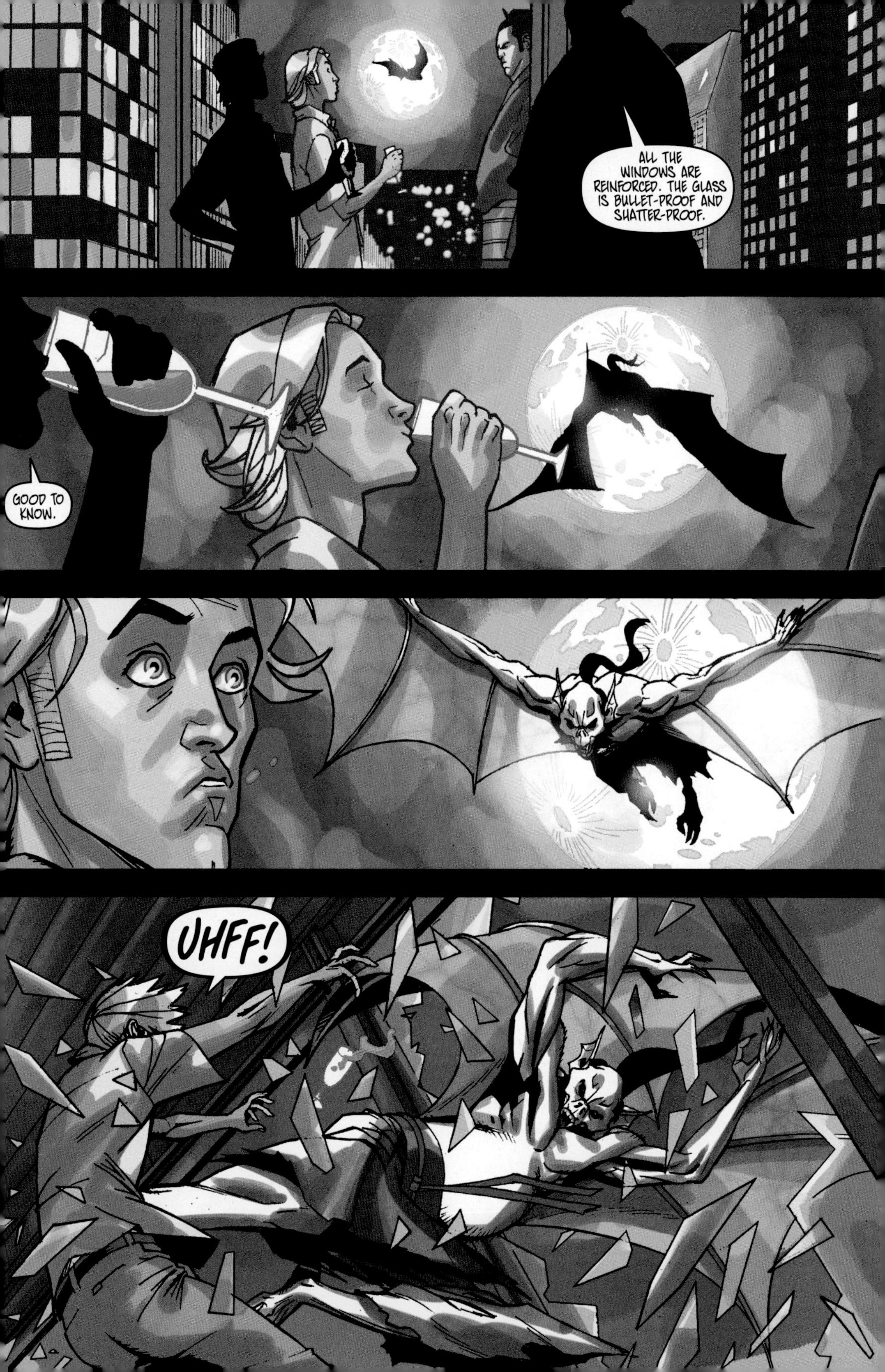
ALL THE WINDOWS ARE REINFORCED. THE GLASS IS BULLET-PROOF AND SHATTER-PROOF.
GOOD TO KNOW.
UHFF!

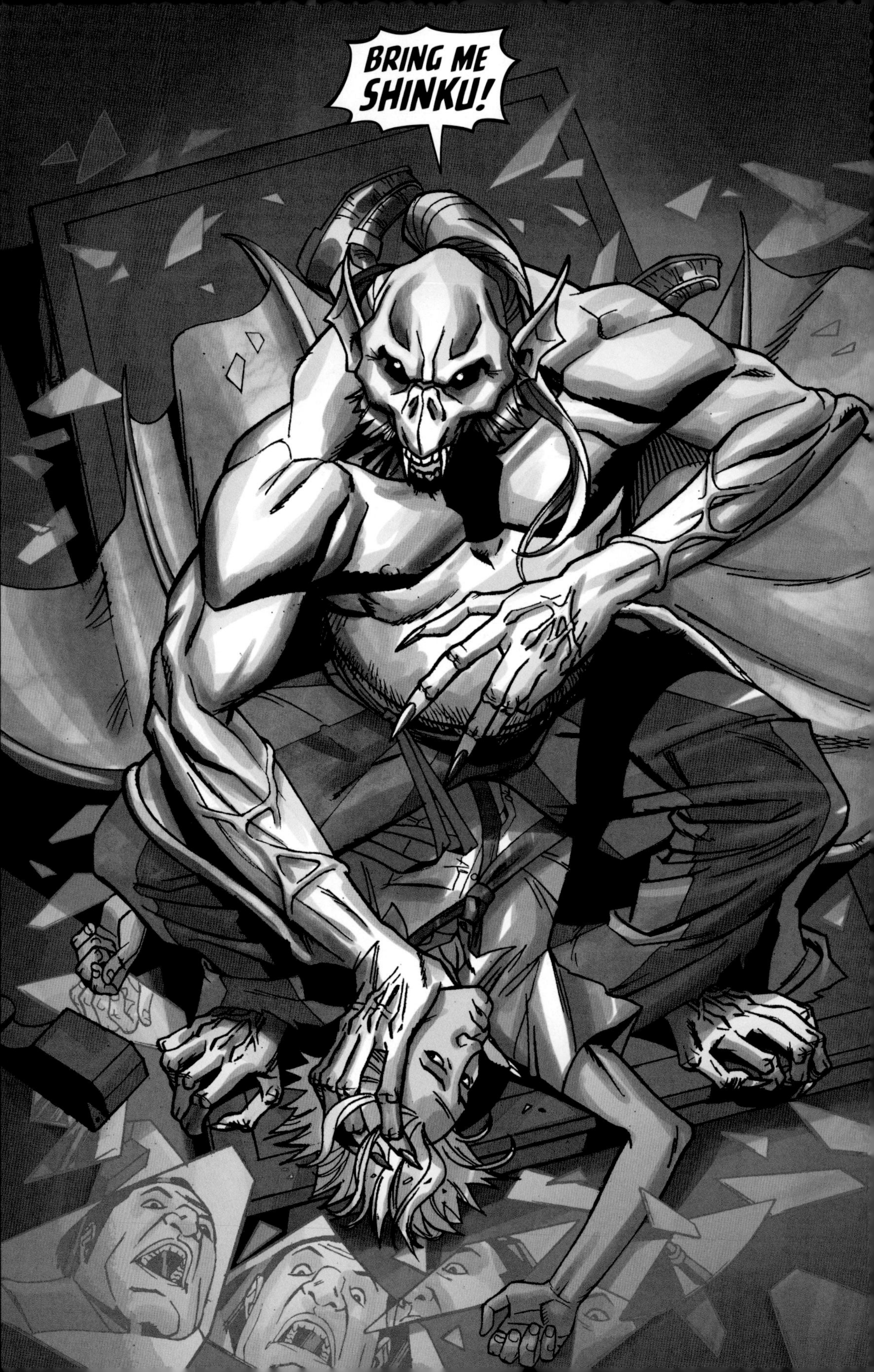
BRING ME SHINKU!

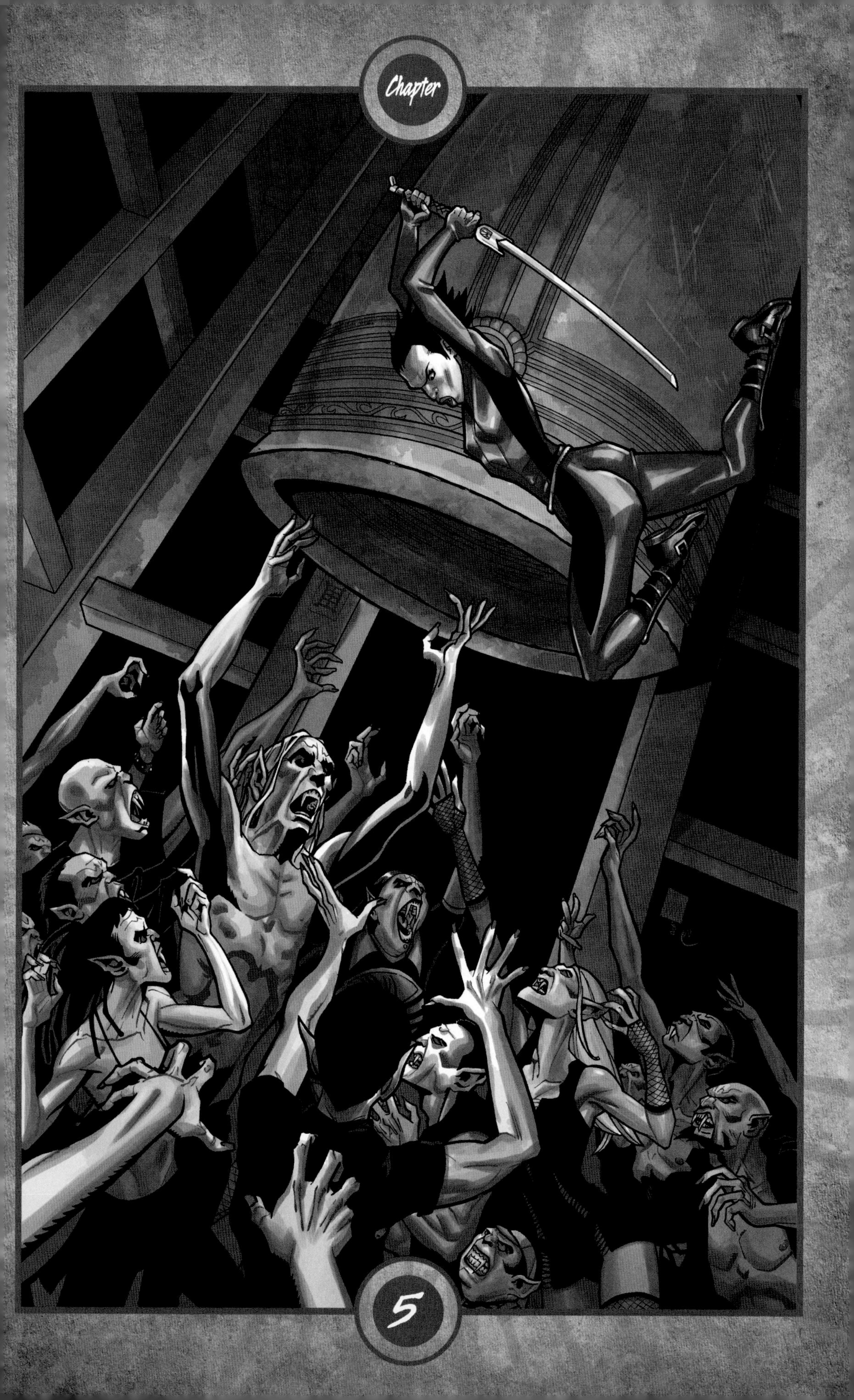
Chapter
5

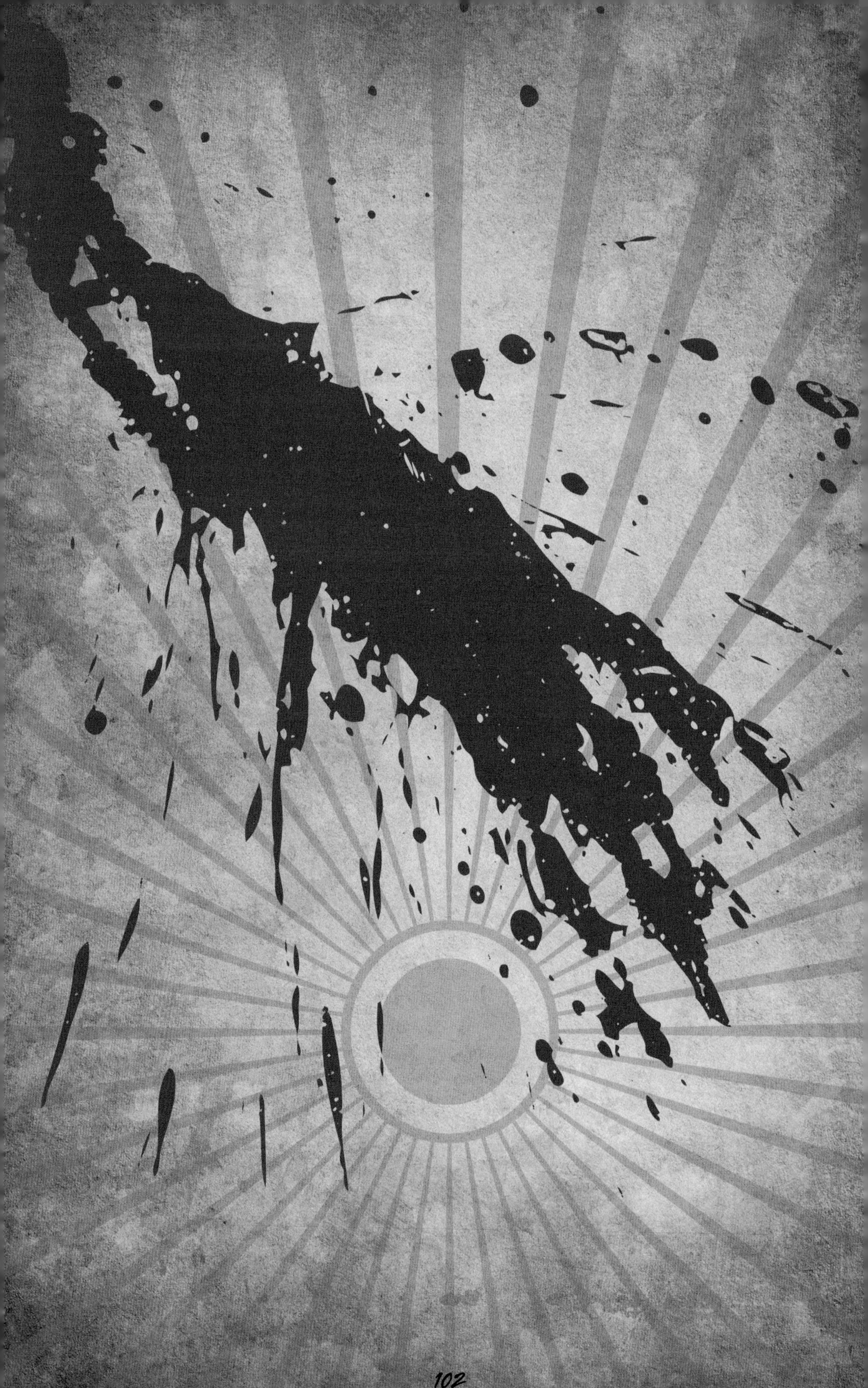

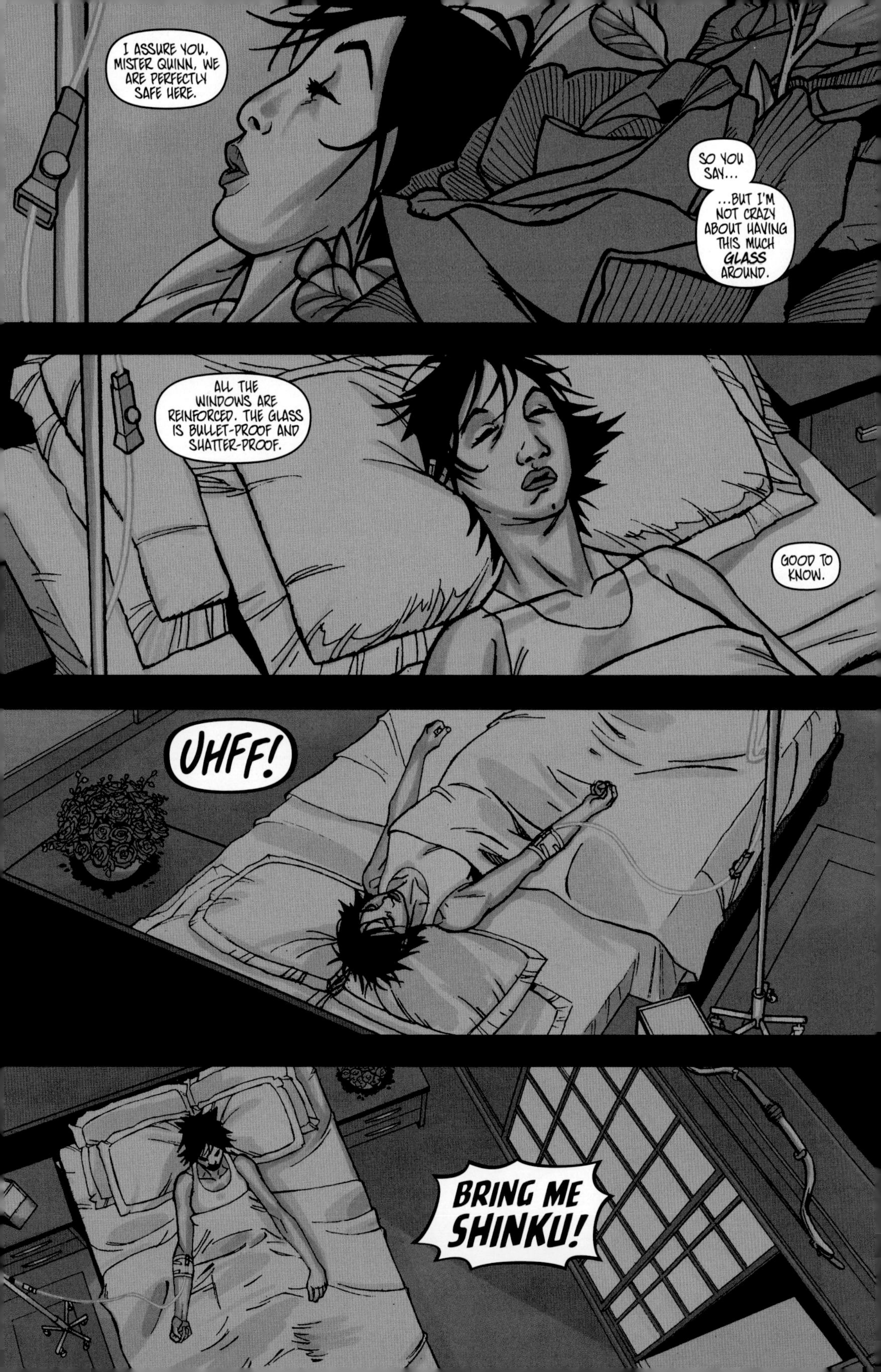
I ASSURE YOU, MISTER QUINN, WE ARE PERFECTLY SAFE HERE.
SO YOU SAY...
...BUT I'M NOT CRAZY ABOUT HAVING THIS MUCH GLASS AROUND.
ALL THE WINDOWS ARE REINFORCED. THE GLASS IS BULLET-PROOF AND SHATTER-PROOF.
GOOD TO KNOW.
UHFF!
BRING ME SHINKU!

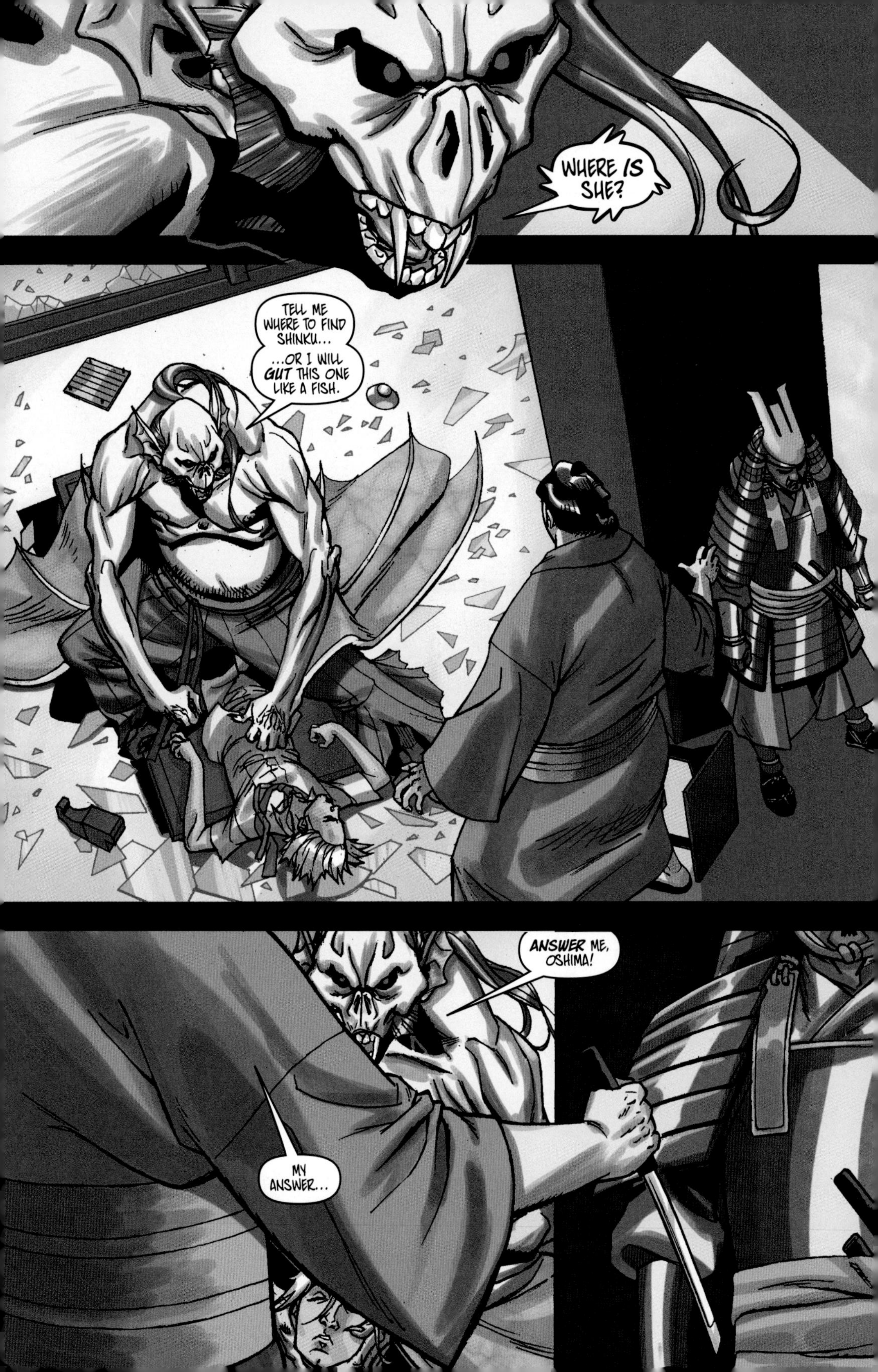
WHERE IS SHE?
TELL ME WHERE TO FIND SHINKU...
...OR I WILL GUT THIS ONE LIKE A FISH.
ANSWER ME, OSHIMA!
MY ANSWER...

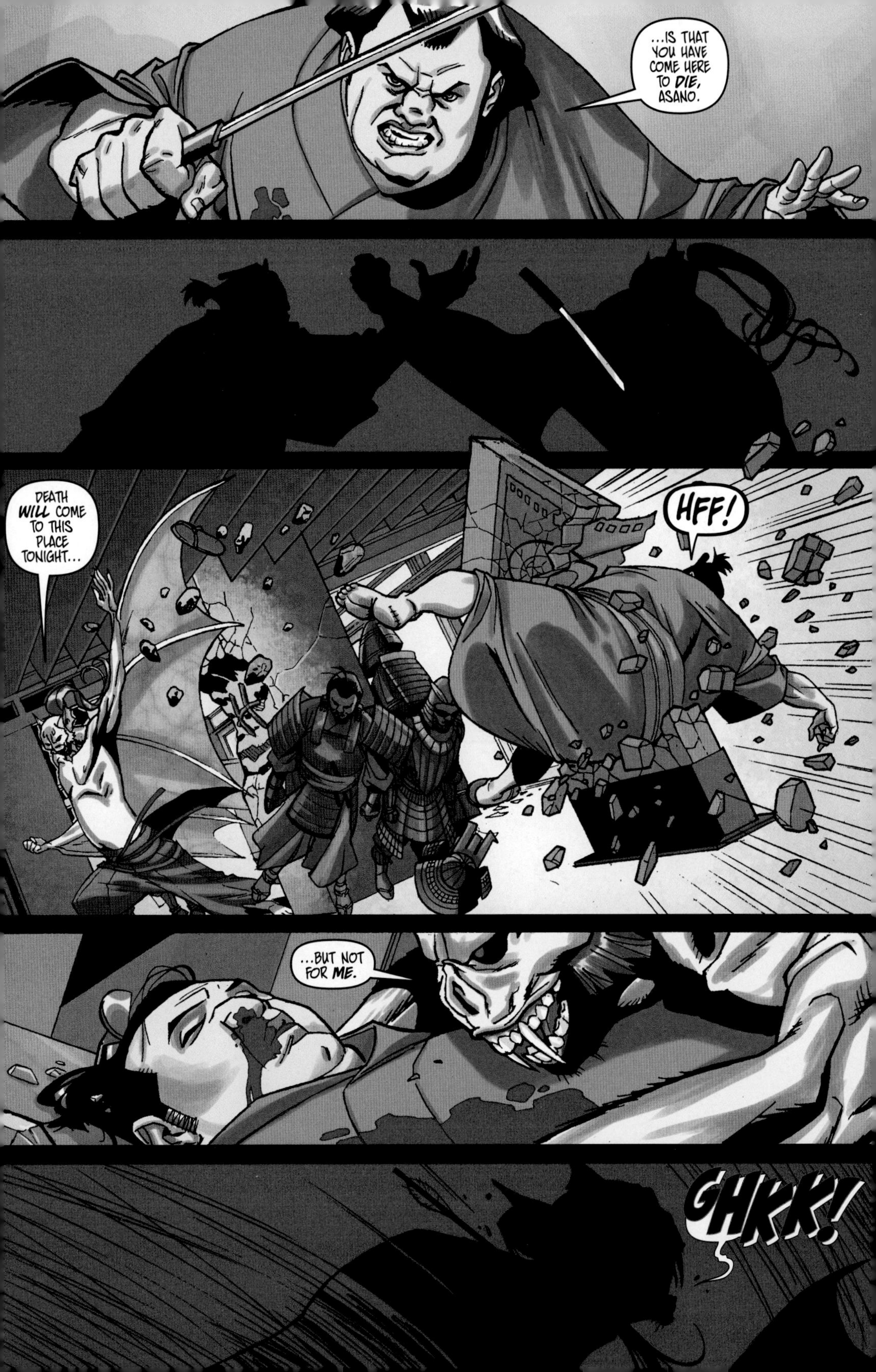
...IS THAT YOU HAVE COME HERE TO **DIE**, ASANO.
DEATH **WILL** COME TO THIS PLACE TONIGHT...
HFF!
...BUT NOT FOR **ME**.
GHKK!

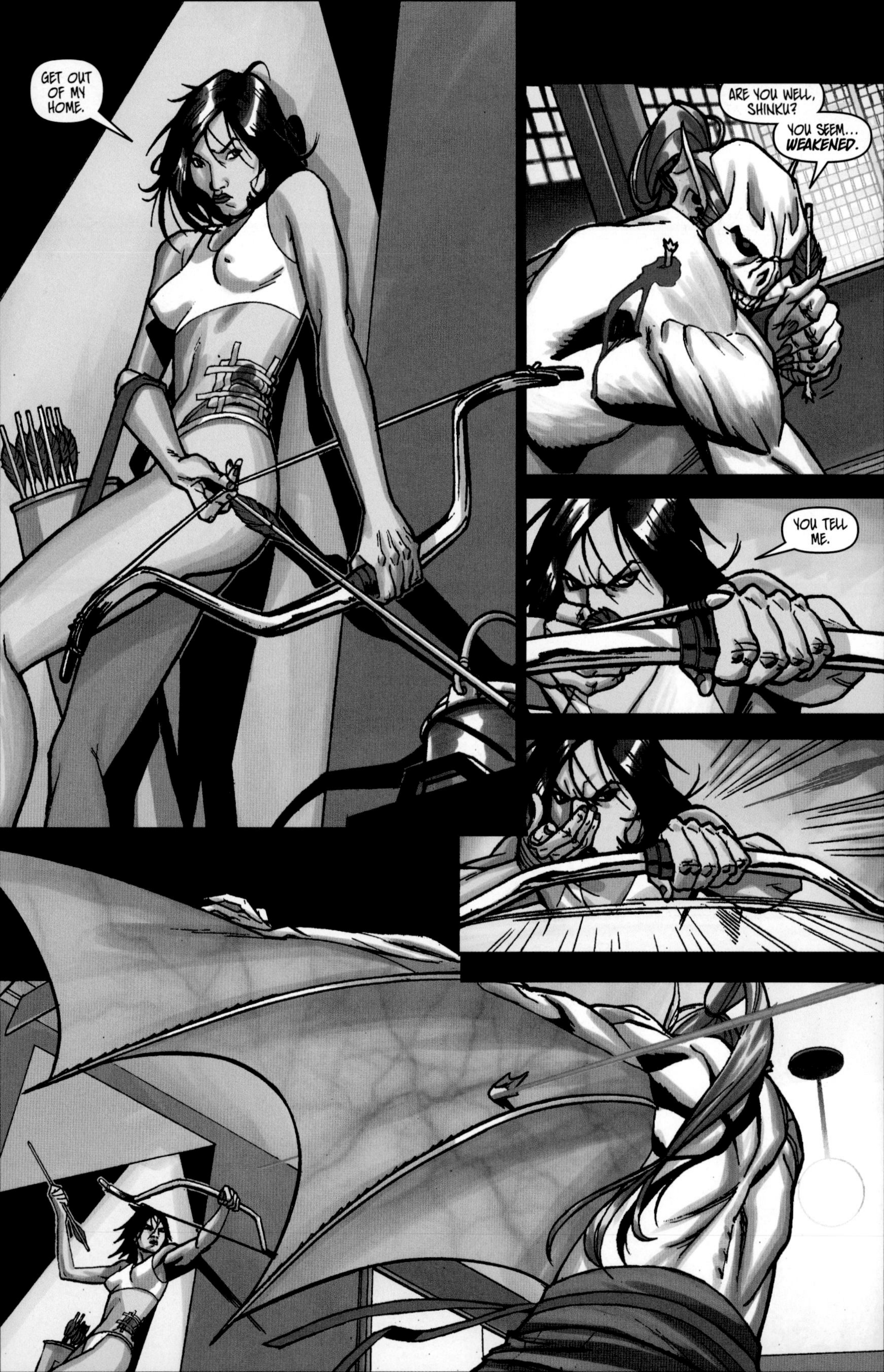
GET OUT OF MY HOME.
ARE YOU WELL, SHINKU?
YOU SEEM... **WEAKENED**.
YOU TELL ME.

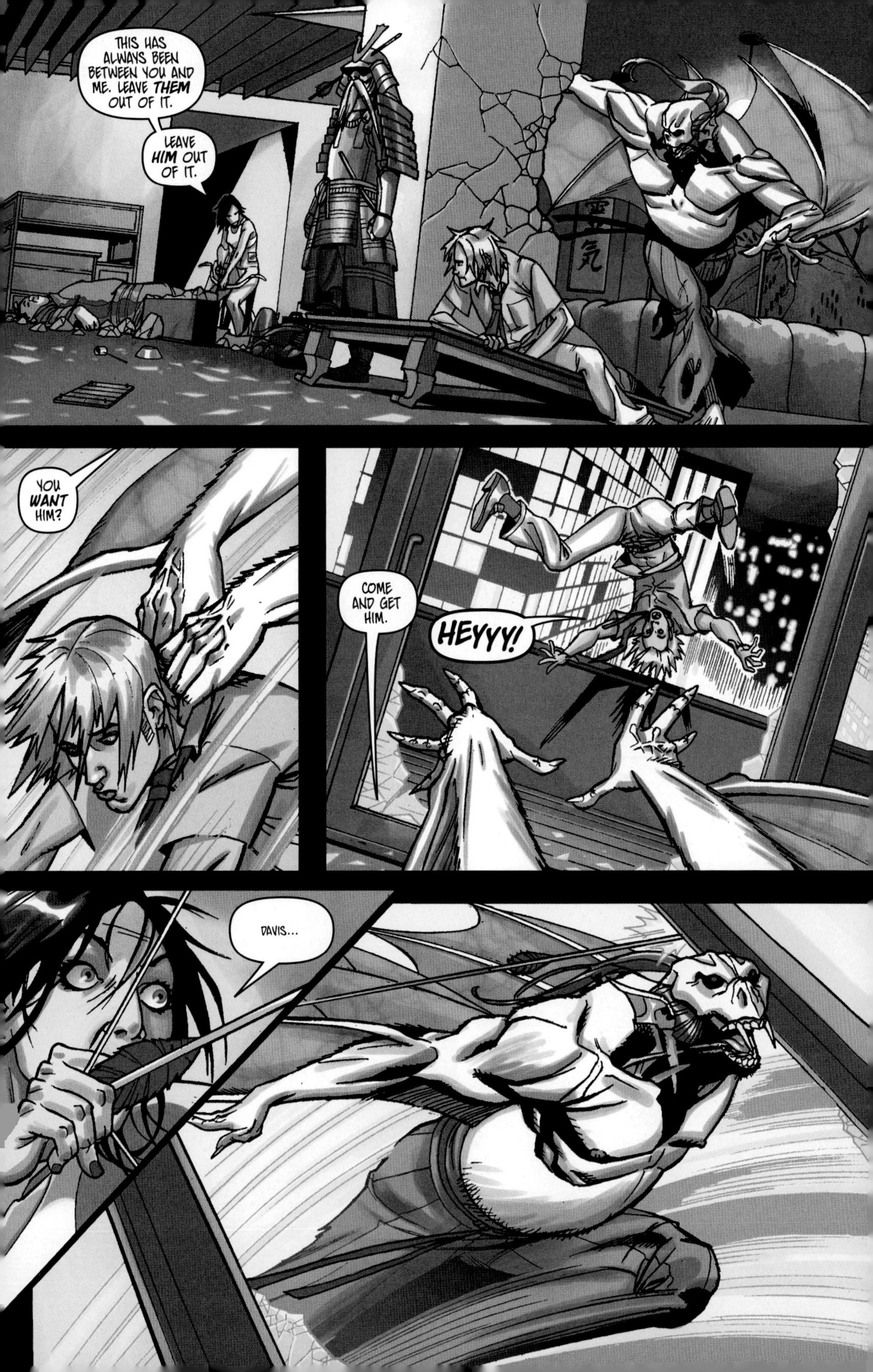
THIS HAS ALWAYS BEEN BETWEEN YOU AND ME. LEAVE THEM OUT OF IT.
LEAVE HIM OUT OF IT.
YOU WANT HIM?
COME AND GET HIM.
HEYYY!
DAVIS...

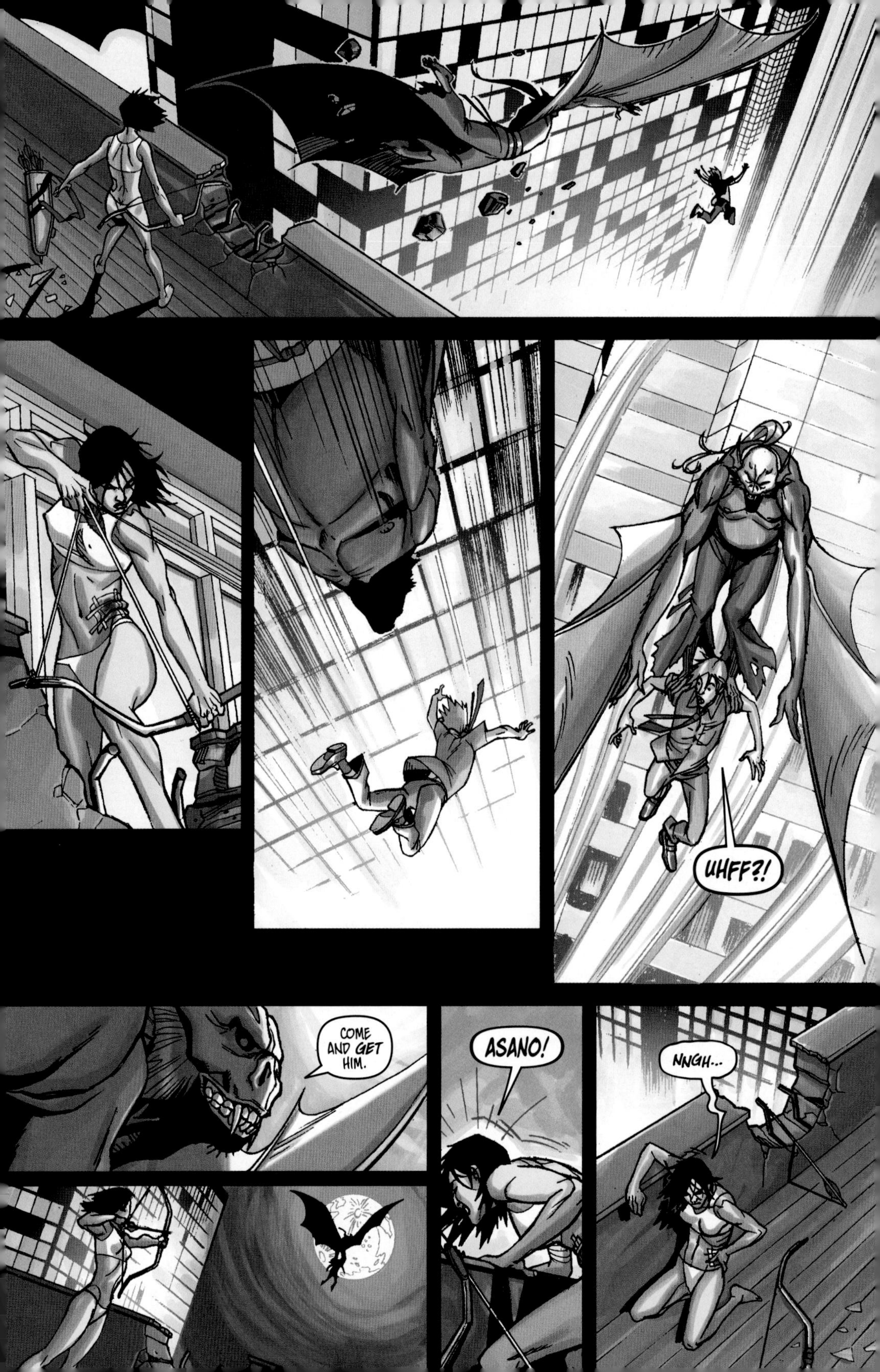
UHFF?!
COME AND GET HIM.
ASANO!
NNGH...

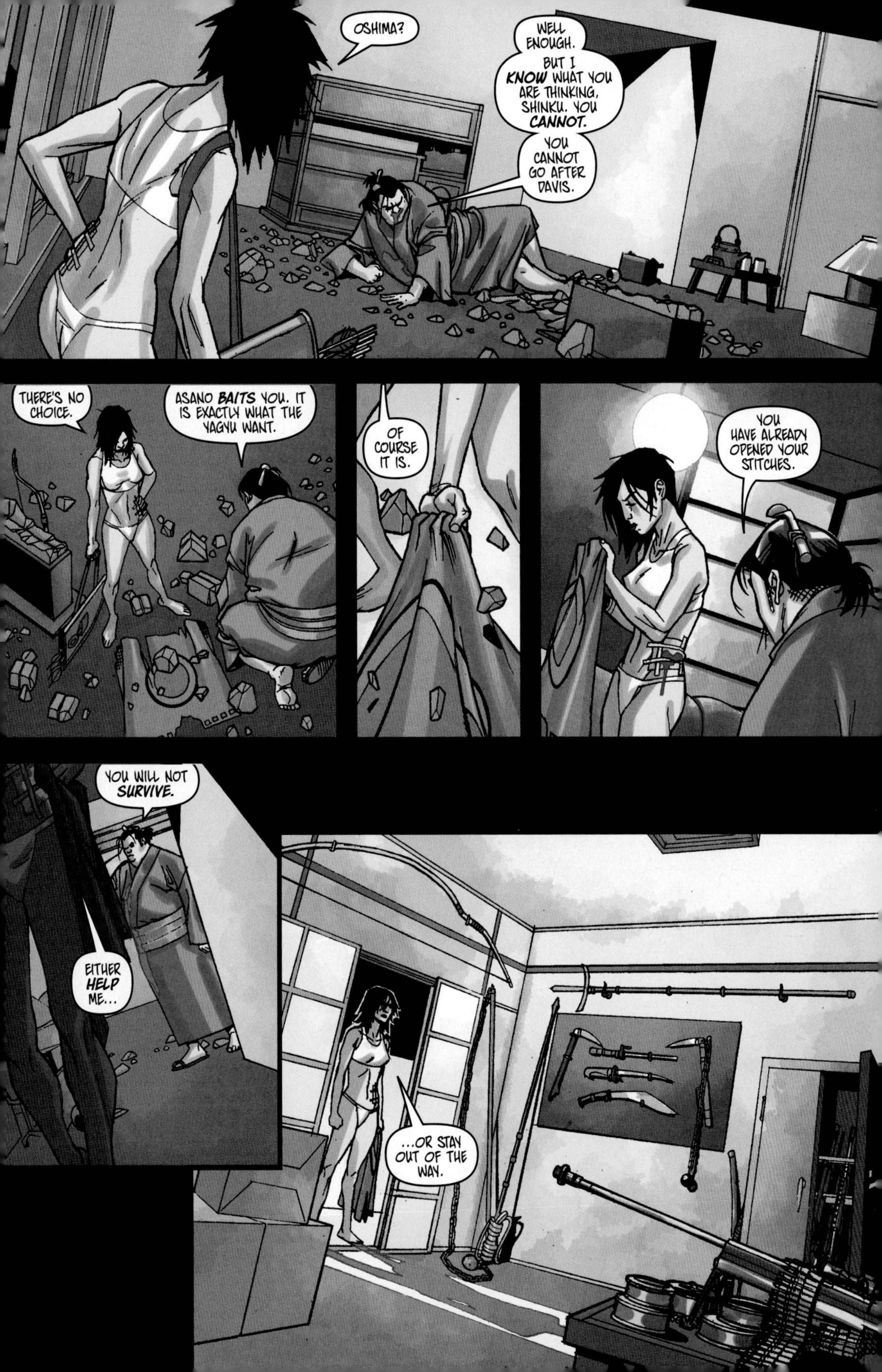
OSHIMA?
WELL ENOUGH.
BUT I KNOW WHAT YOU ARE THINKING, SHINKU. YOU CANNOT.
YOU CANNOT GO AFTER DAVIS.
THERE'S NO CHOICE.
ASANO BAITS YOU. IT IS EXACTLY WHAT THE YAGYU WANT.
OF COURSE IT IS.
YOU HAVE ALREADY OPENED YOUR STITCHES.
YOU WILL NOT SURVIVE.
EITHER HELP ME...
...OR STAY OUT OF THE WAY.

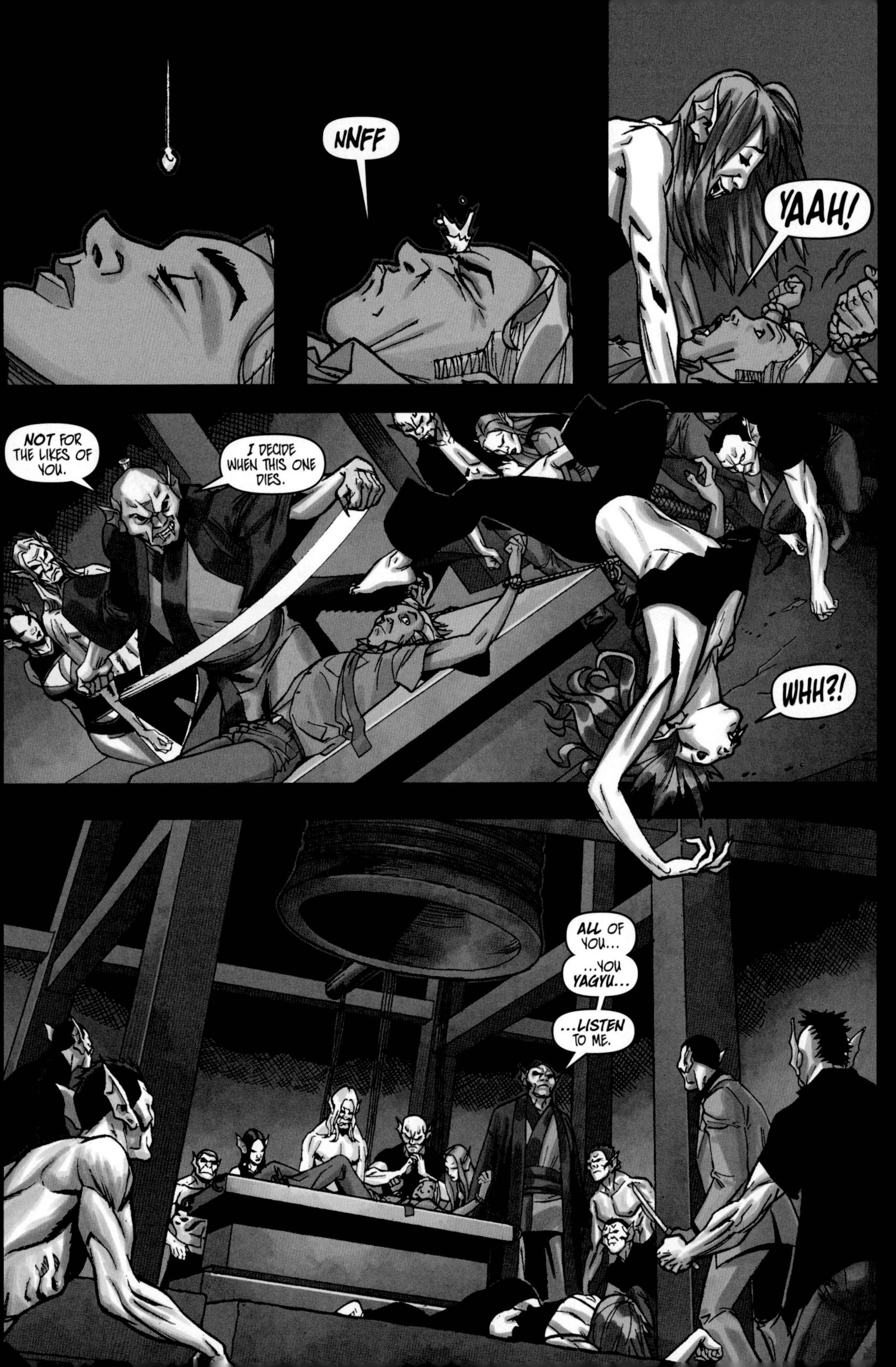
NNFF
YAAH!
NOT FOR THE LIKES OF YOU.
I DECIDE WHEN THIS ONE DIES.
WHH?!
ALL OF YOU...
...YOU YAGYU...
...LISTEN TO ME.

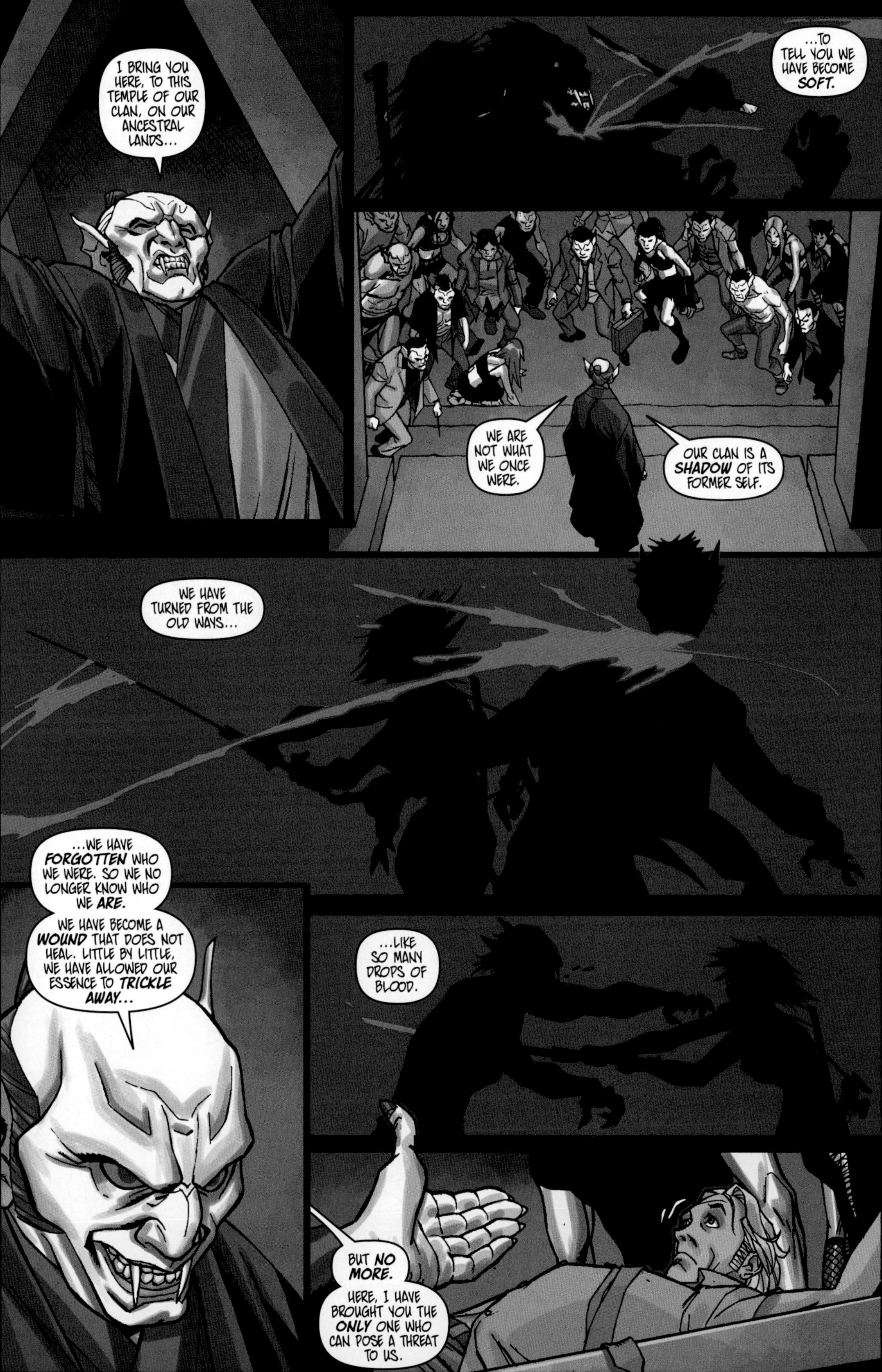
I BRING YOU HERE, TO THIS TEMPLE OF OUR CLAN, ON OUR ANCESTRAL LANDS...
...TO TELL YOU WE HAVE BECOME **SOFT.**
WE ARE NOT WHAT WE ONCE WERE.
OUR CLAN IS A **SHADOW** OF ITS FORMER SELF.
WE HAVE TURNED FROM THE OLD WAYS...
...WE HAVE **FORGOTTEN** WHO WE WERE. SO WE NO LONGER KNOW WHO WE **ARE.**
WE HAVE BECOME A **WOUND** THAT DOES NOT HEAL. LITTLE BY LITTLE, WE HAVE ALLOWED OUR ESSENCE TO **TRICKLE AWAY...**
...LIKE SO MANY DROPS OF BLOOD.
BUT **NO MORE.**
HERE, I HAVE BROUGHT YOU THE **ONLY** ONE WHO CAN POSE A THREAT TO US.

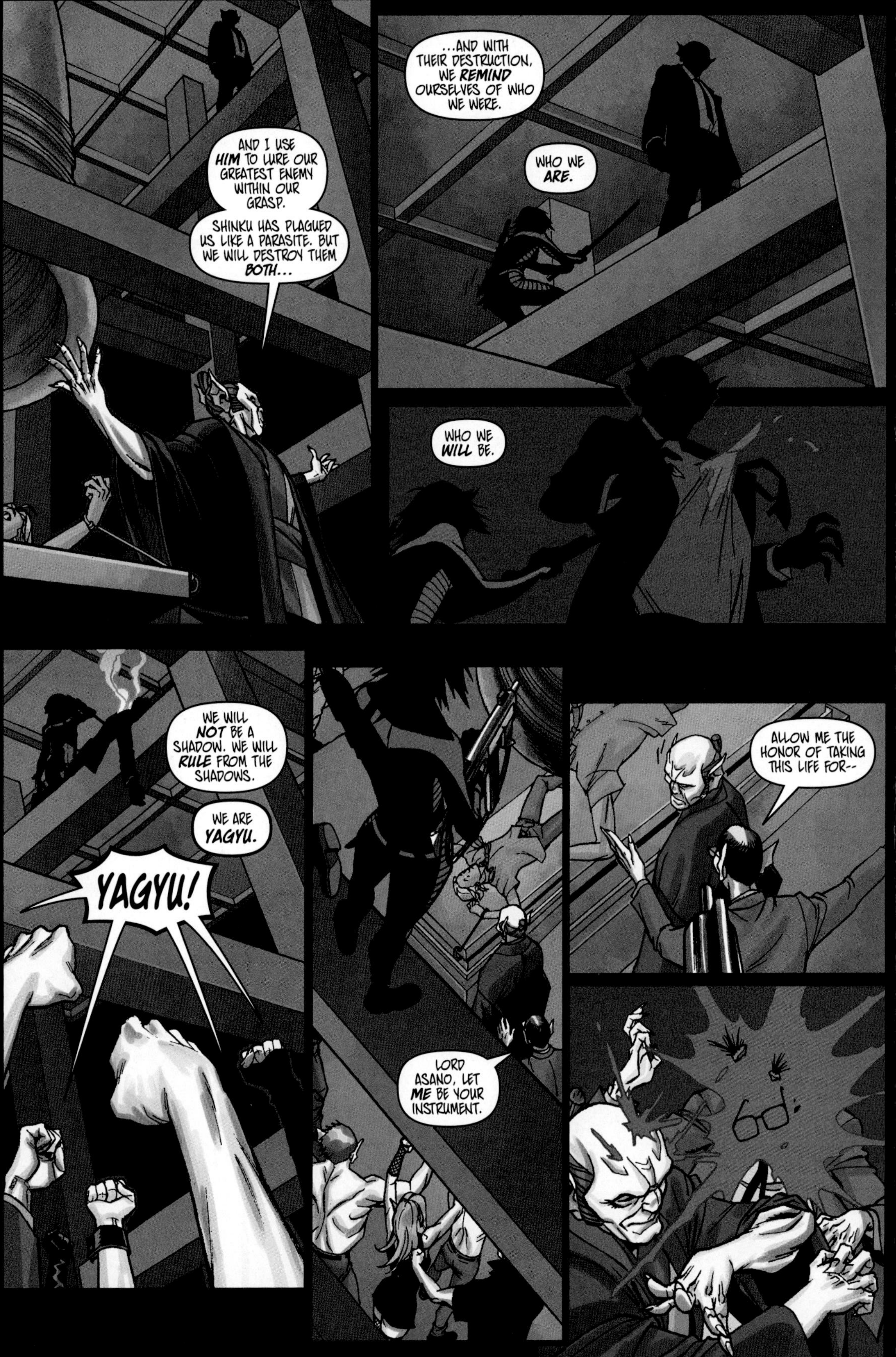
AND I USE *HIM* TO LURE OUR GREATEST ENEMY WITHIN OUR GRASP.
SHINKU HAS PLAGUED US LIKE A PARASITE. BUT WE WILL DESTROY THEM *BOTH*...
...AND WITH THEIR DESTRUCTION, WE *REMIND* OURSELVES OF WHO WE WERE.
WHO WE *ARE.*
WHO WE *WILL* BE.
WE WILL *NOT* BE A SHADOW. WE WILL *RULE* FROM THE SHADOWS.
WE ARE *YAGYU.*
YAGYU!
LORD ASANO, LET *ME* BE YOUR INSTRUMENT.
ALLOW ME THE HONOR OF TAKING THIS LIFE FOR--

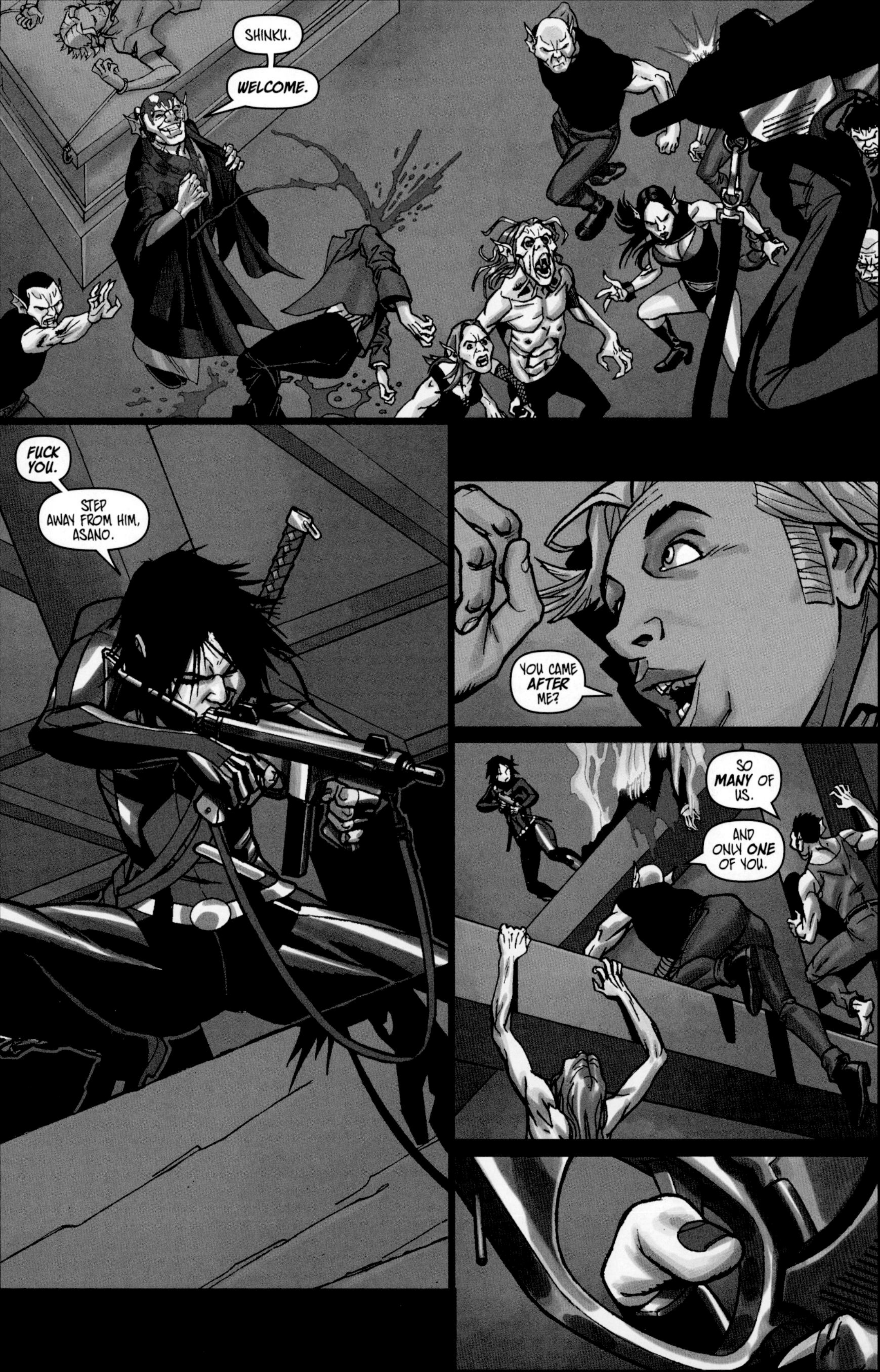
SHINKU.
WELCOME.
FUCK YOU.
STEP AWAY FROM HIM, ASANO.
YOU CAME AFTER ME?
SO MANY OF US.
AND ONLY ONE OF YOU.

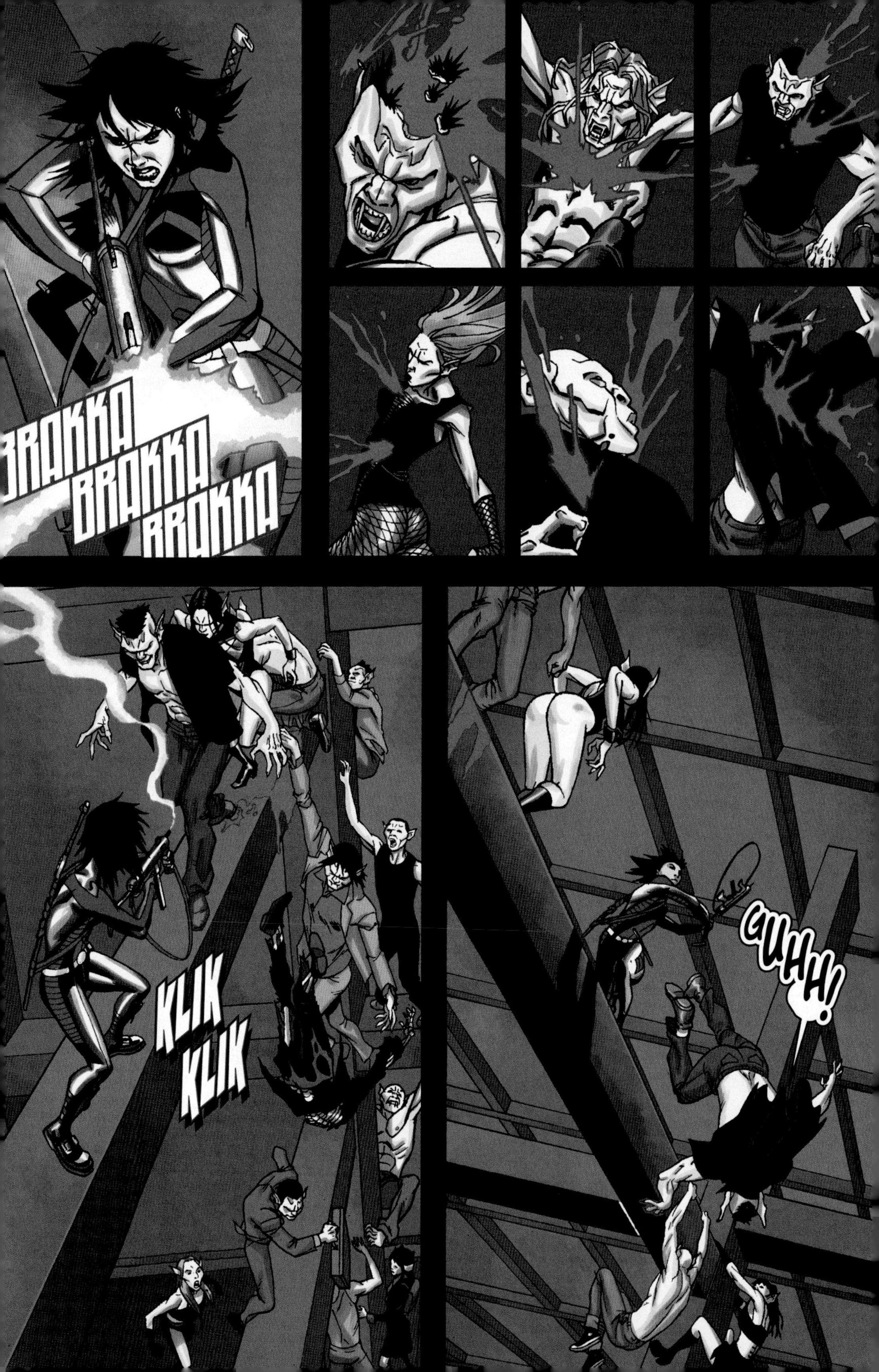
BRAKKA
BRAKKA
BRAKKA
KLIK
KLIK
GUHH!

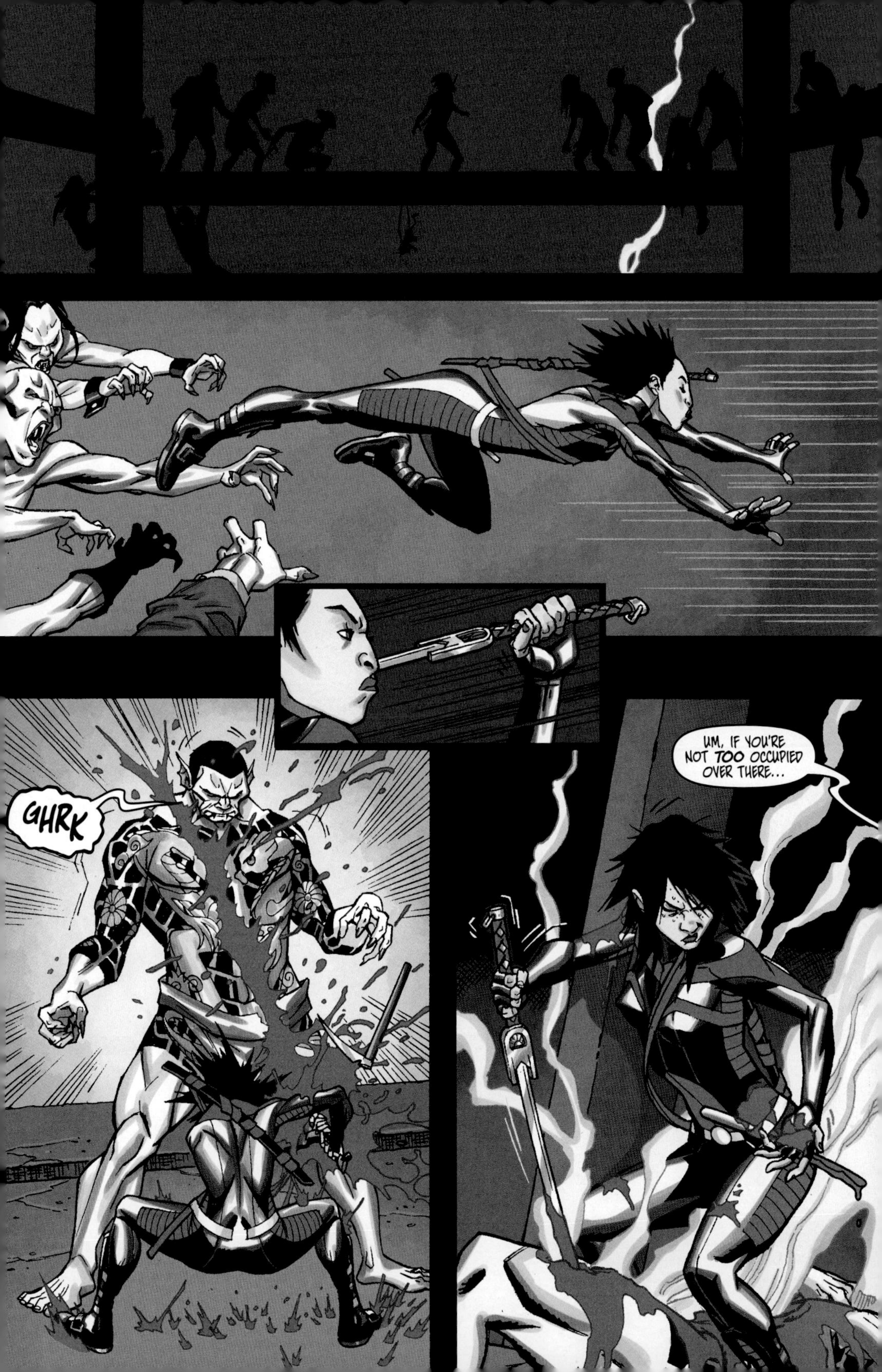
GHRK
UM, IF YOU'RE NOT TOO OCCUPIED OVER THERE...

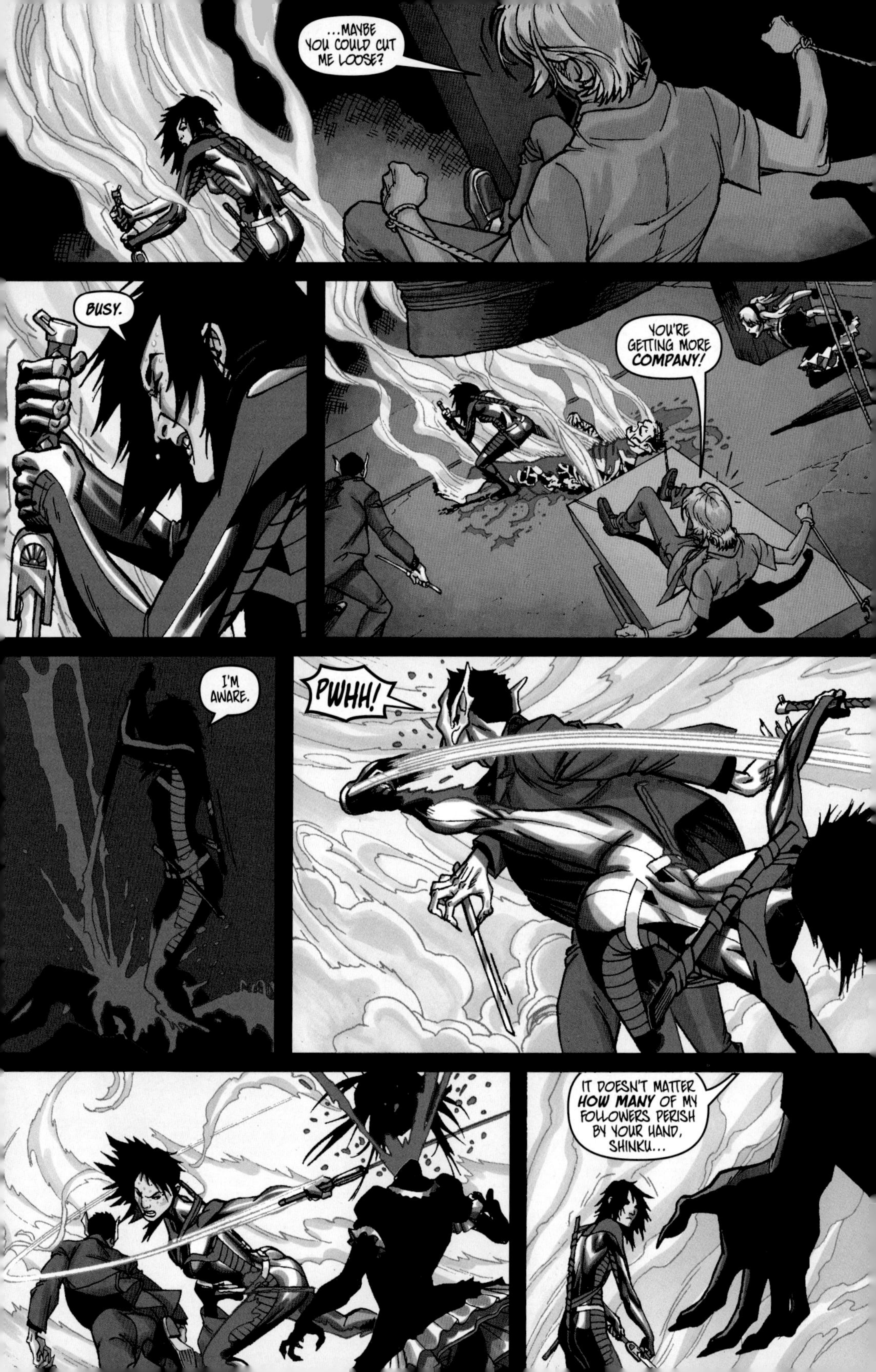
...MAYBE YOU COULD CUT ME LOOSE?
BUSY.
YOU'RE GETTING MORE **COMPANY!**
I'M AWARE.
PWHH!
IT DOESN'T MATTER **HOW MANY** OF MY FOLLOWERS PERISH BY YOUR HAND, SHINKU...

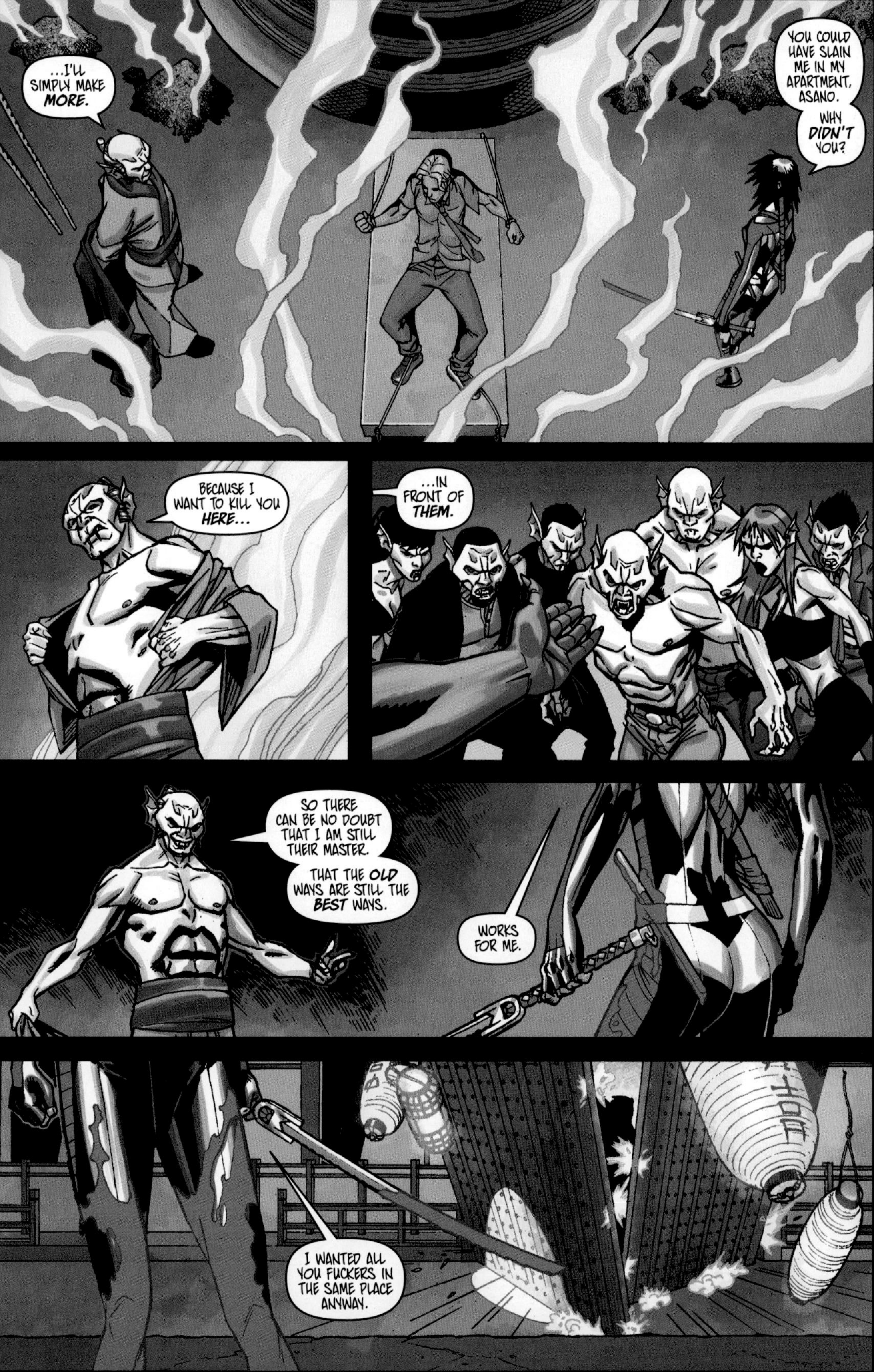
...I'LL SIMPLY MAKE MORE.
YOU COULD HAVE SLAIN ME IN MY APARTMENT, ASANO.
WHY DIDN'T YOU?
BECAUSE I WANT TO KILL YOU HERE...
...IN FRONT OF THEM.
SO THERE CAN BE NO DOUBT THAT I AM STILL THEIR MASTER.
THAT THE OLD WAYS ARE STILL THE BEST WAYS.
WORKS FOR ME.
I WANTED ALL YOU FUCKERS IN THE SAME PLACE ANYWAY.

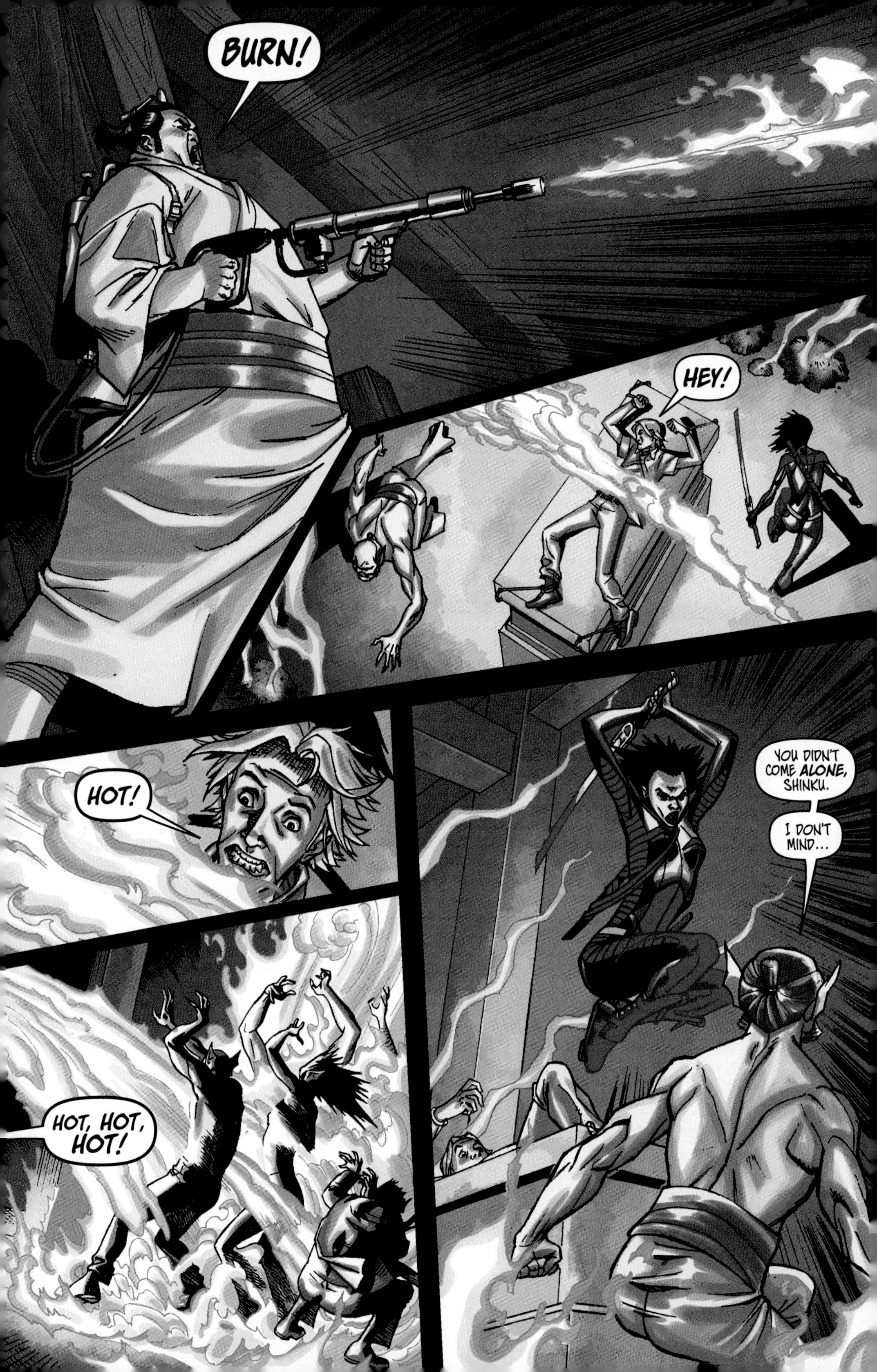
BURN!
HEY!
HOT!
YOU DIDN'T COME ALONE, SHINKU.
I DON'T MIND...
HOT, HOT, HOT!

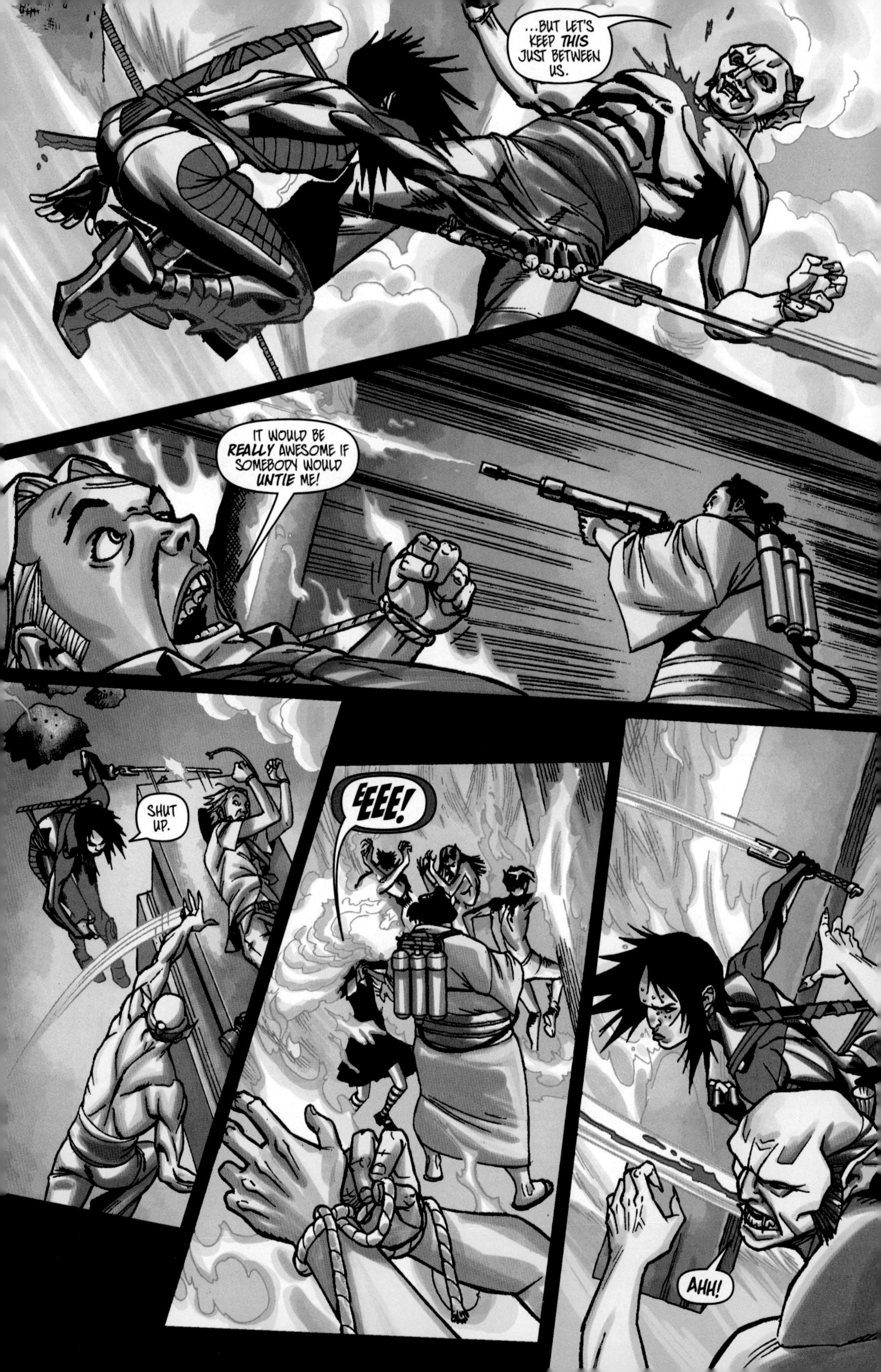
...BUT LET'S KEEP THIS JUST BETWEEN US.
IT WOULD BE REALLY AWESOME IF SOMEBODY WOULD UNTIE ME!
SHUT UP.
EEEE!
AHH!

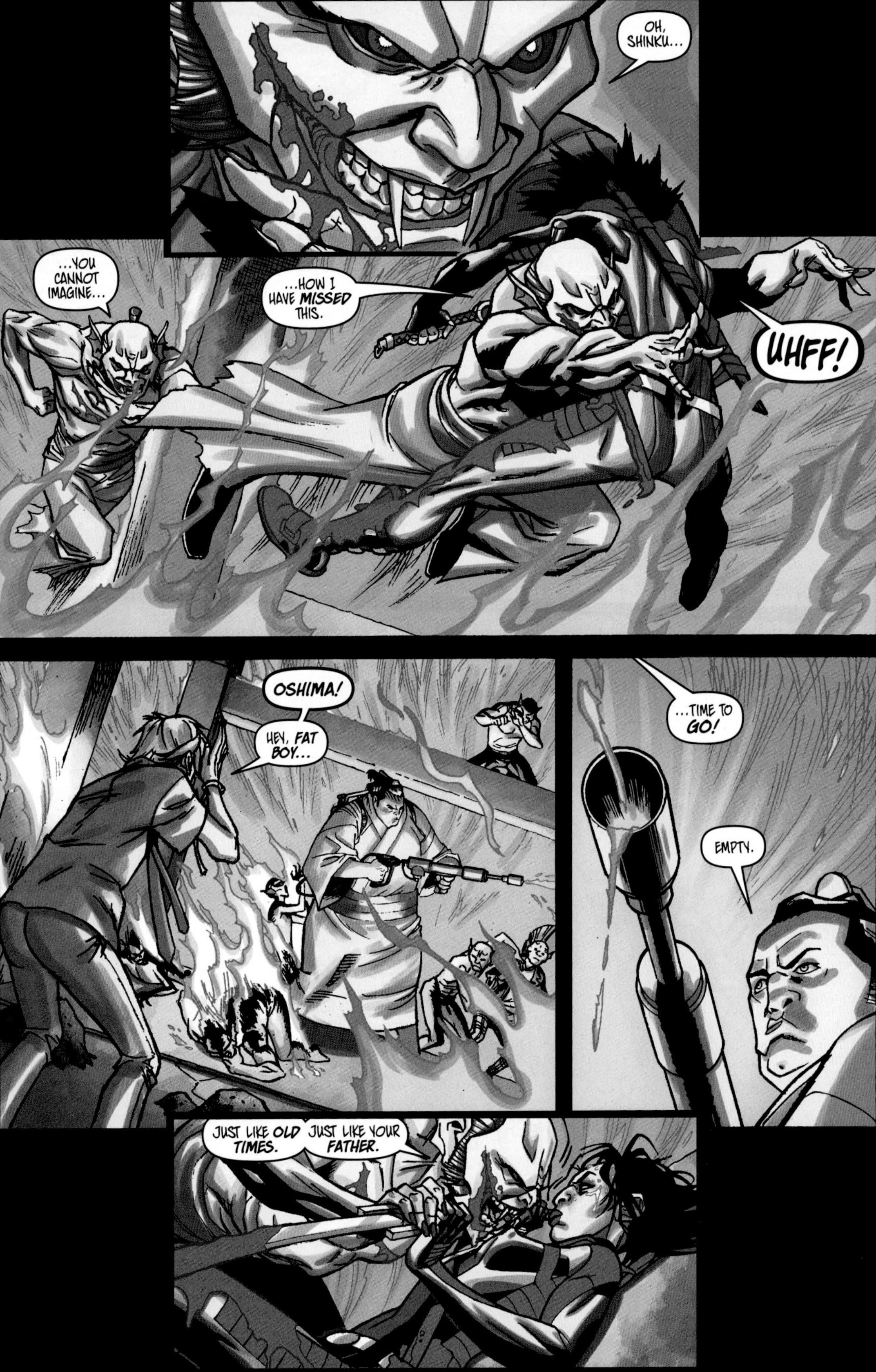
OH, SHINKU...
...YOU CANNOT IMAGINE...
...HOW I HAVE MISSED THIS.
UHFF!
OSHIMA!
HEY, FAT BOY...
...TIME TO GO!
EMPTY.
JUST LIKE OLD TIMES.
JUST LIKE YOUR FATHER.

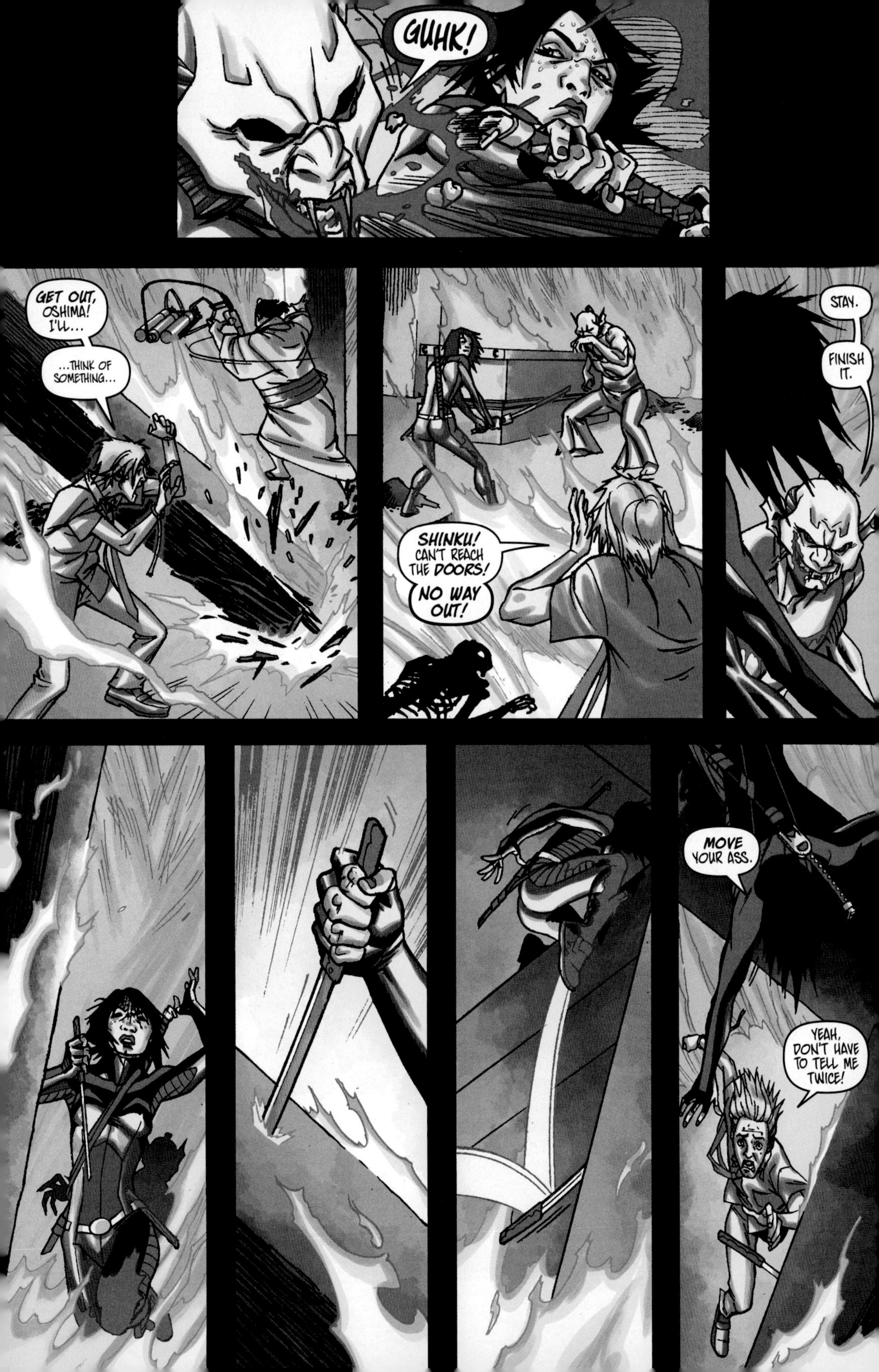

GUHK!
GET OUT, OSHIMA! I'LL...
...THINK OF SOMETHING...
SHINKU! CAN'T REACH THE DOORS!
NO WAY OUT!
STAY.
FINISH IT.
MOVE YOUR ASS.
YEAH, DON'T HAVE TO TELL ME TWICE!

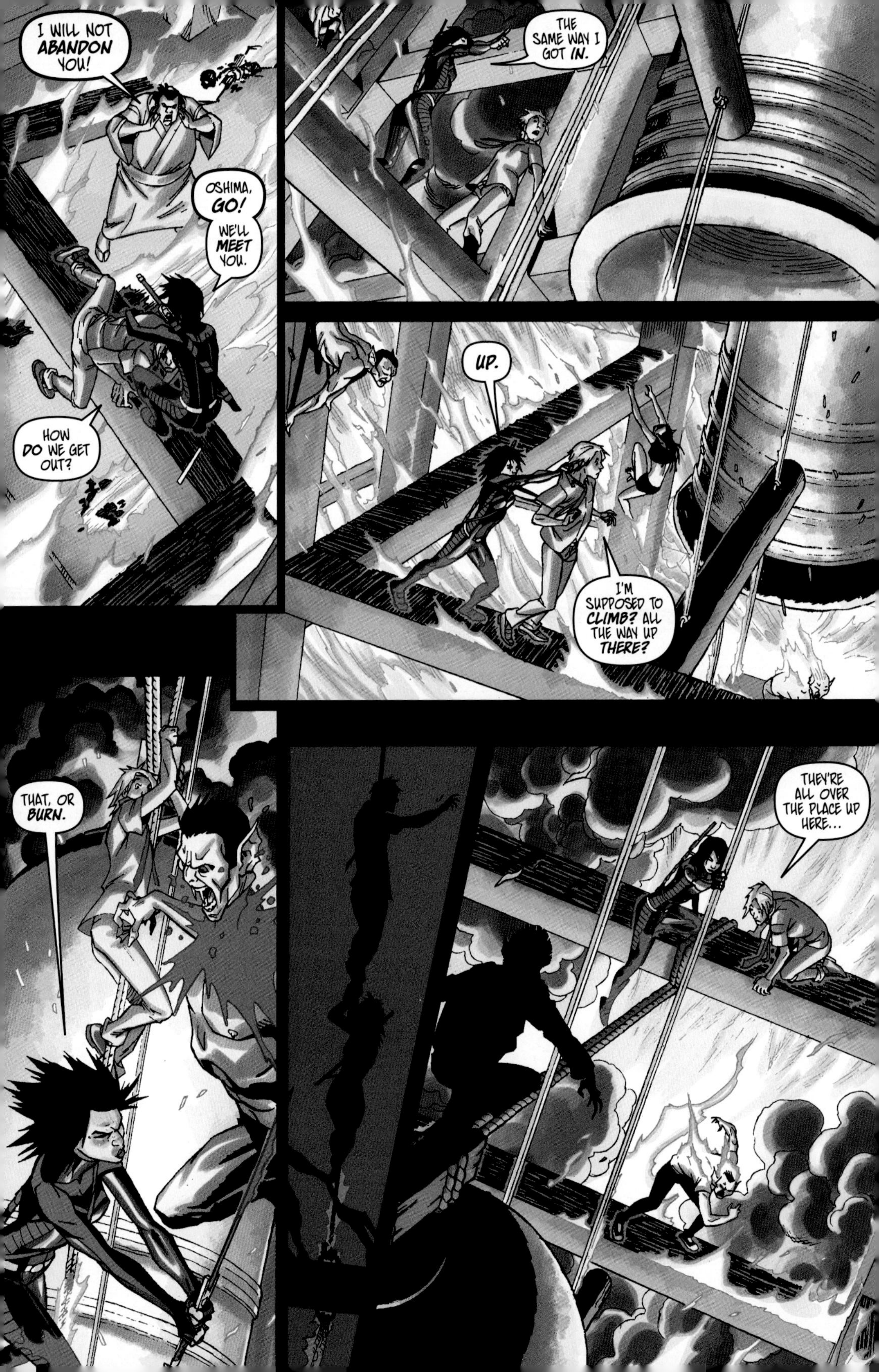
I WILL NOT ABANDON YOU!
OSHIMA, GO!
WE'LL MEET YOU.
HOW DO WE GET OUT?
THE SAME WAY I GOT IN.
UP.
I'M SUPPOSED TO CLIMB? ALL THE WAY UP THERE?
THAT, OR BURN.
THEY'RE ALL OVER THE PLACE UP HERE...

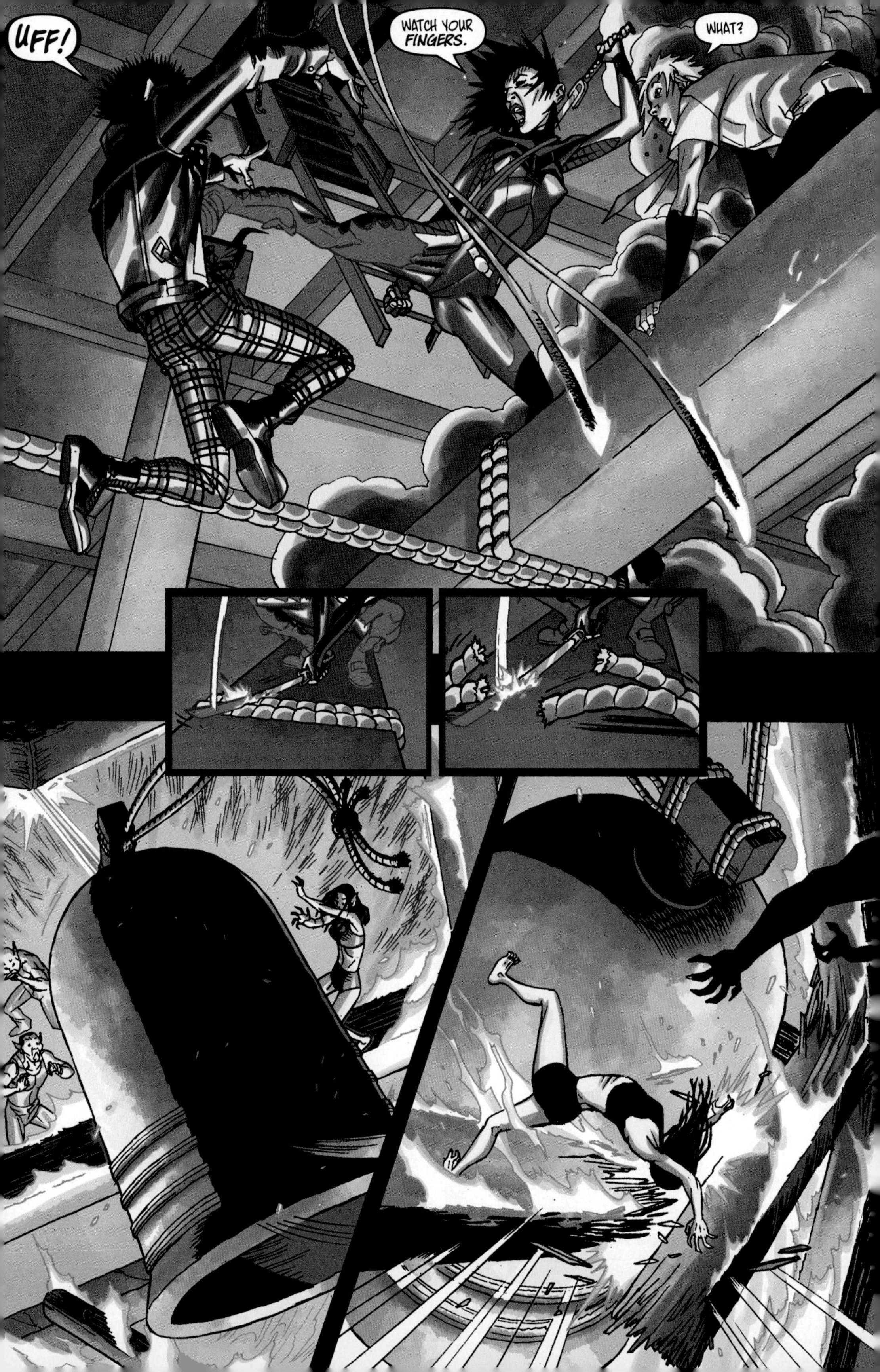
UFF!
WATCH YOUR FINGERS.
WHAT?

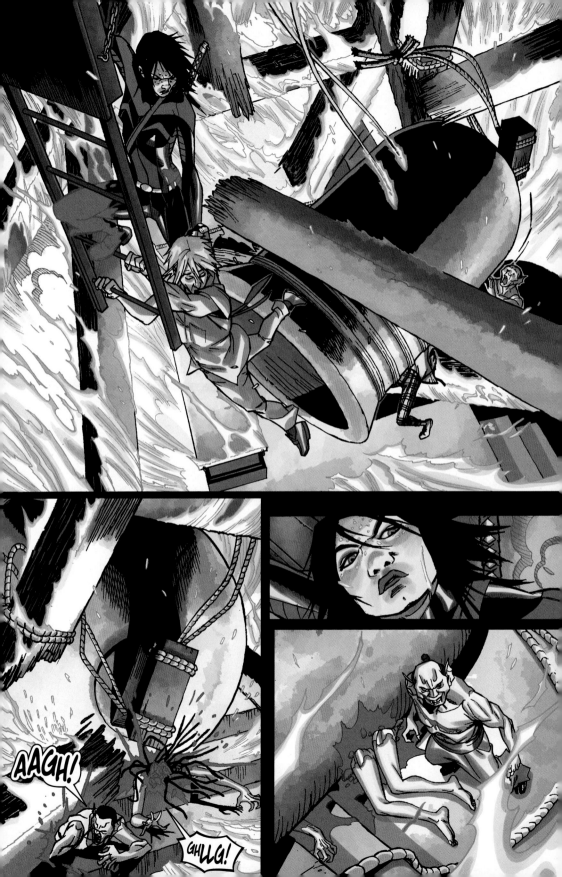

AACH!

GHLLG!

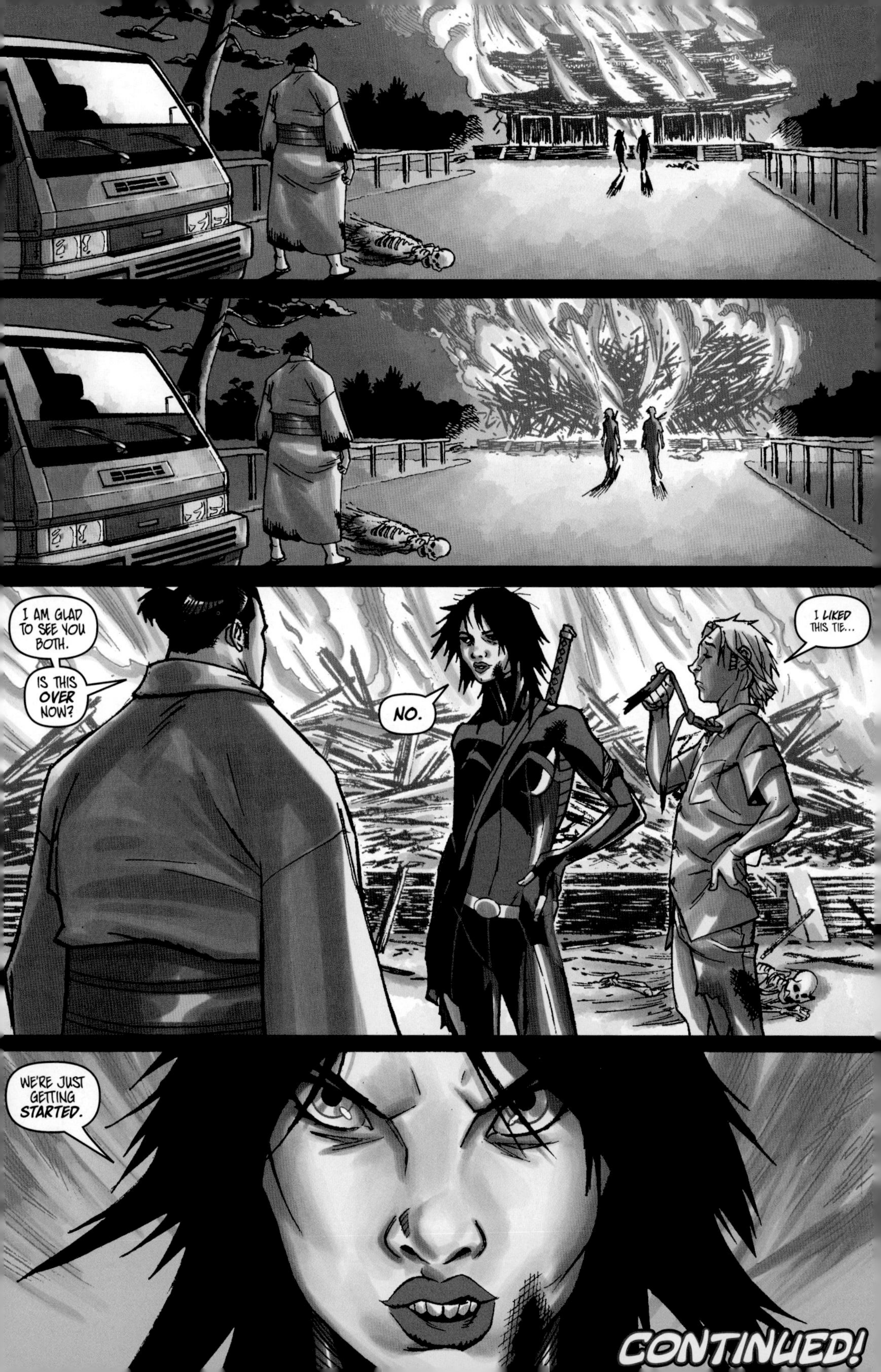
I AM GLAD TO SEE YOU BOTH.
IS THIS OVER NOW?
NO.
I LIKED THIS TIE...
WE'RE JUST GETTING STARTED.
CONTINUED!

Gallery

Alternate covers and pinups

art by Lee Moder, Matthew Waite & Michael Atiyeh

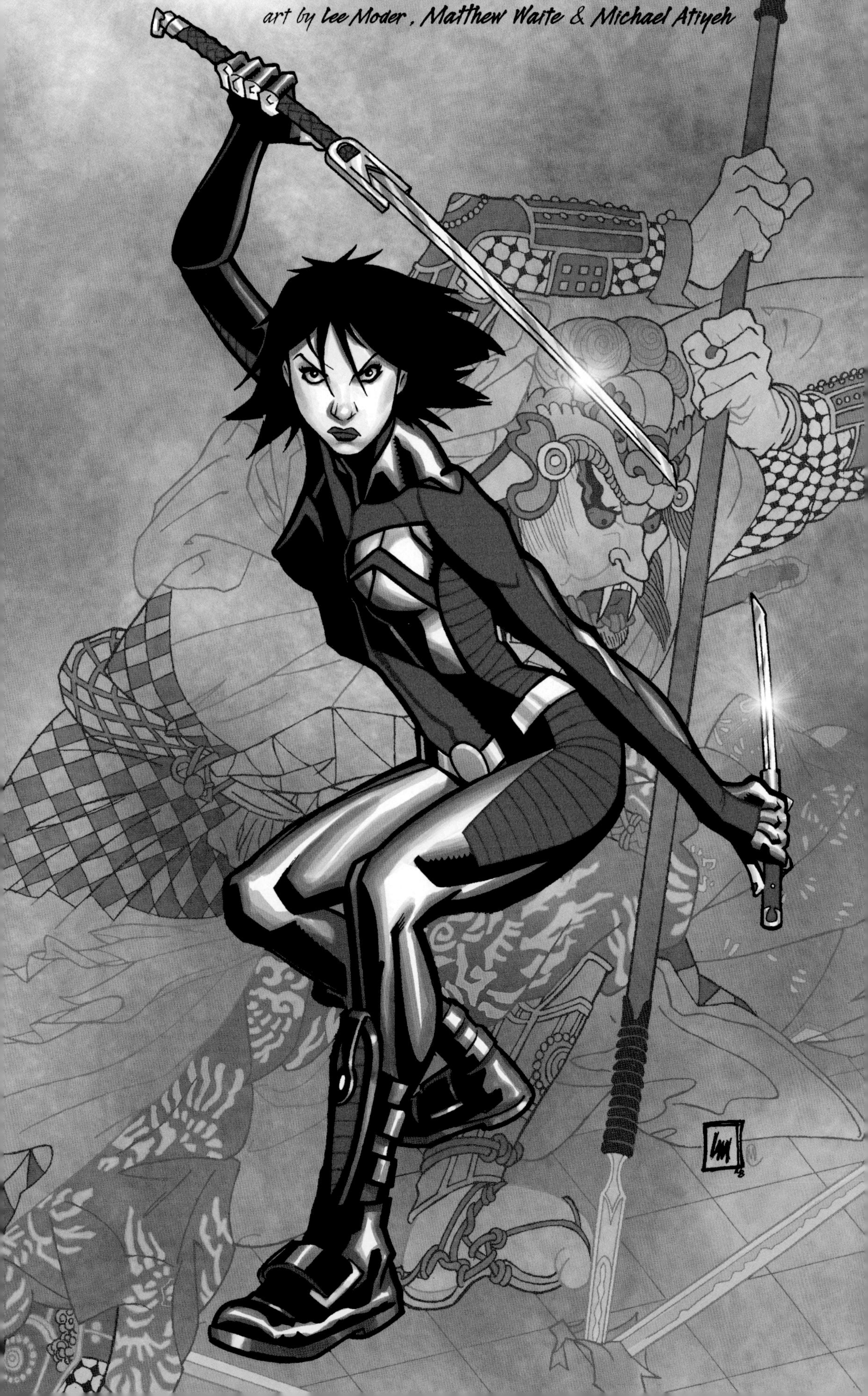

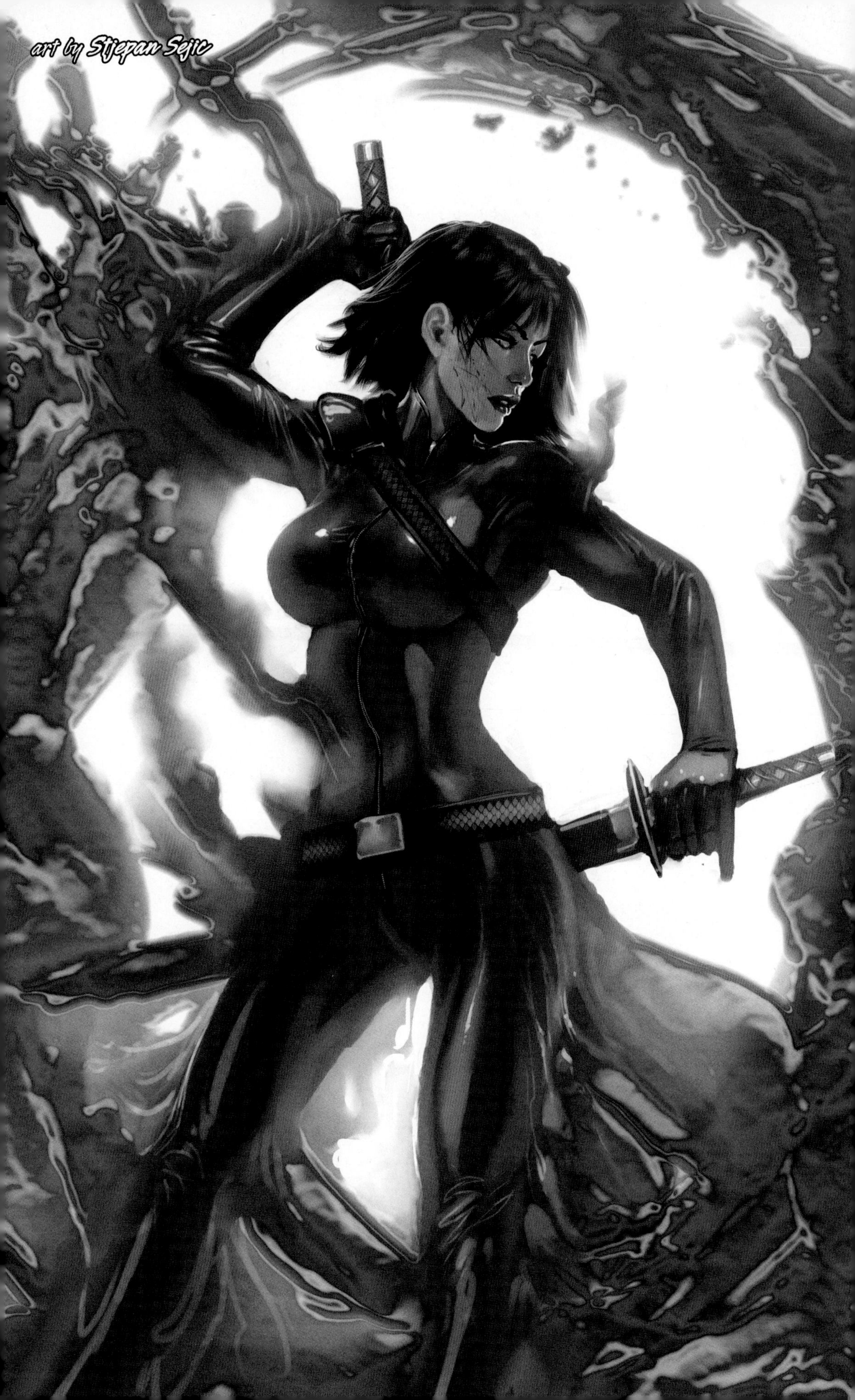
art by Stjepan Sejic

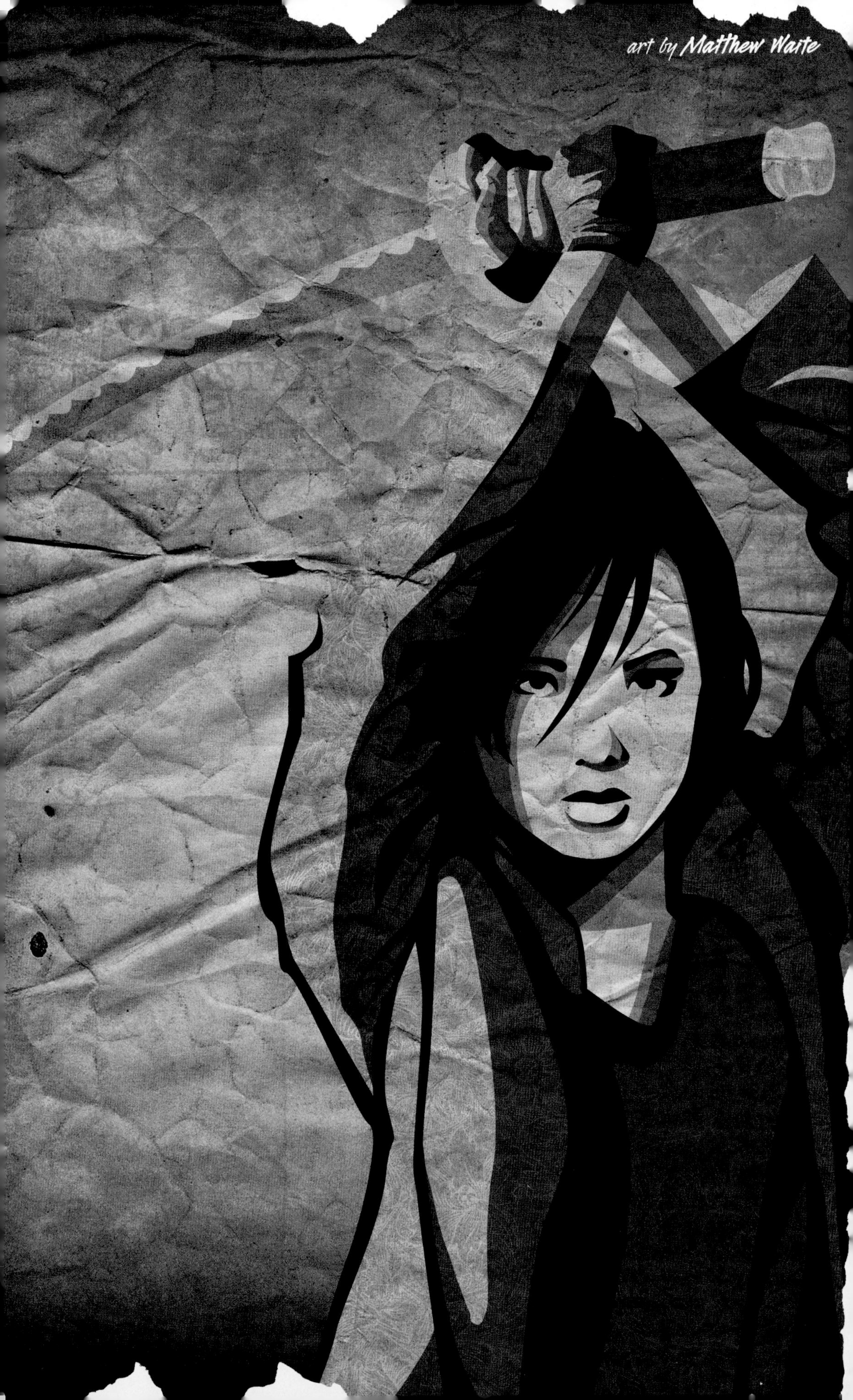
art by Matthew Waite

art by Michael Borkowski

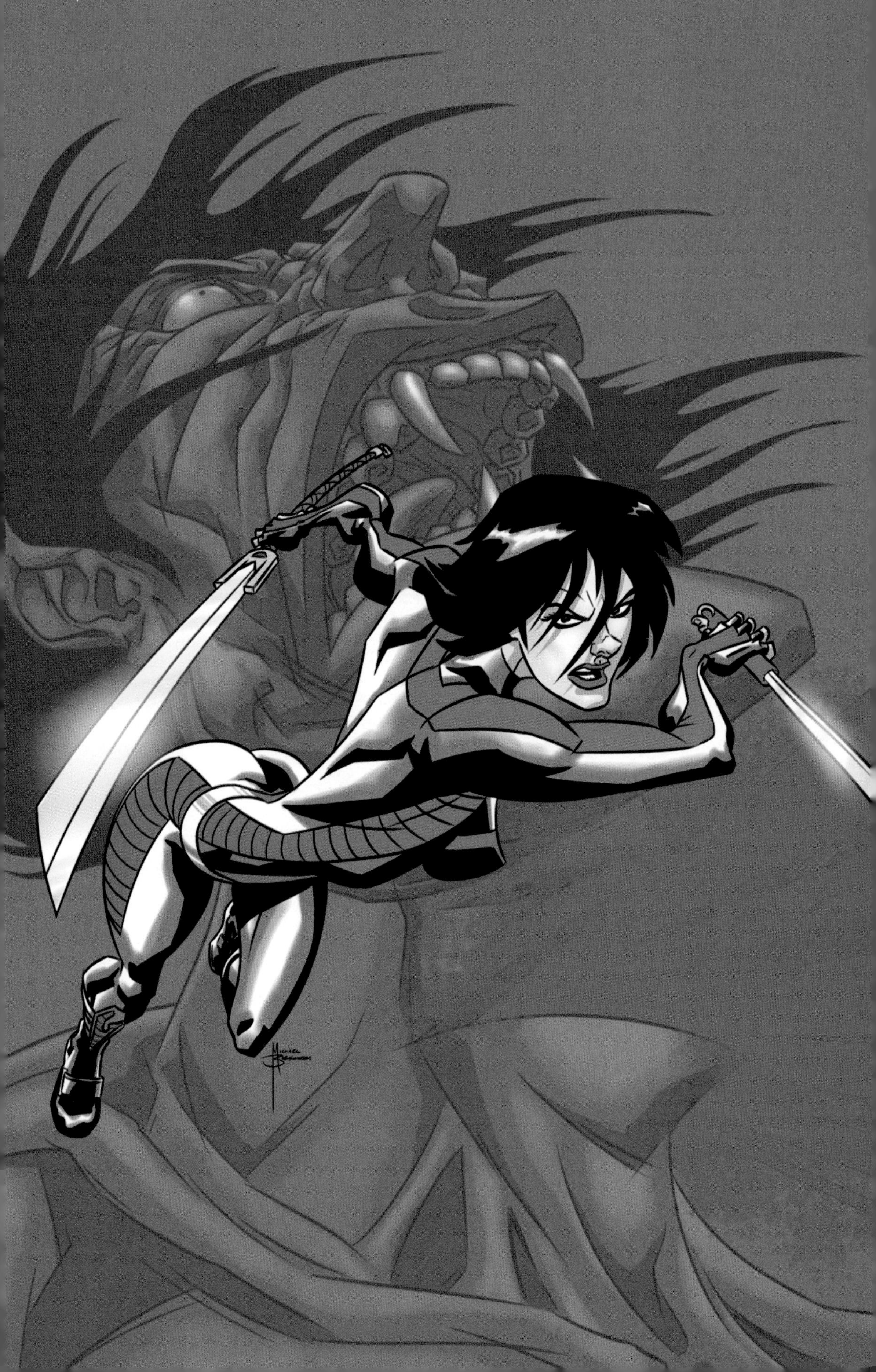

art by **Scott Zitta**

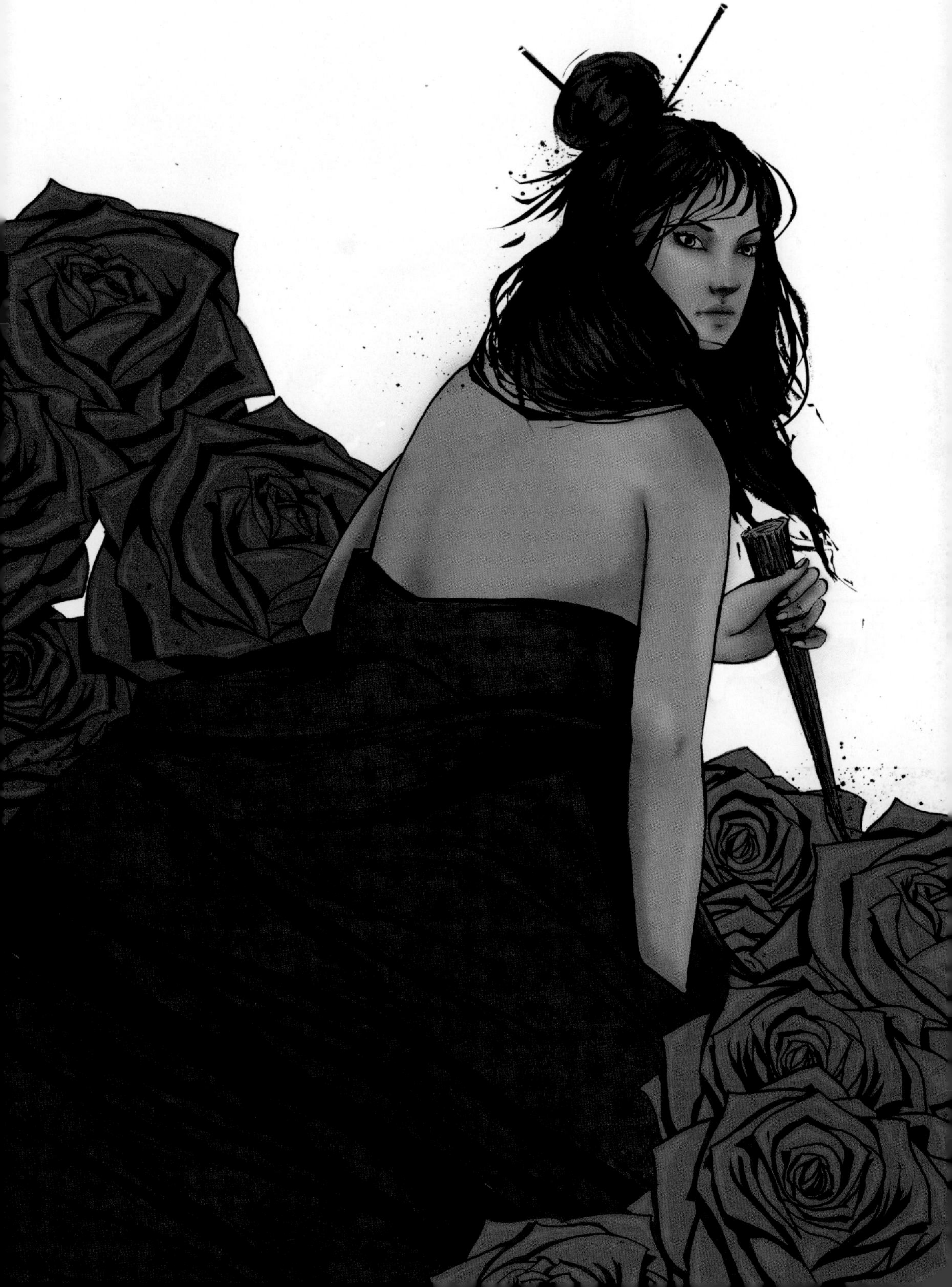

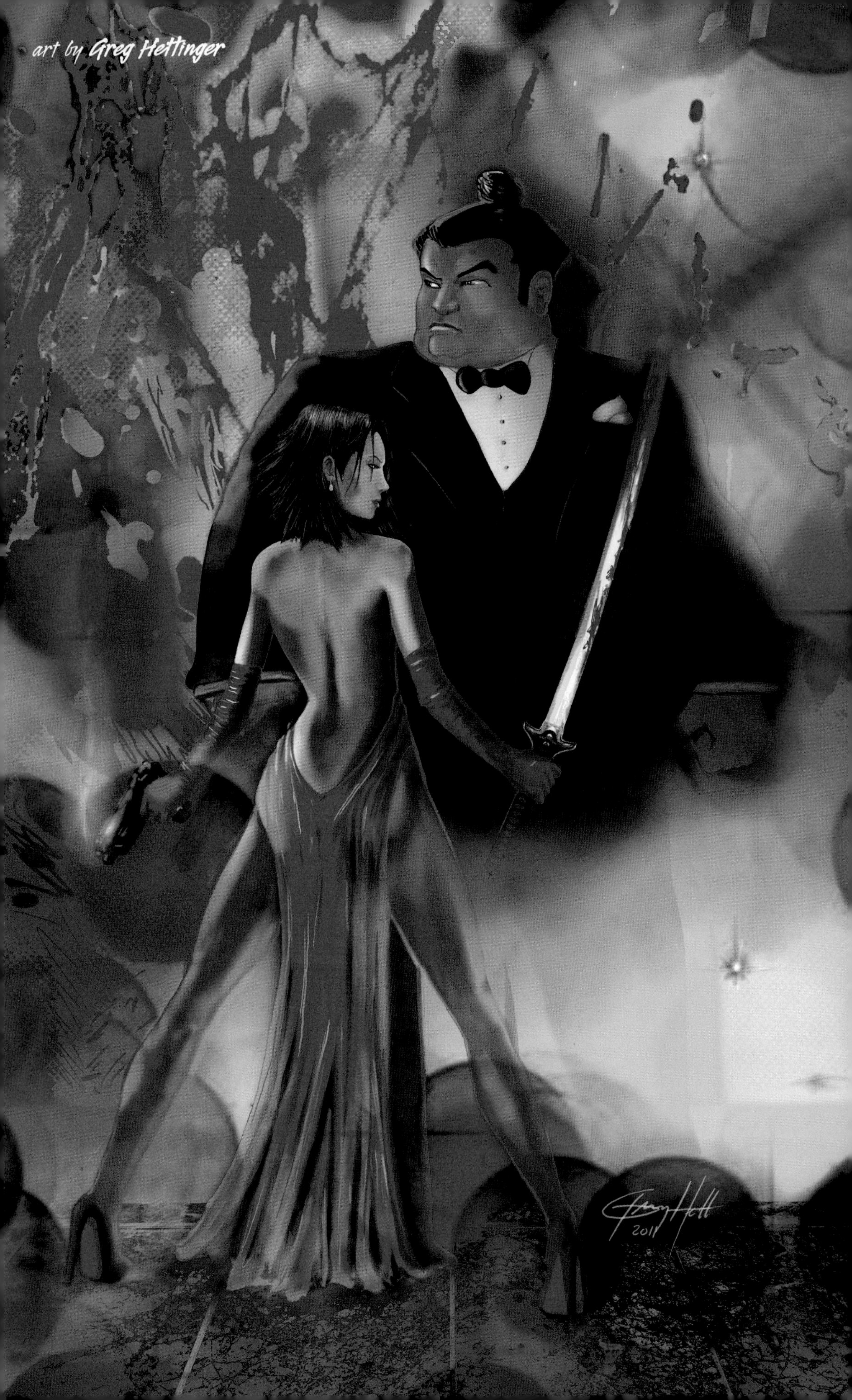
art by Greg Hettinger
2011

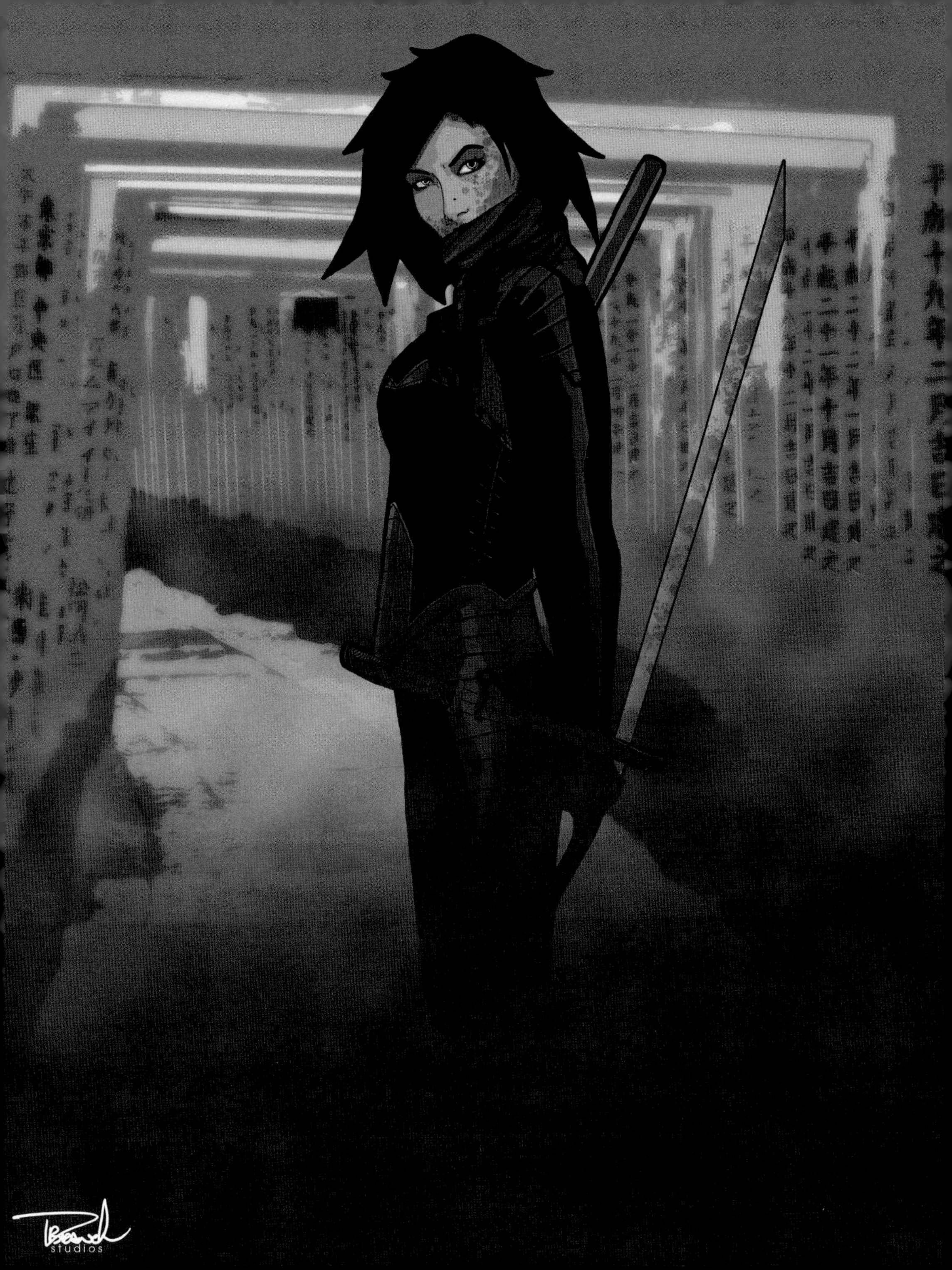

Sketchbook

Artwork by Lee Moder

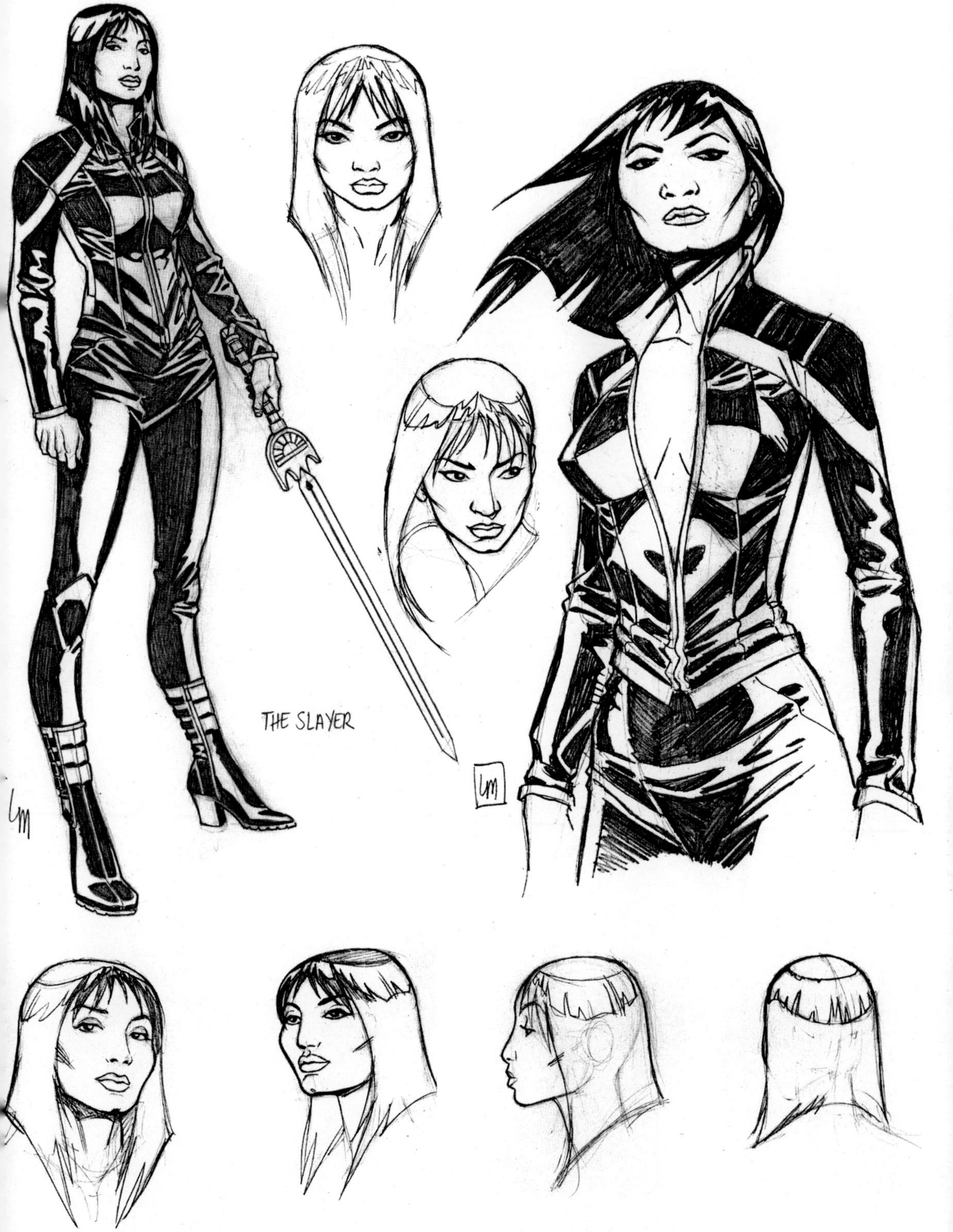
THE SLAYER

The design of the vampire hunter was settled upon almost immediately, taking its cue from motorcycle leathers. The sword design was revised subtly, to reflect a more Japanese-style blade.

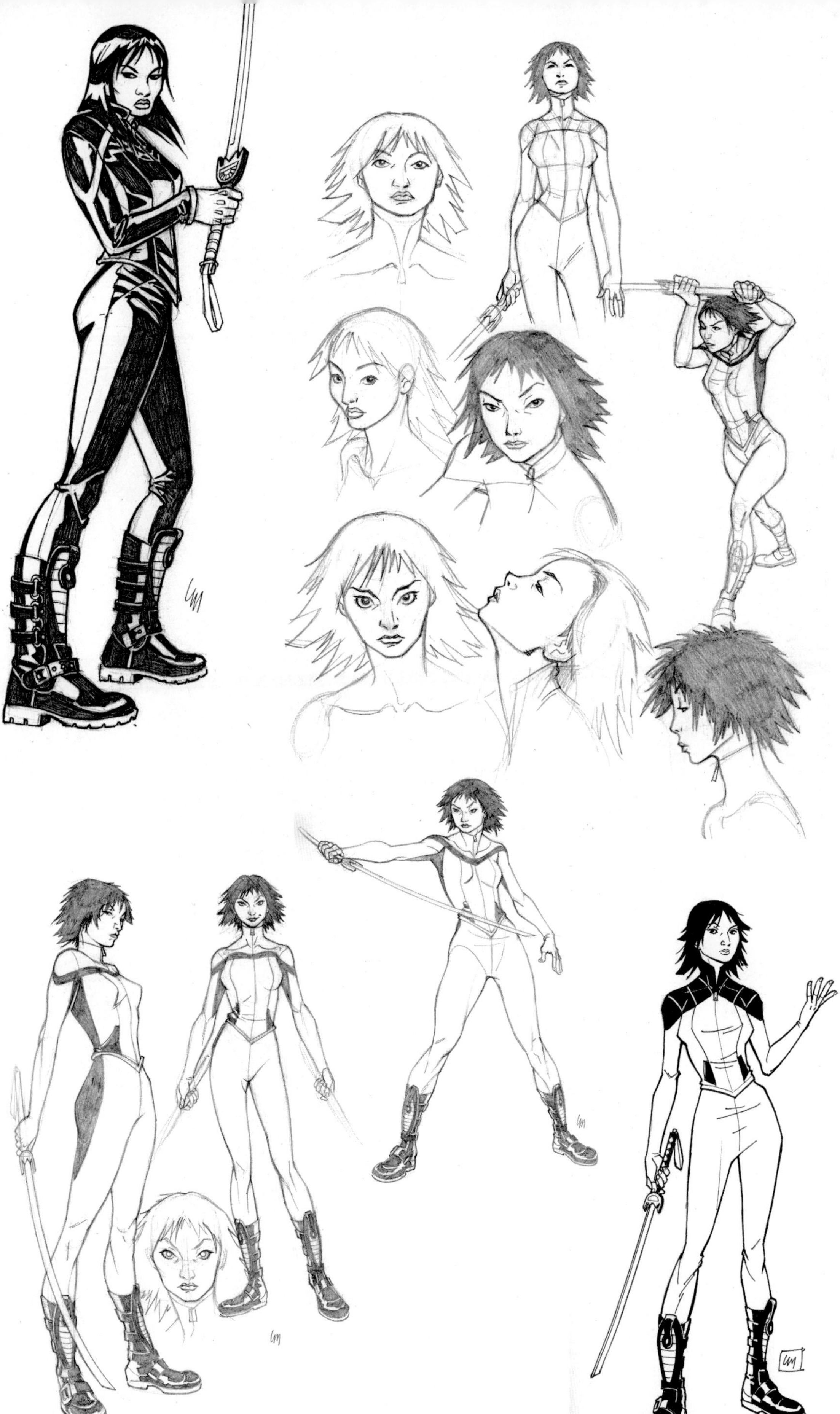

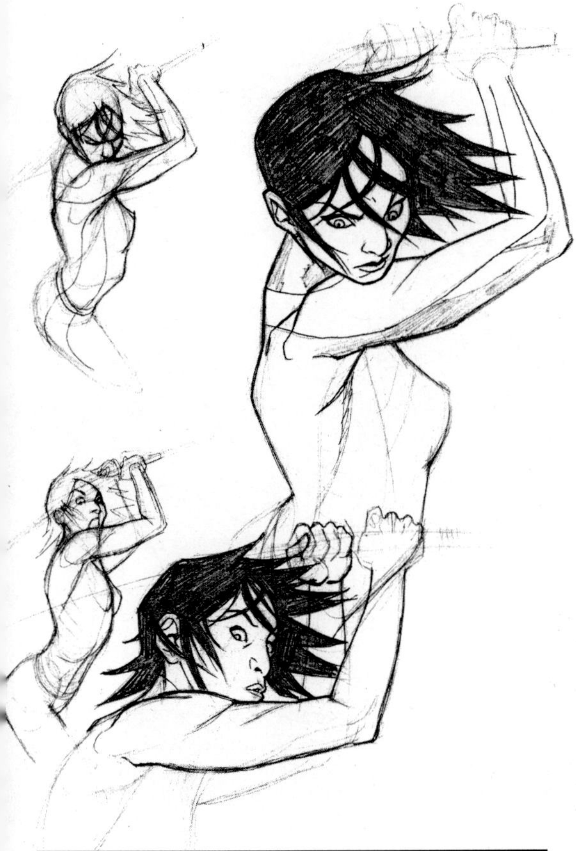

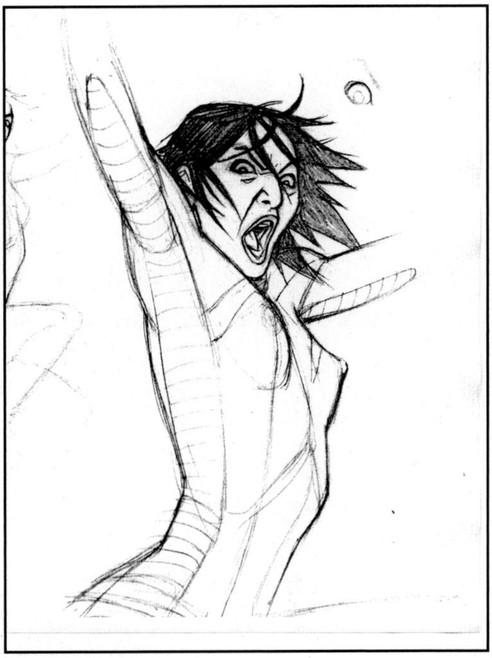

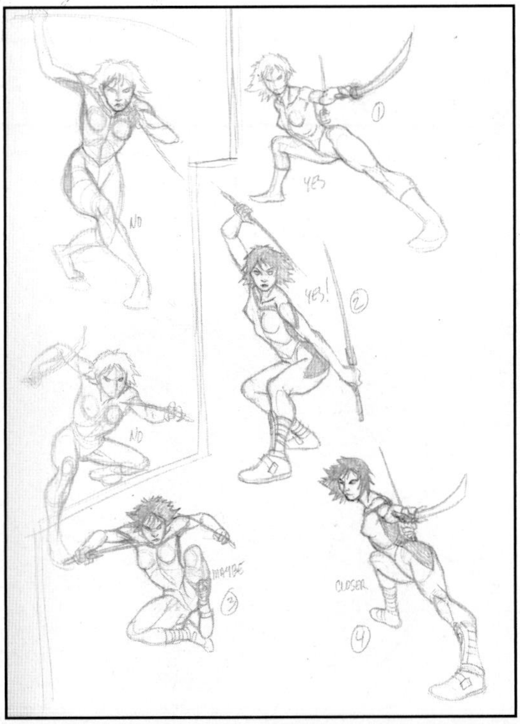
1
YES
NO
YES!
2
NO
MAYBE
3
CLOSER
4

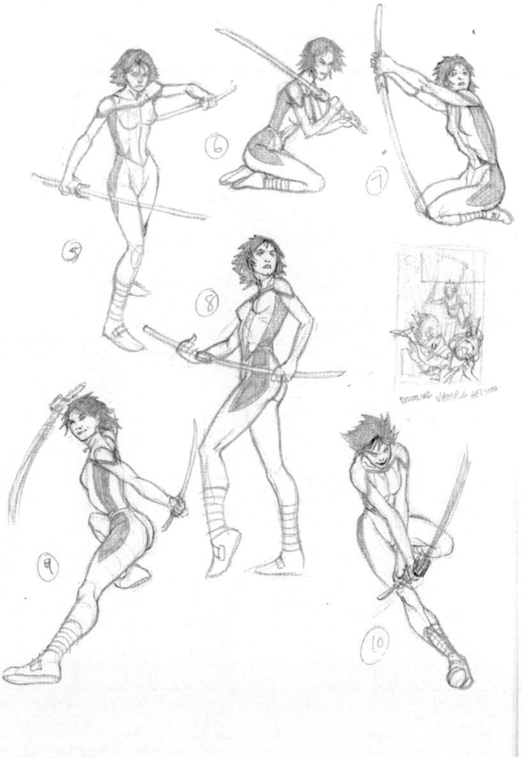
6
7
5
8
9
10

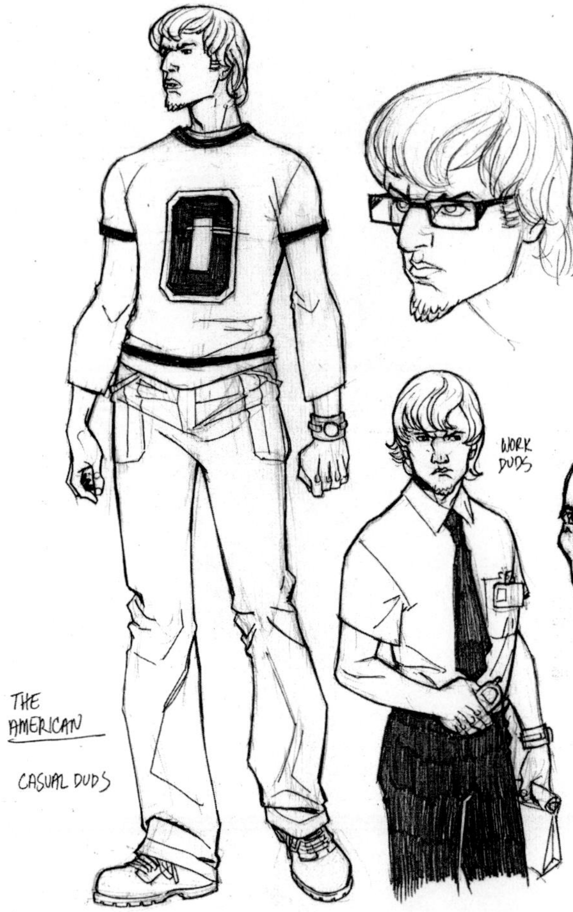

WORK DUDS
THE AMERICAN
CASUAL DUDS

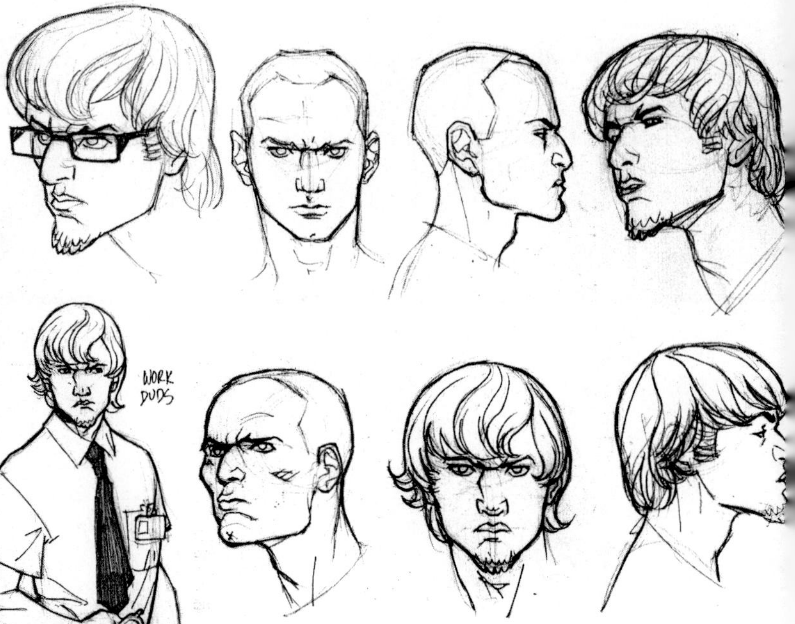

An American living and working in Tokyo, Davis is intended to be the initial point-of-view character for the audience. The first designs gave the character a more intense look that was deemed too harsh.

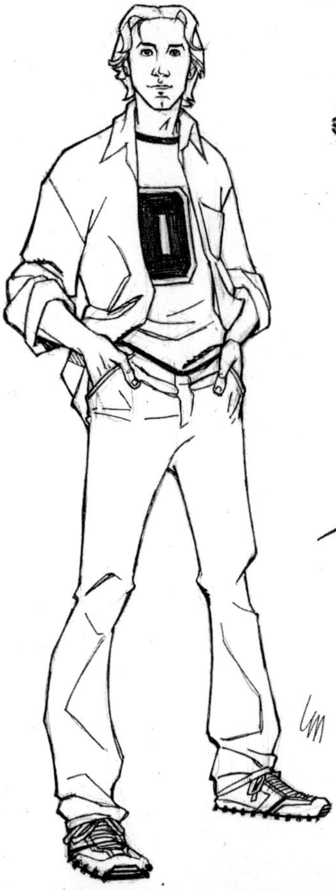

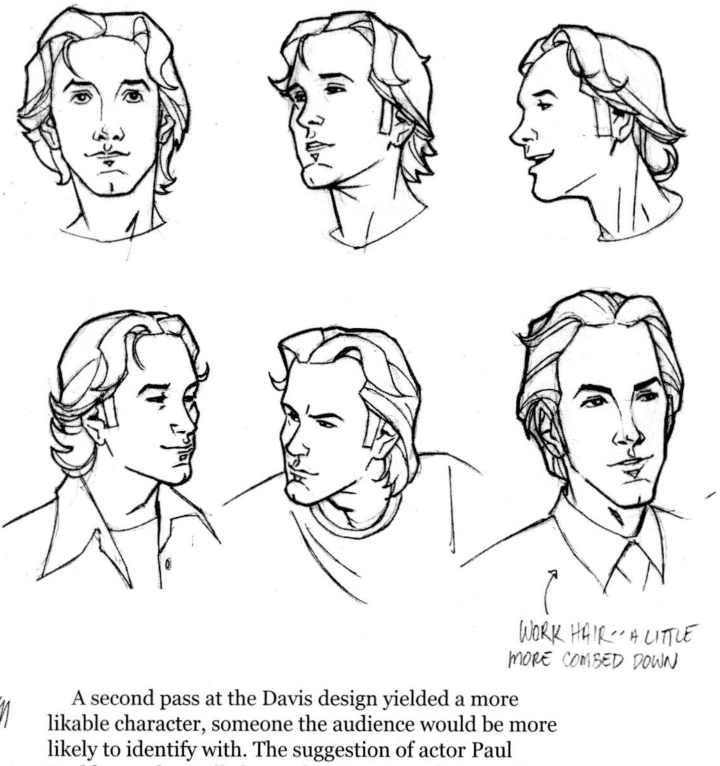

WORK HAIR -- A LITTLE MORE COMBED DOWN

A second pass at the Davis design yielded a more likable character, someone the audience would be more likely to identify with. The suggestion of actor Paul Rudd, not physically but rather in terms of personality, helped nail the character's look.

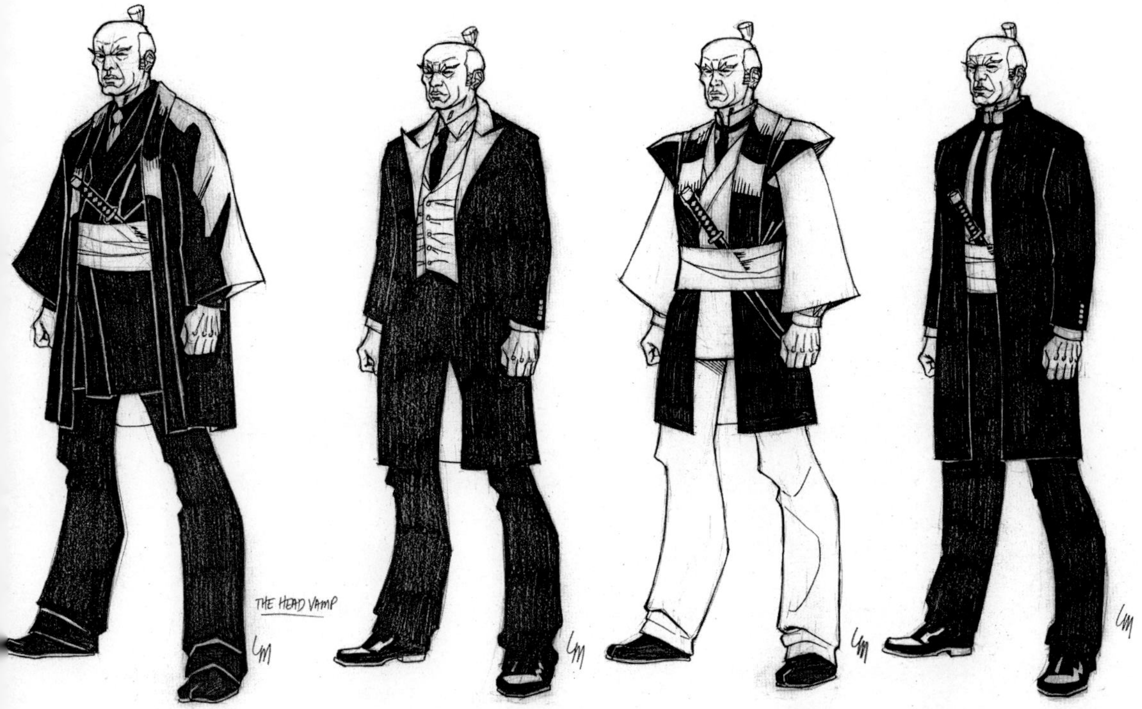
THE HEAD VAMP

Various costume designs were produced for Asano, leader of the Yagyu vampire clan, combining modern aspects with flourishes from the past. The timeless look reflects the character's centuries-long lifespan.

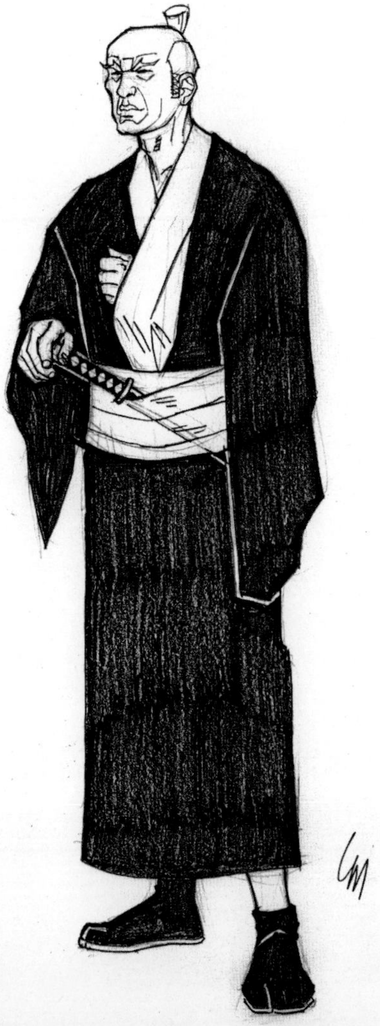

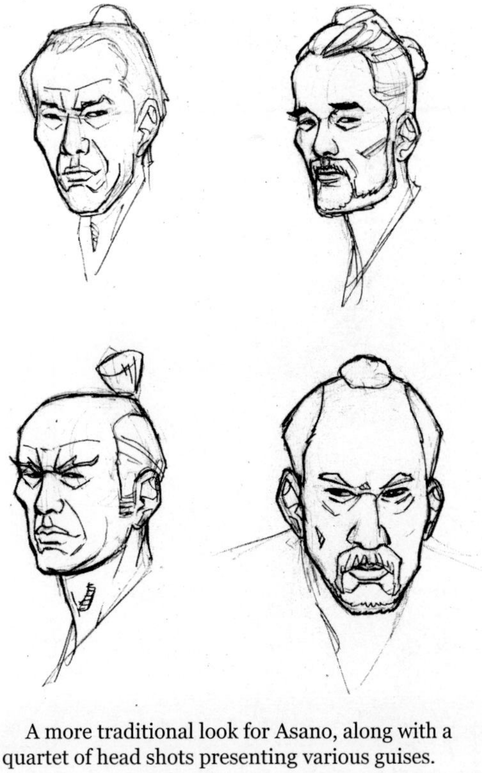

A more traditional look for Asano, along with a quartet of head shots presenting various guises.

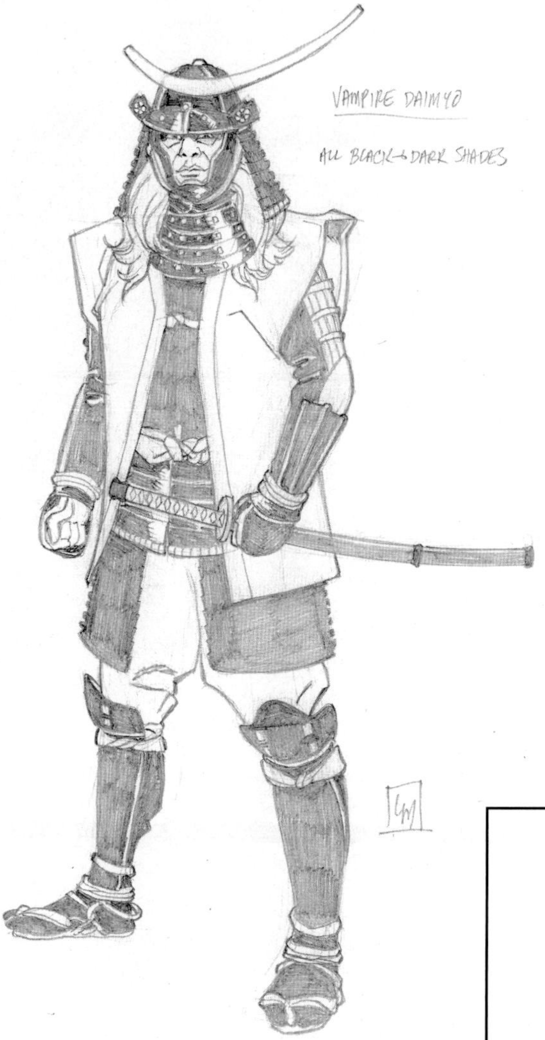
VAMPIRE DAIMYO
ALL BLACK & DARK SHADES

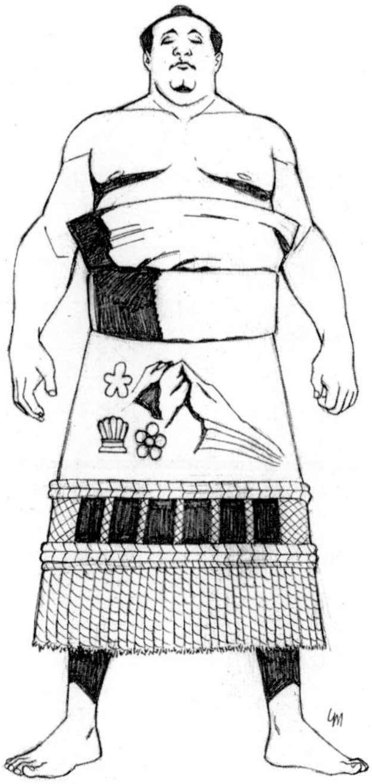

Above, character design for Oshima. At left and below, samurai designs.

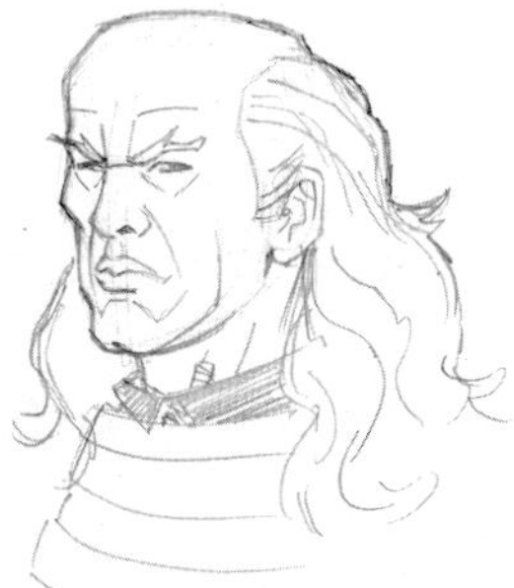

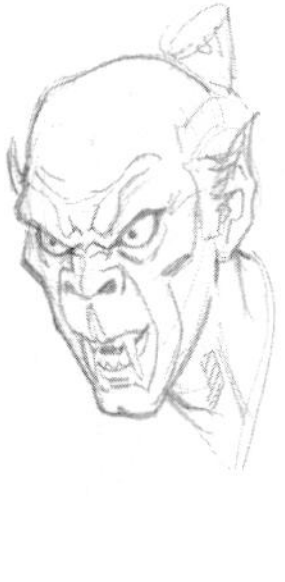

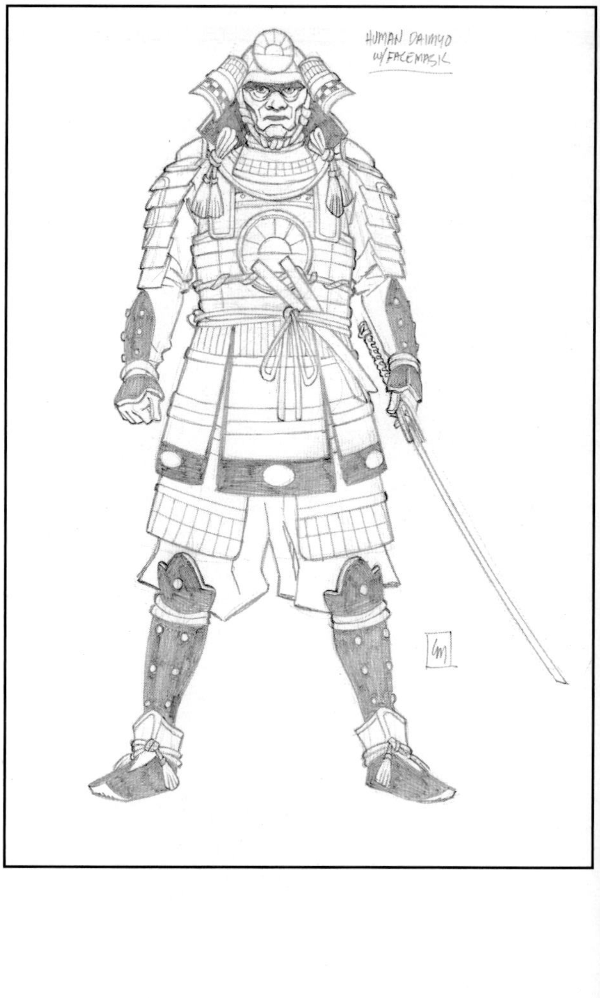
HUMAN DAIMYO
w/FACEMASK

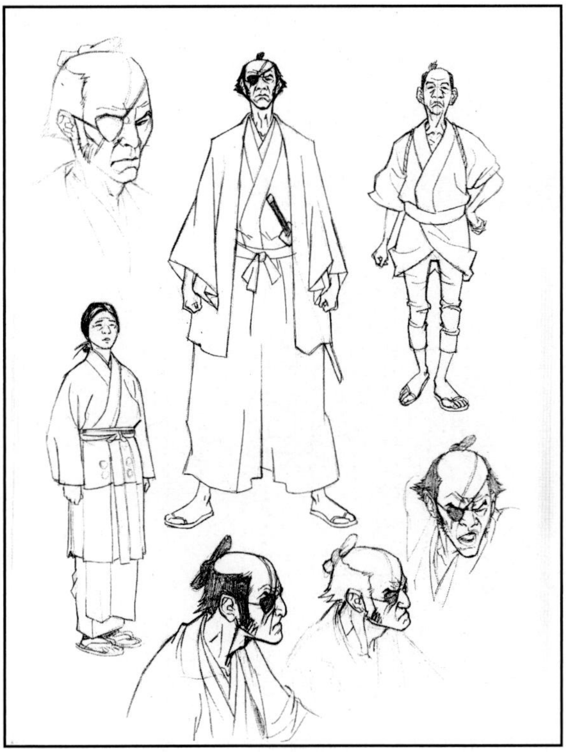

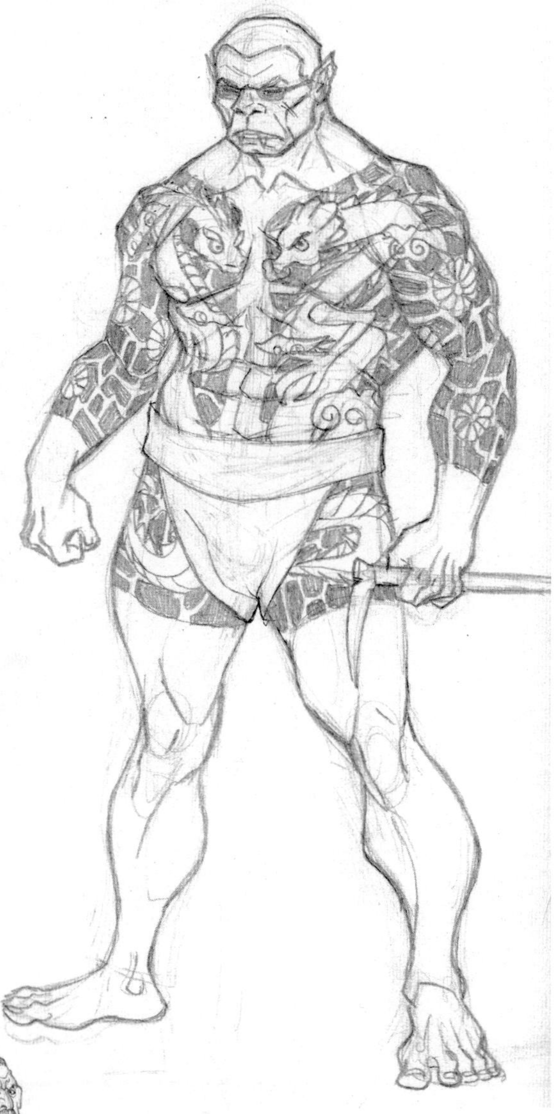

Above, samurai and peasant designs.
At right and below, vampire designs.

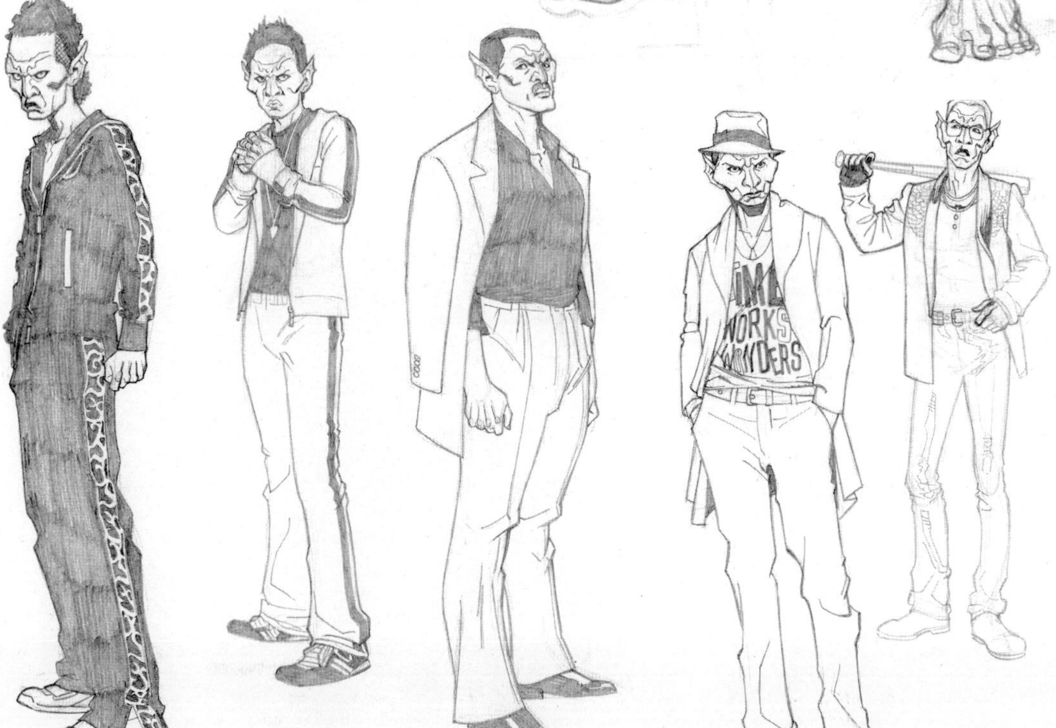

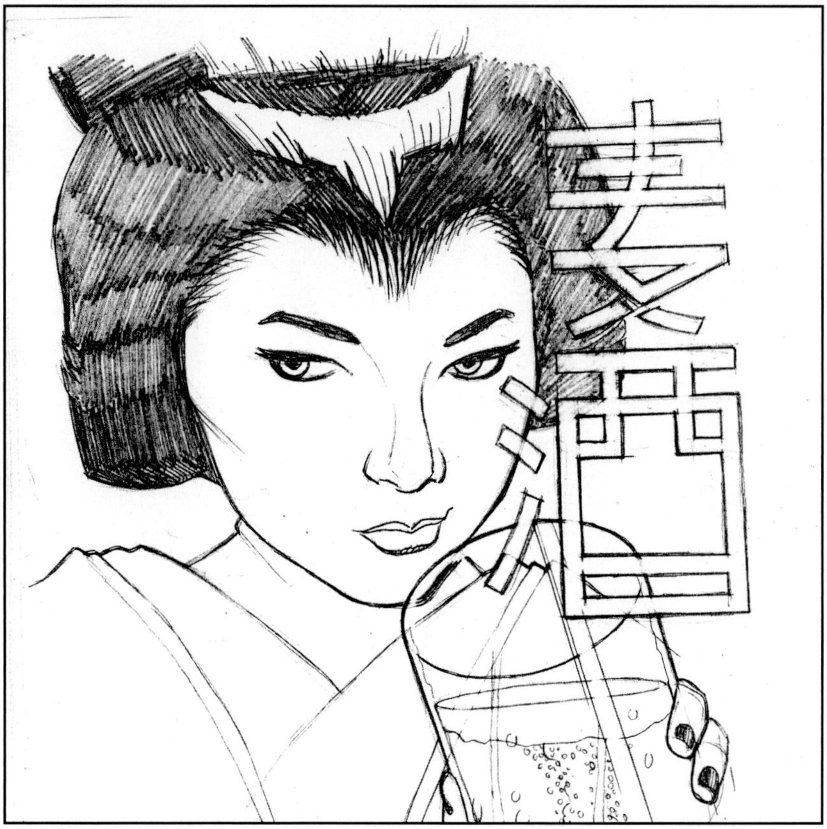

Above, cover element. Below, daimyo character sketch.

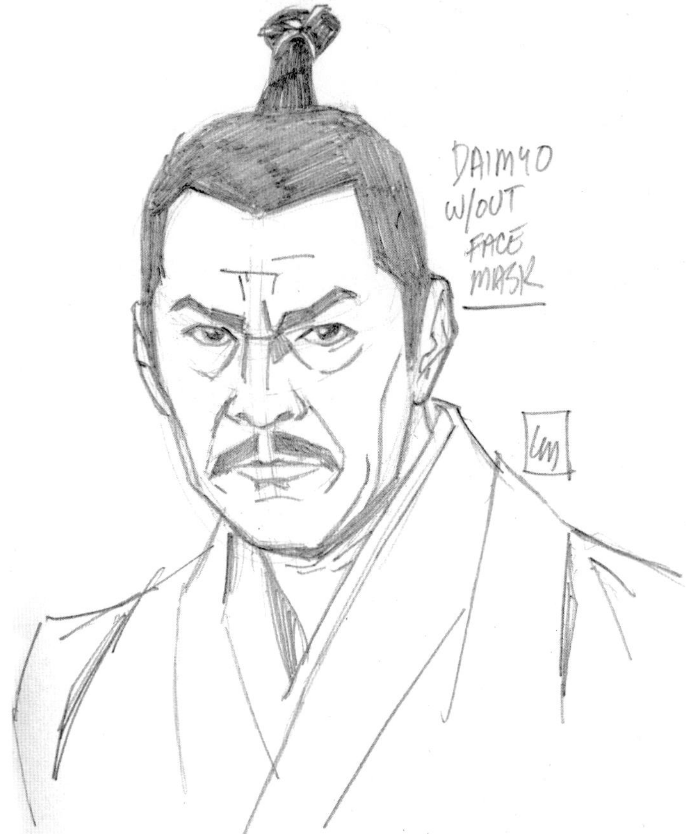
DAIMYO
W/OUT
FACE
MASK

Designs for Asano's bat guise,
and the vampire ronin Sakura.

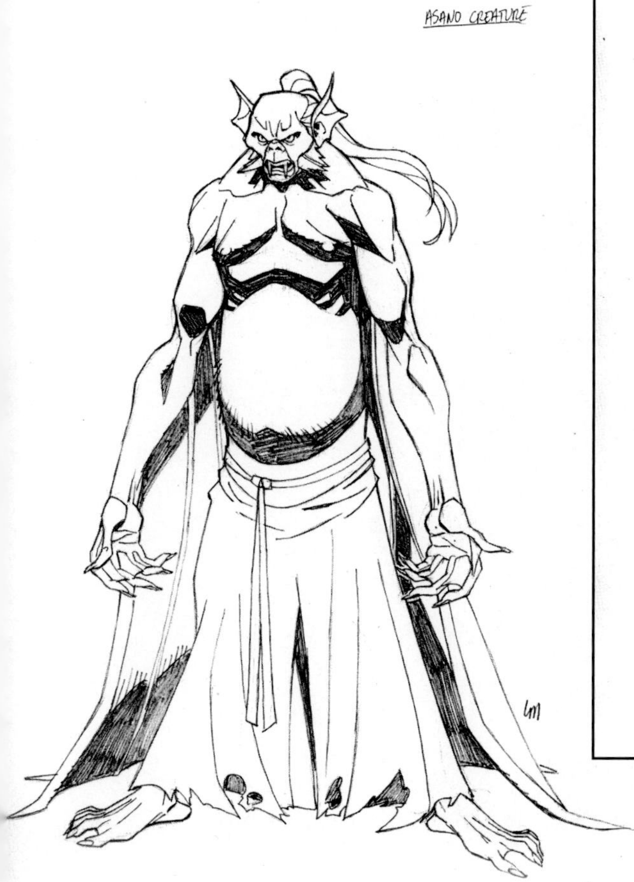
ASANO CREATURE

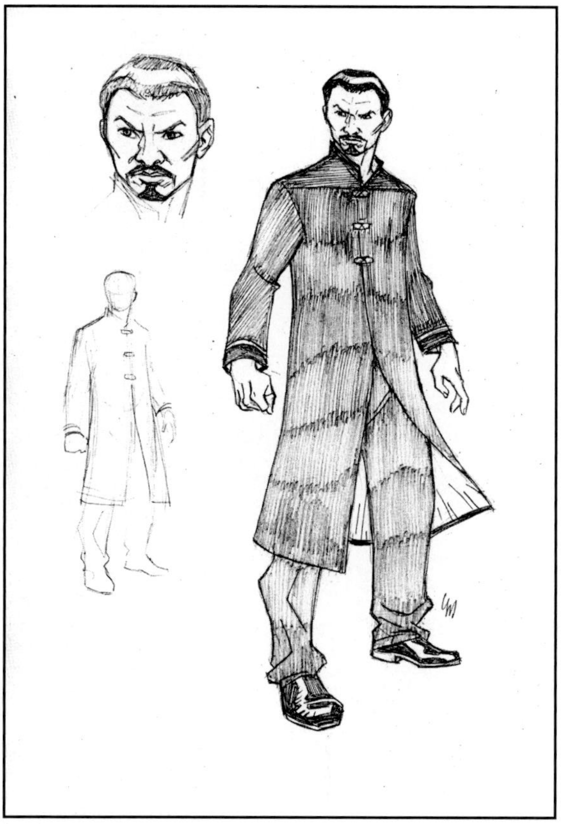

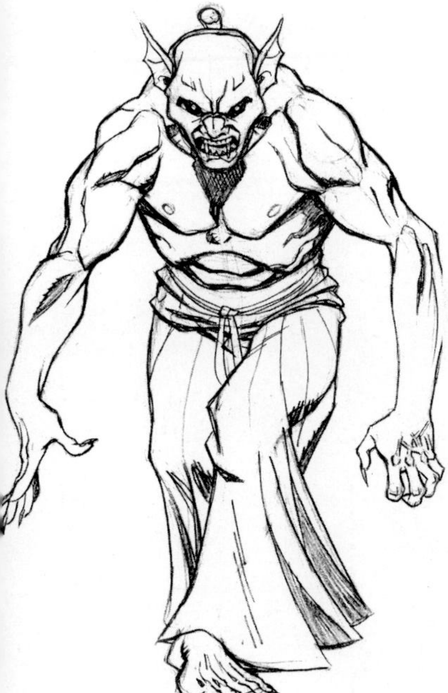

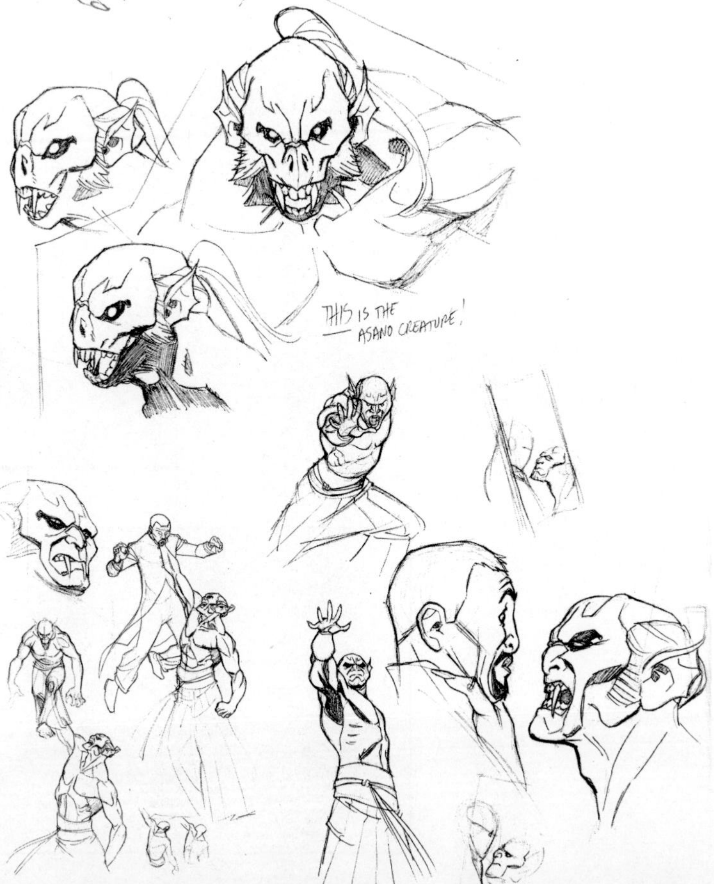
THIS IS THE ASANO CREATURE!

Cover layouts, and more finished expression studies.

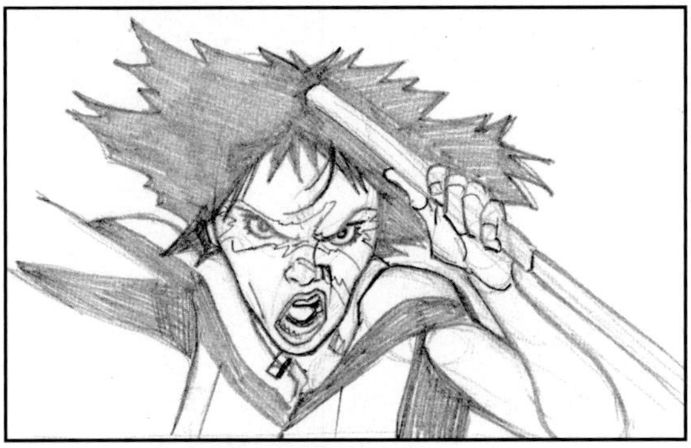

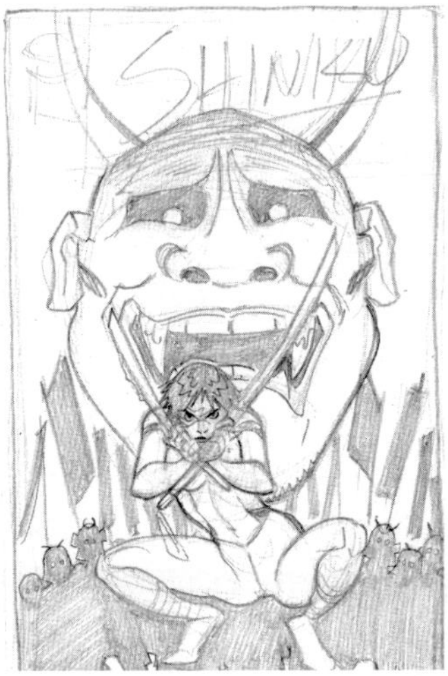
SHINKU

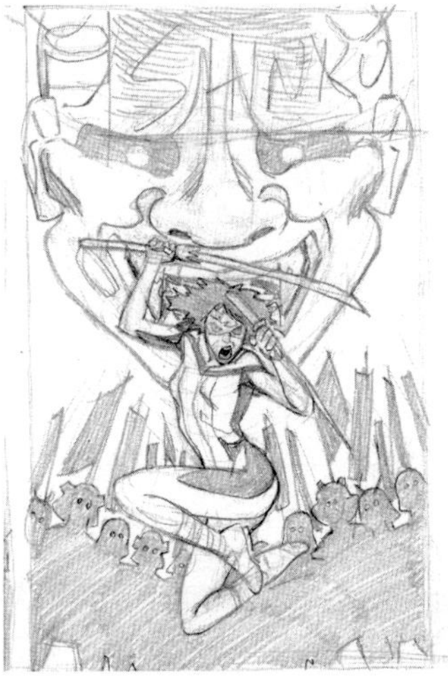
SHINKU

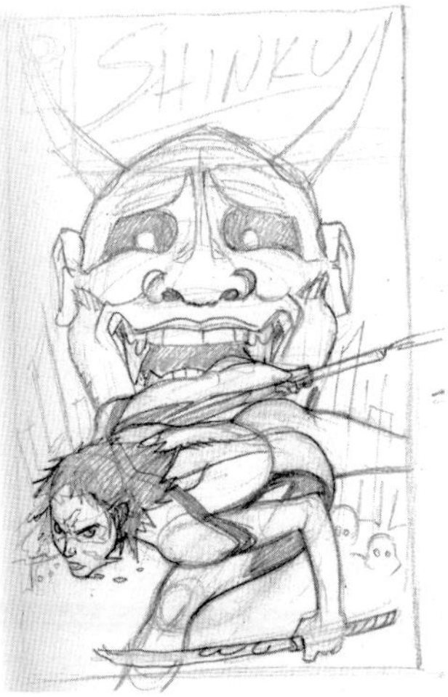
SHINKU

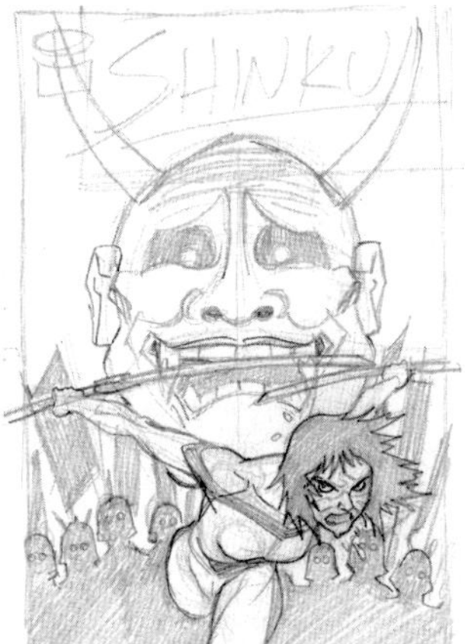
SHINKU

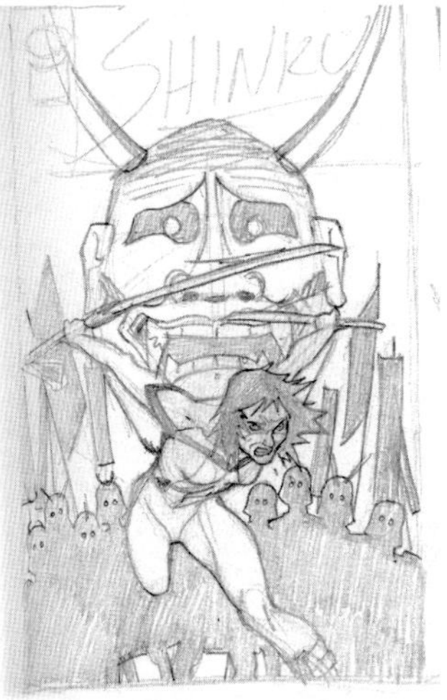
SHINKU

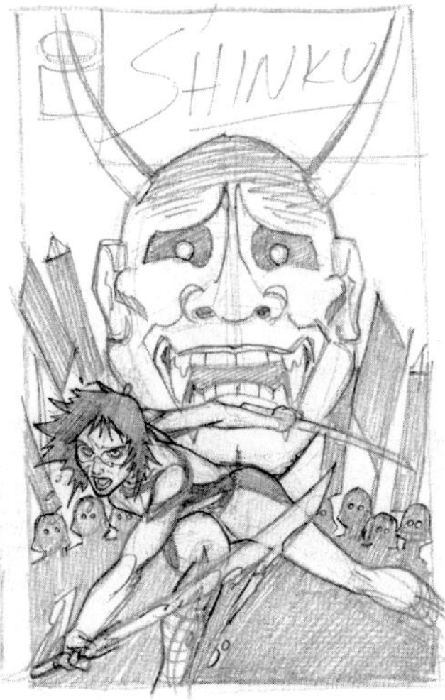
SHINKU

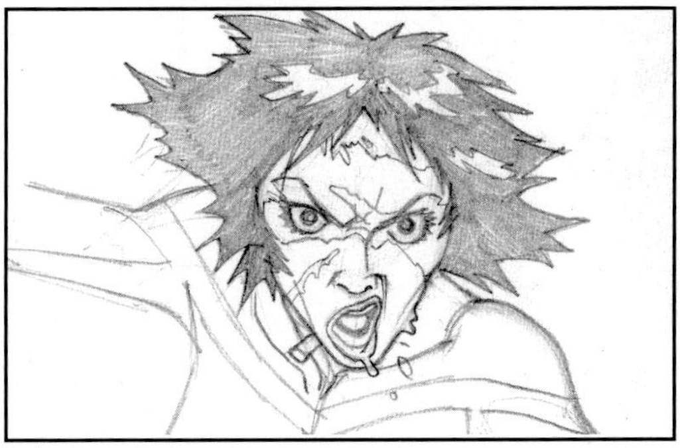

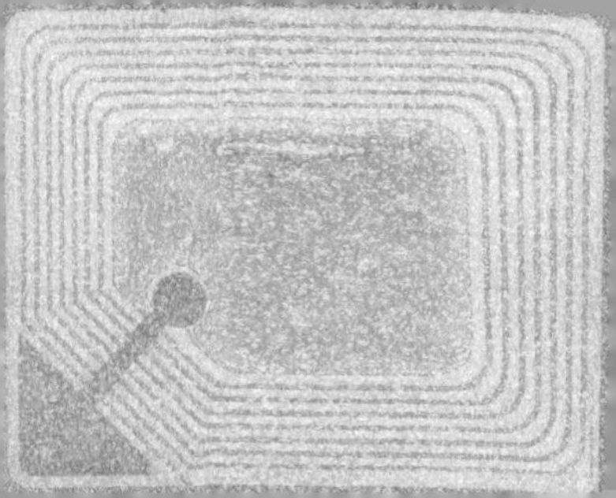

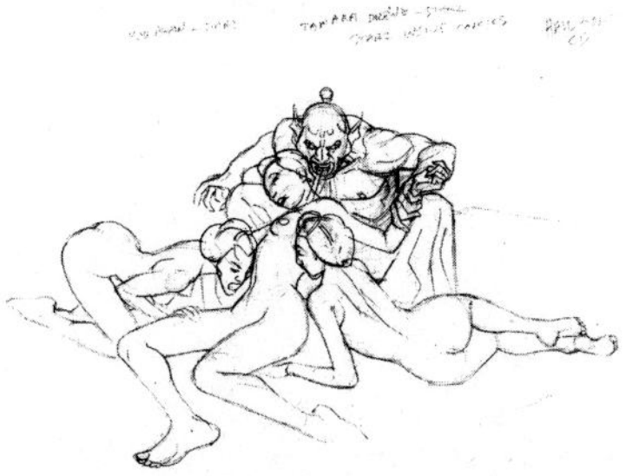

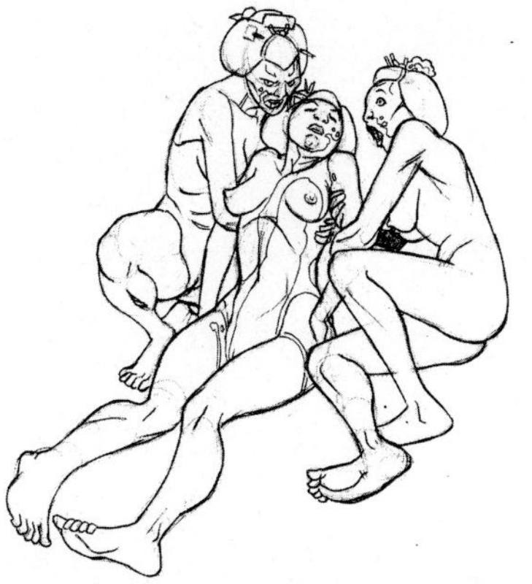

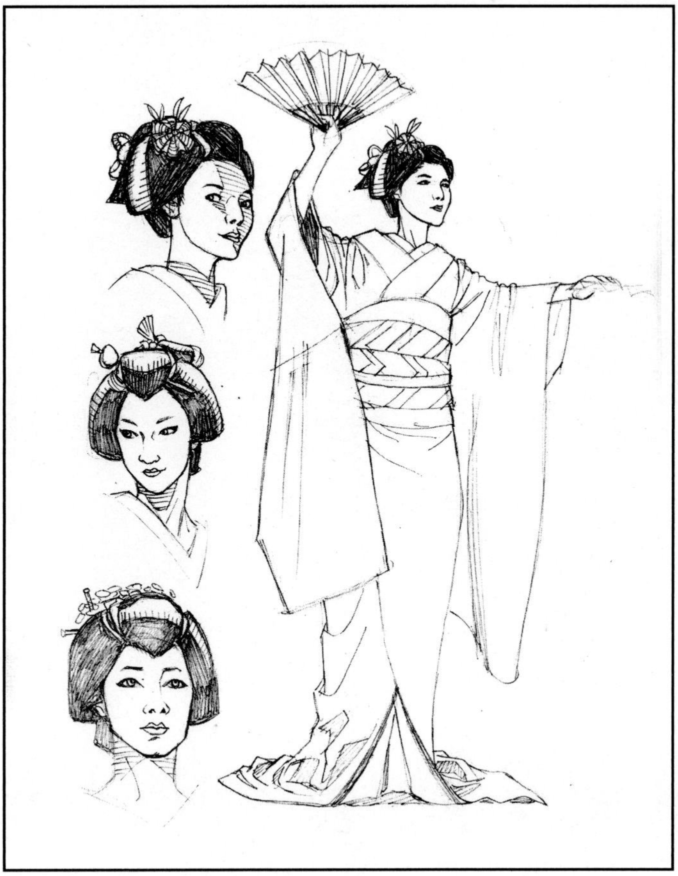

Above, Asano's brides. Below, Shinku layout and color experiment.

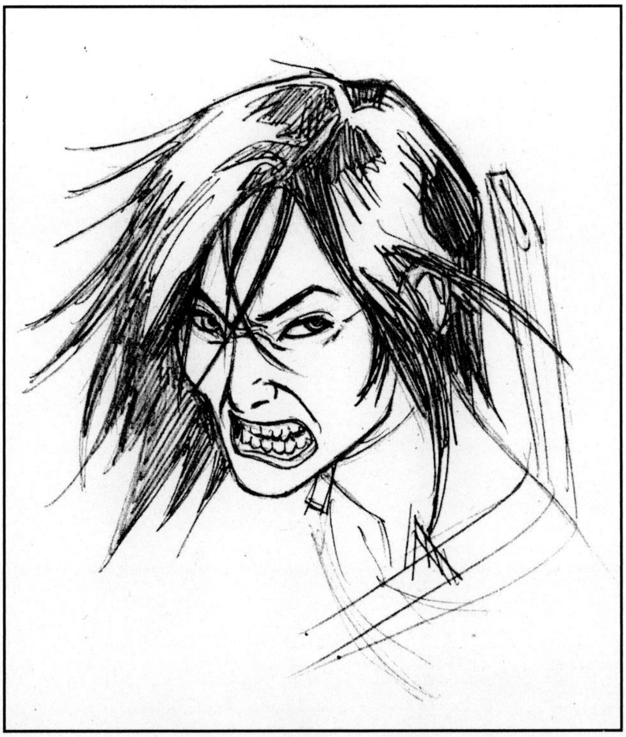

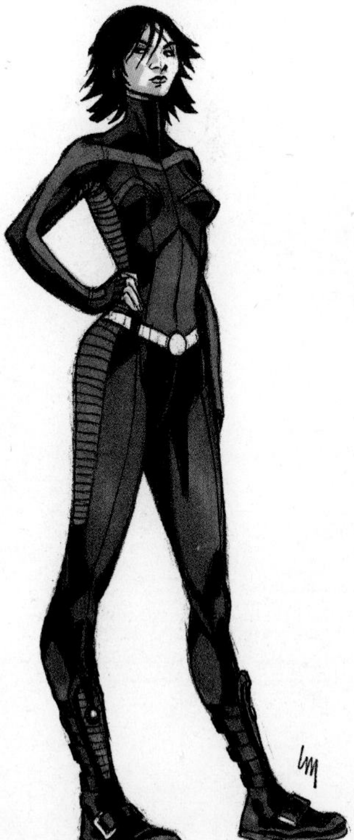

Back cover illustration, color by **Michael Atiyeh**.

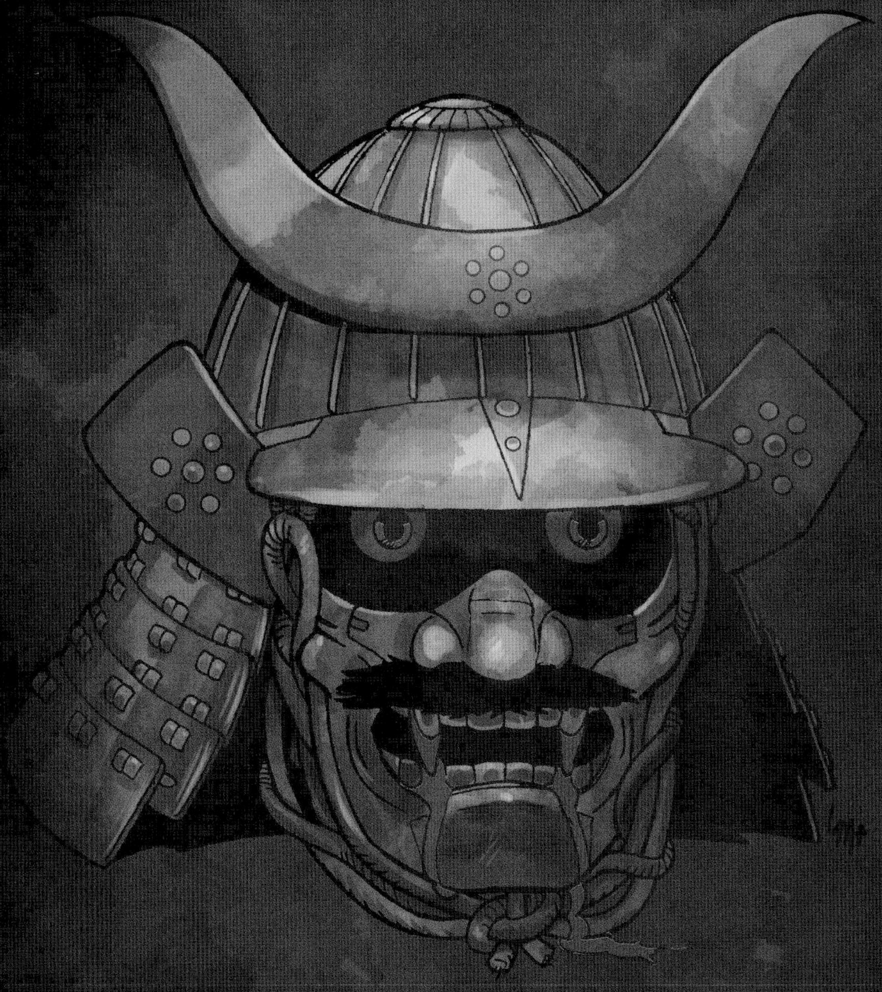

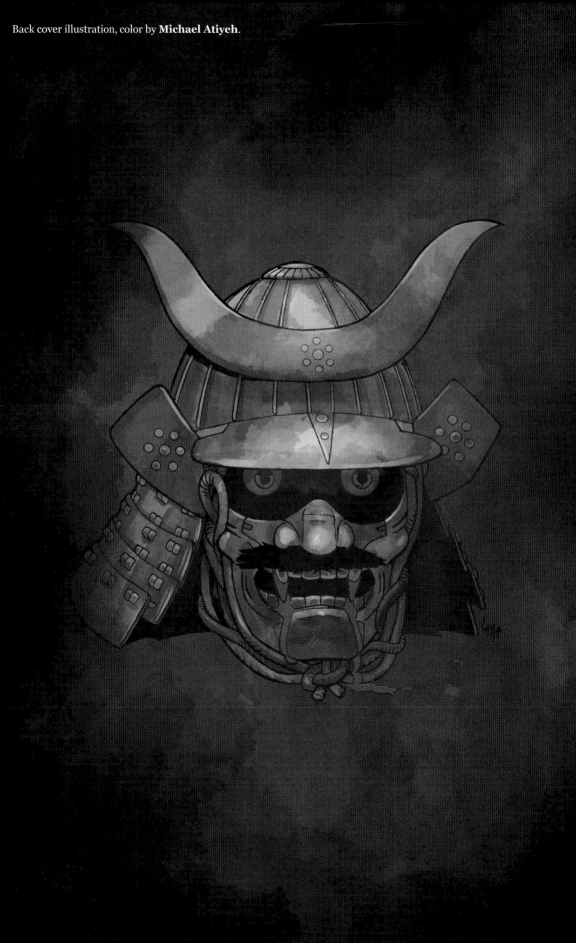

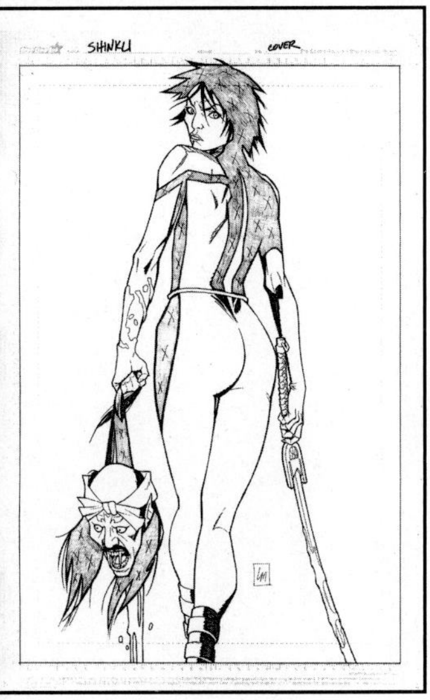
SHINKU
COVER

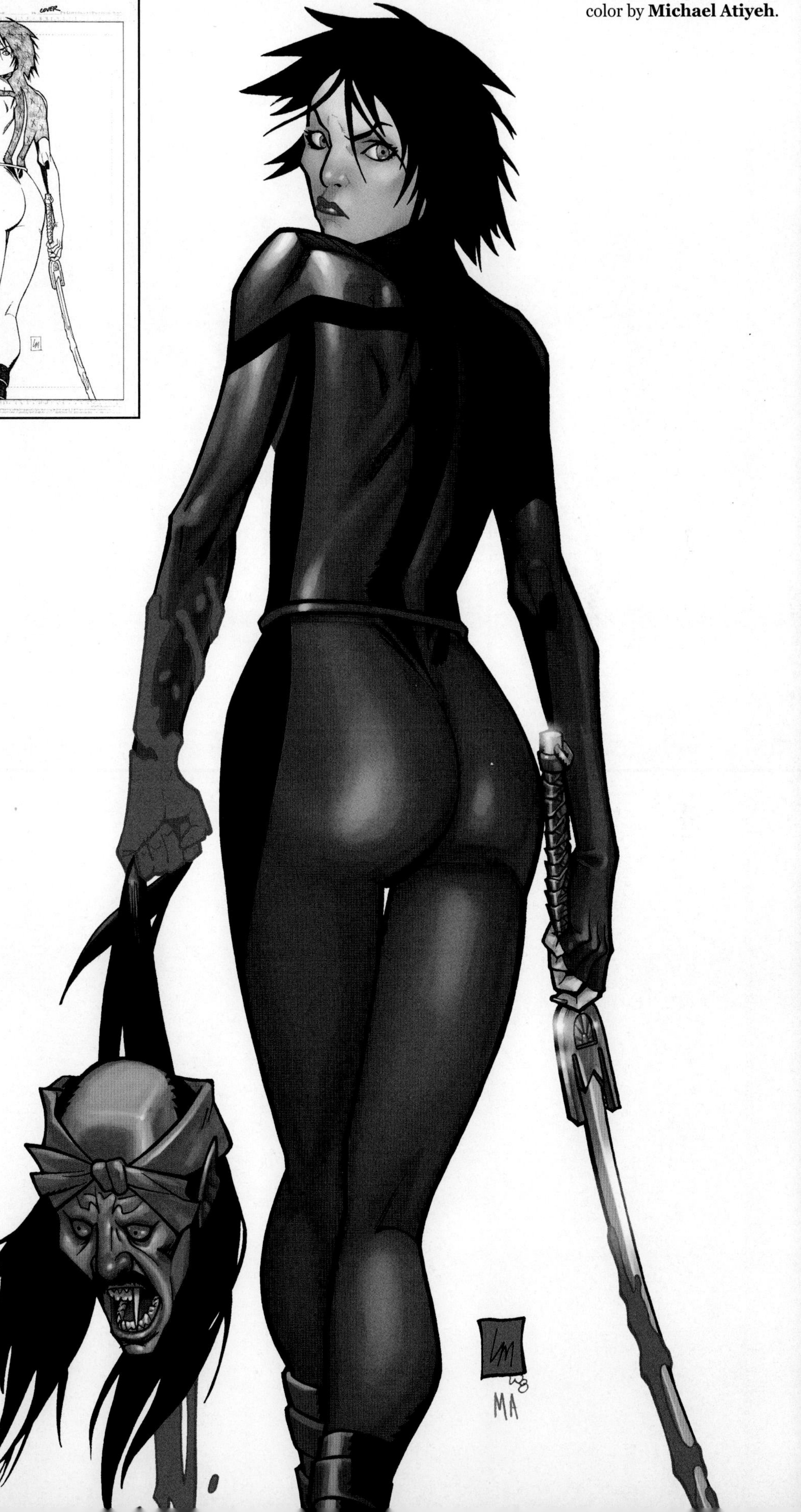

Back cover illustration, with pencils inset, color by **Michael Atiyeh**.

Ashcan

The following "ashcan" pages offer up the original vision for *Shinku*: a black, white and red book, like Matt Wagner's *Grendel* anthologies utilizing the same color scheme. The ashcan contained nine story pages and some character designs, and we produced a few hundred copies at a local printer that's literally housed in a barn a few miles from my home. I took copies to the Baltimore Comic Con, where I gave one to Joe Keatinge, then Image's marketing guy, now a damn fine writer of comics in his own right.

Joe's copy found its way into the hands of Image publisher Eric Stephenson, who approached me about bringing *Shinku* to Image. Eventually, at Eric's suggestion, *Shinku* became a full-color book. I asked my friend Mike Atiyeh if he wanted to color the series, making the offer more as a courtesy than anything else, because I assumed Mike's schedule was jammed with other freelance work. And it was. But Mike vowed to make room, and created the "marker comp" color style that has become a *Shinku* hallmark.

That wasn't even a glimmer when the ashcan was produced, though. The pages that follow are subtly different from those that saw print in the color issue #1. Lee Moder eventually redrew a handful of these panels, changing expressions or posture. But the biggest departure is that the Davis character was called Aaron at this point ... at least until someone reminded me that "Aaron" was also the name of the protagonist in my creator-owned *Dragon Prince* series, also drawn by Lee.

We experimented with a few treatments of the spot red, before settling on the more minimal version seen here. This is a glimpse at what might have been.

–Ron Marz

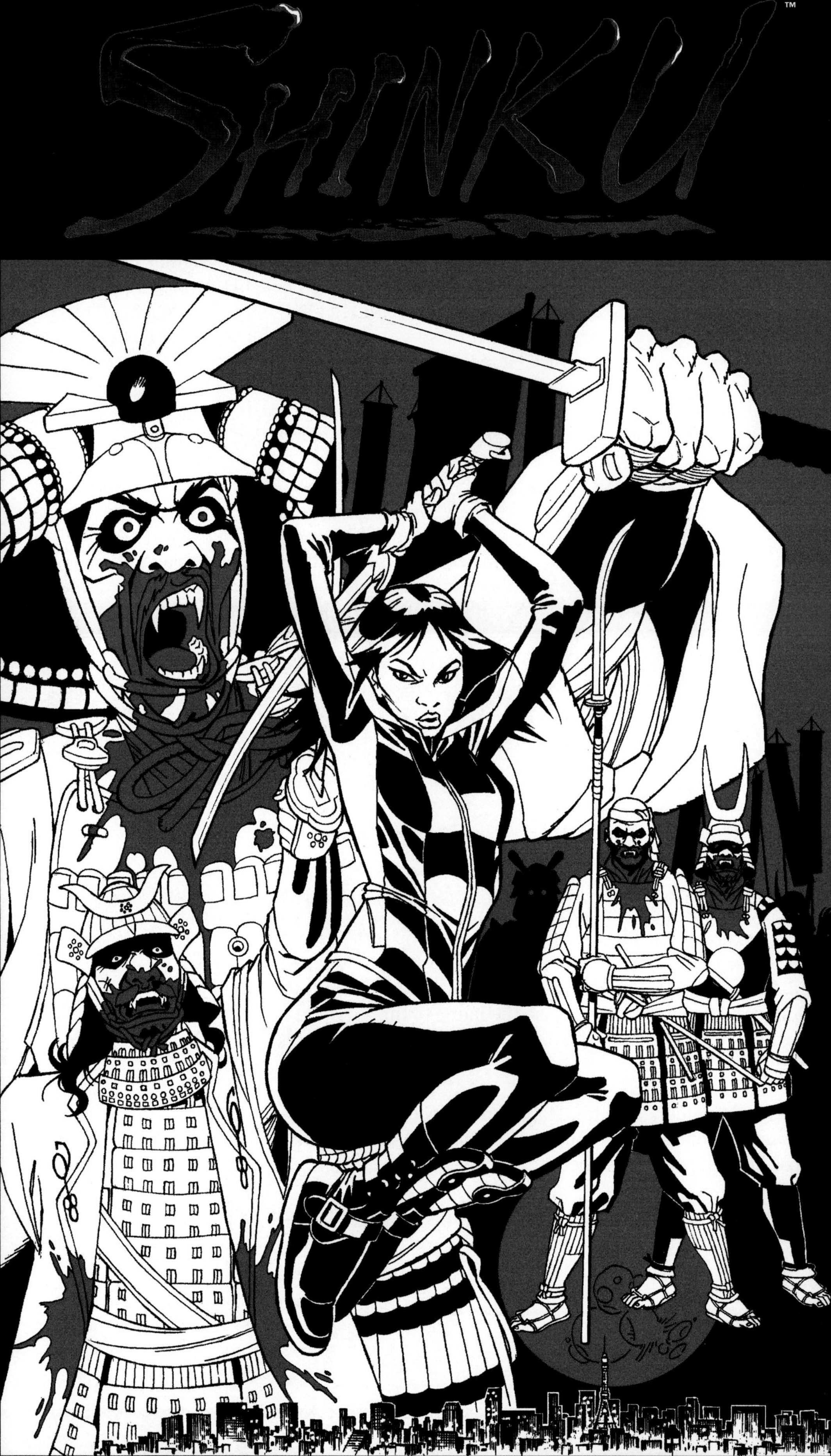
SHINKU™

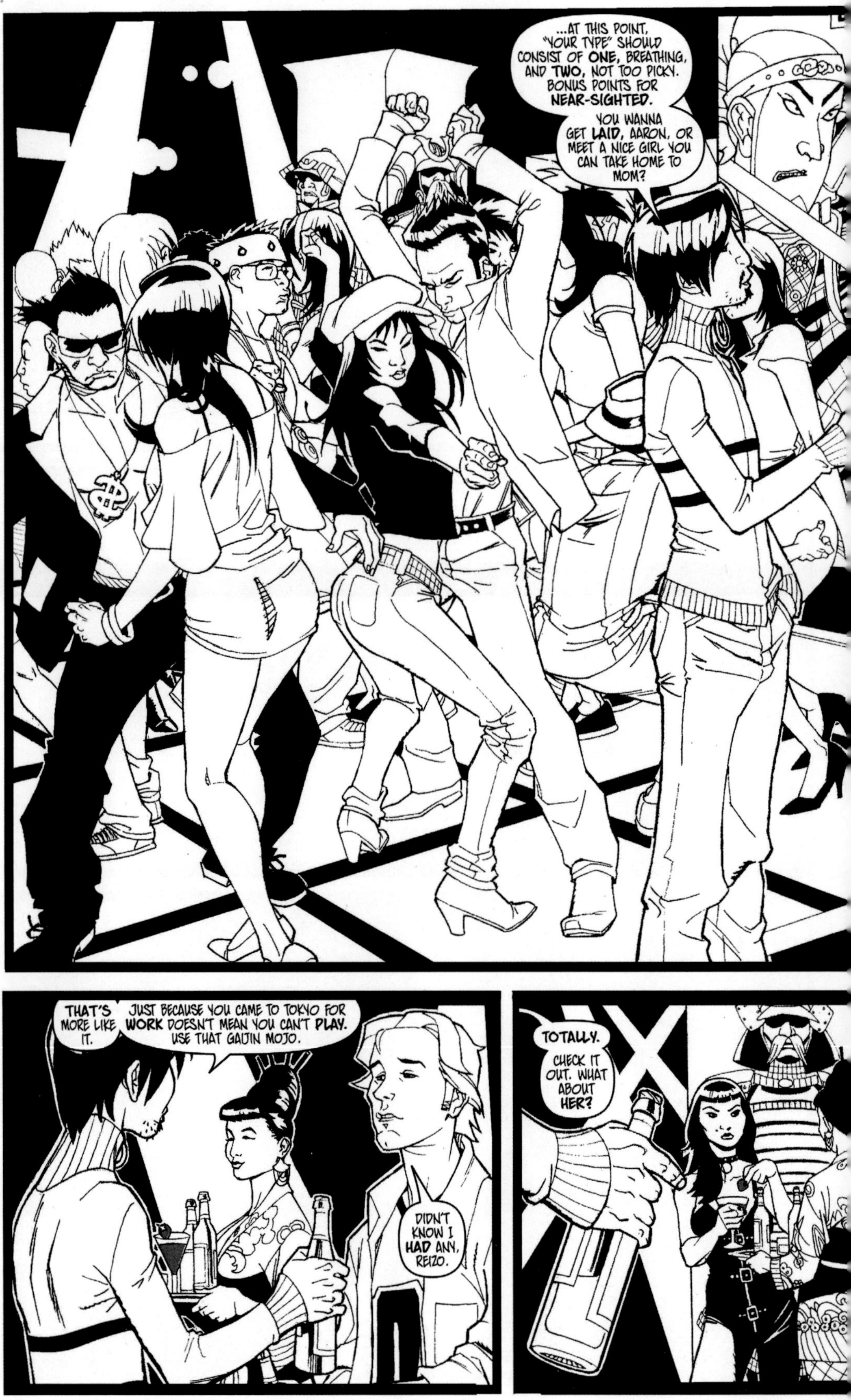
...AT THIS POINT, "YOUR TYPE" SHOULD CONSIST OF ONE, BREATHING, AND TWO, NOT TOO PICKY. BONUS POINTS FOR NEAR-SIGHTED.
YOU WANNA GET LAID, AARON, OR MEET A NICE GIRL YOU CAN TAKE HOME TO MOM?
THAT'S MORE LIKE IT.
JUST BECAUSE YOU CAME TO TOKYO FOR WORK DOESN'T MEAN YOU CAN'T PLAY. USE THAT GAIJIN MOJO.
DIDN'T KNOW I HAD ANY, REIZO.
TOTALLY.
CHECK IT OUT. WHAT ABOUT HER?

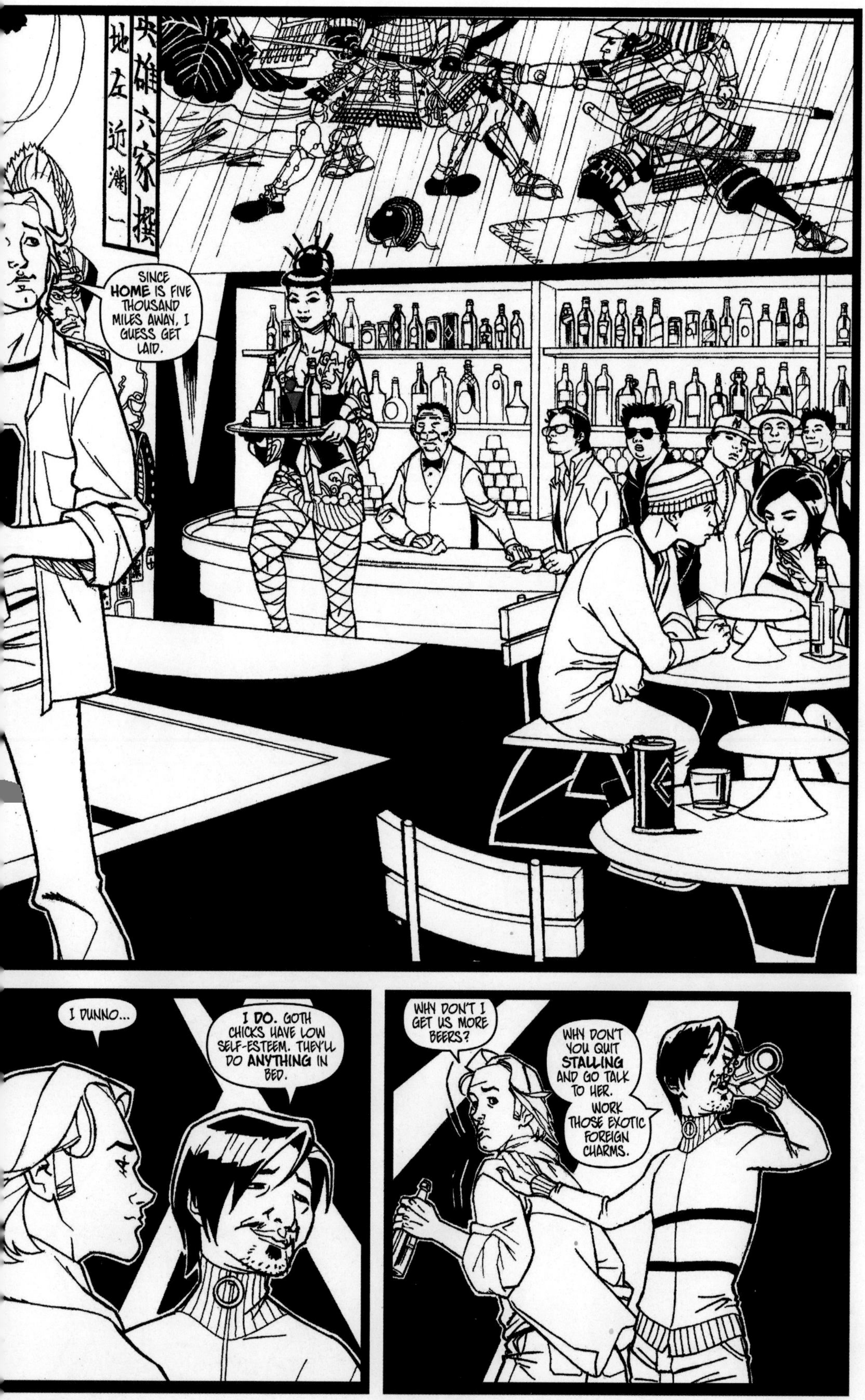
SINCE HOME IS FIVE THOUSAND MILES AWAY, I GUESS GET LAID.
I DUNNO...
I DO. GOTH CHICKS HAVE LOW SELF-ESTEEM. THEY'LL DO ANYTHING IN BED.
WHY DON'T I GET US MORE BEERS?
WHY DON'T YOU QUIT STALLING AND GO TALK TO HER.
WORK THOSE EXOTIC FOREIGN CHARMS.

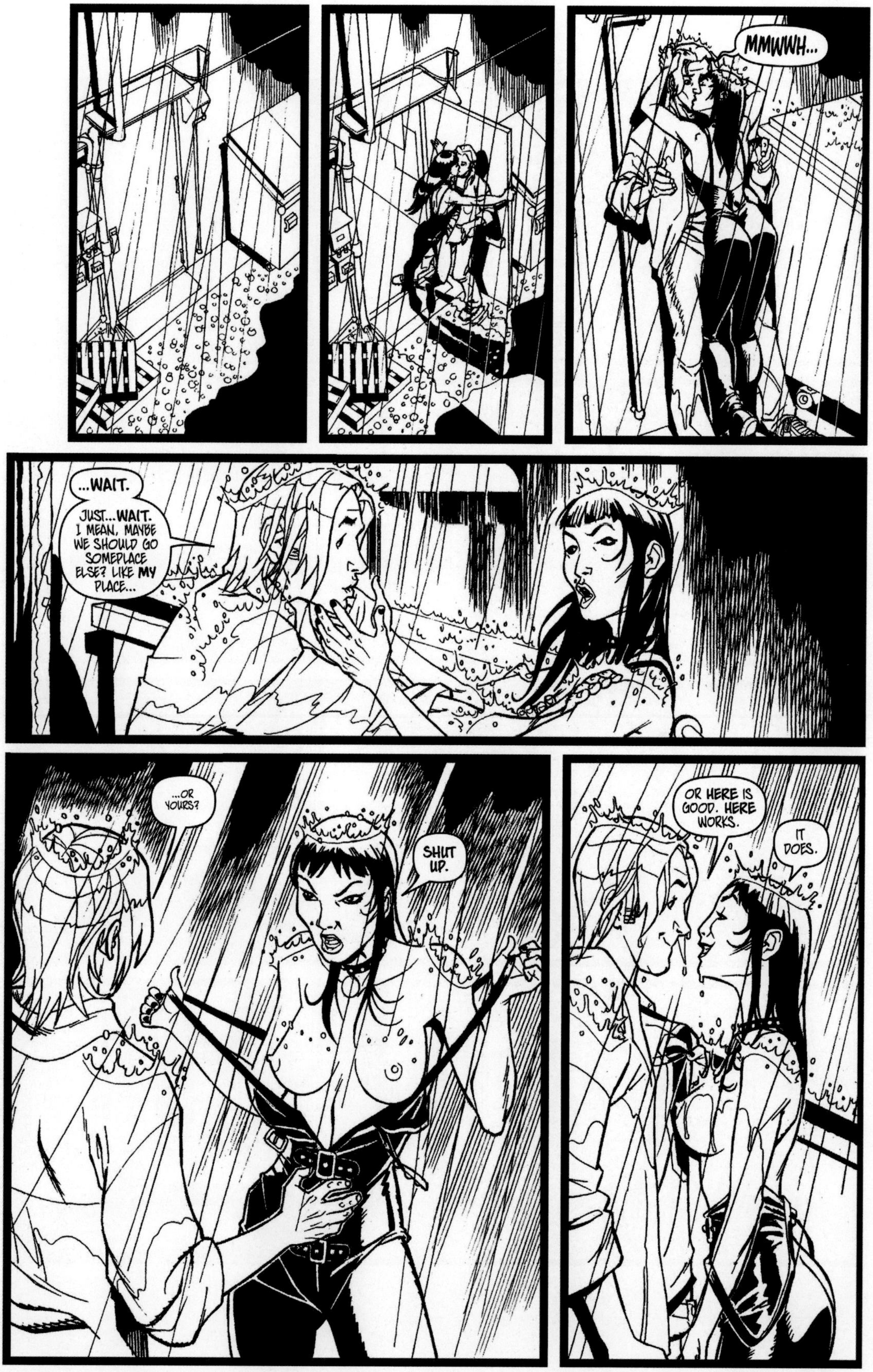
MMWWH...
...WAIT.
JUST...WAIT. I MEAN, MAYBE WE SHOULD GO SOMEPLACE ELSE? LIKE MY PLACE...
...OR YOURS?
SHUT UP.
OR HERE IS GOOD. HERE WORKS.
IT DOES.

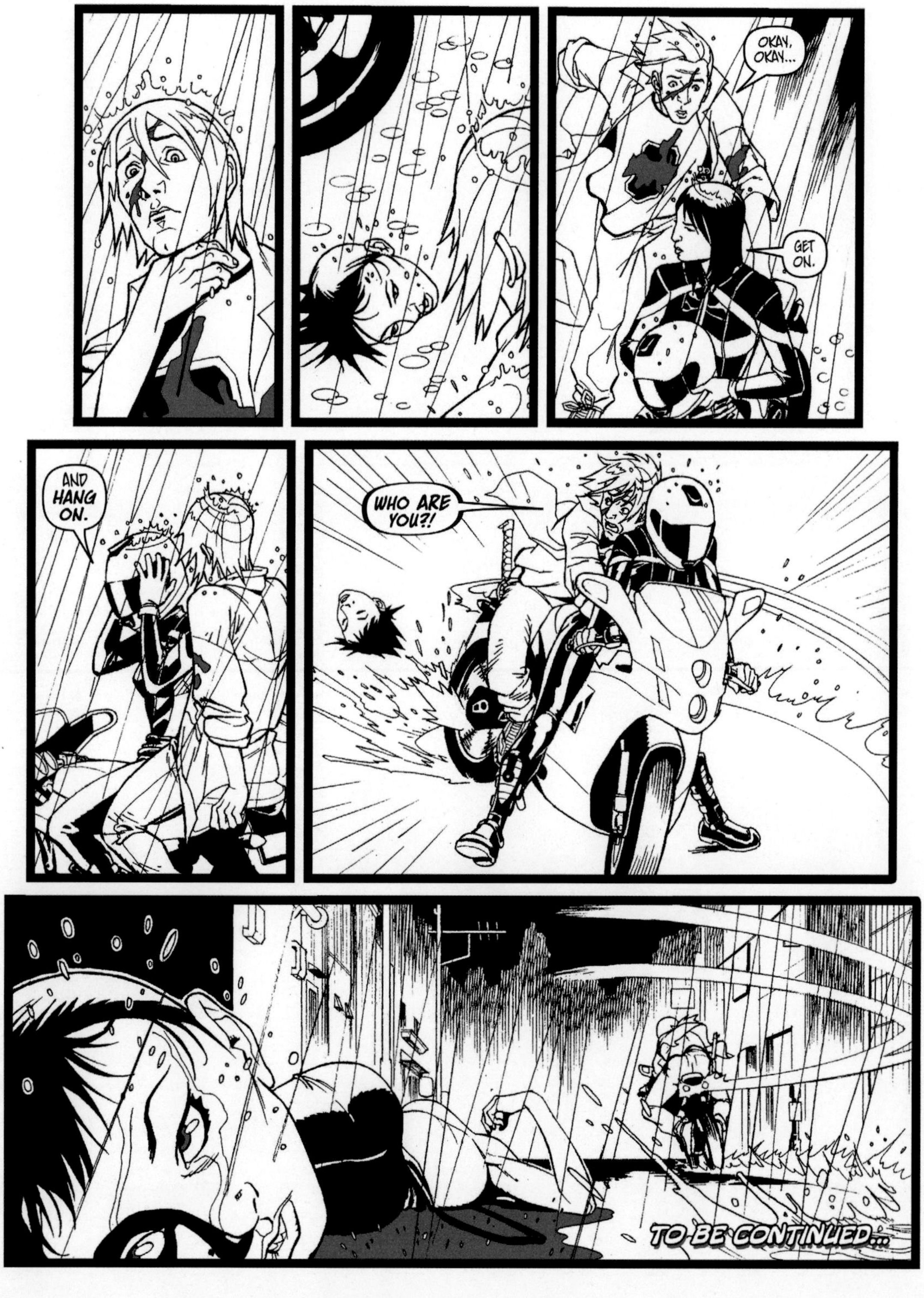
OKAY, OKAY...
GET ON.
AND HANG ON.
WHO ARE YOU?!
TO BE CONTINUED...

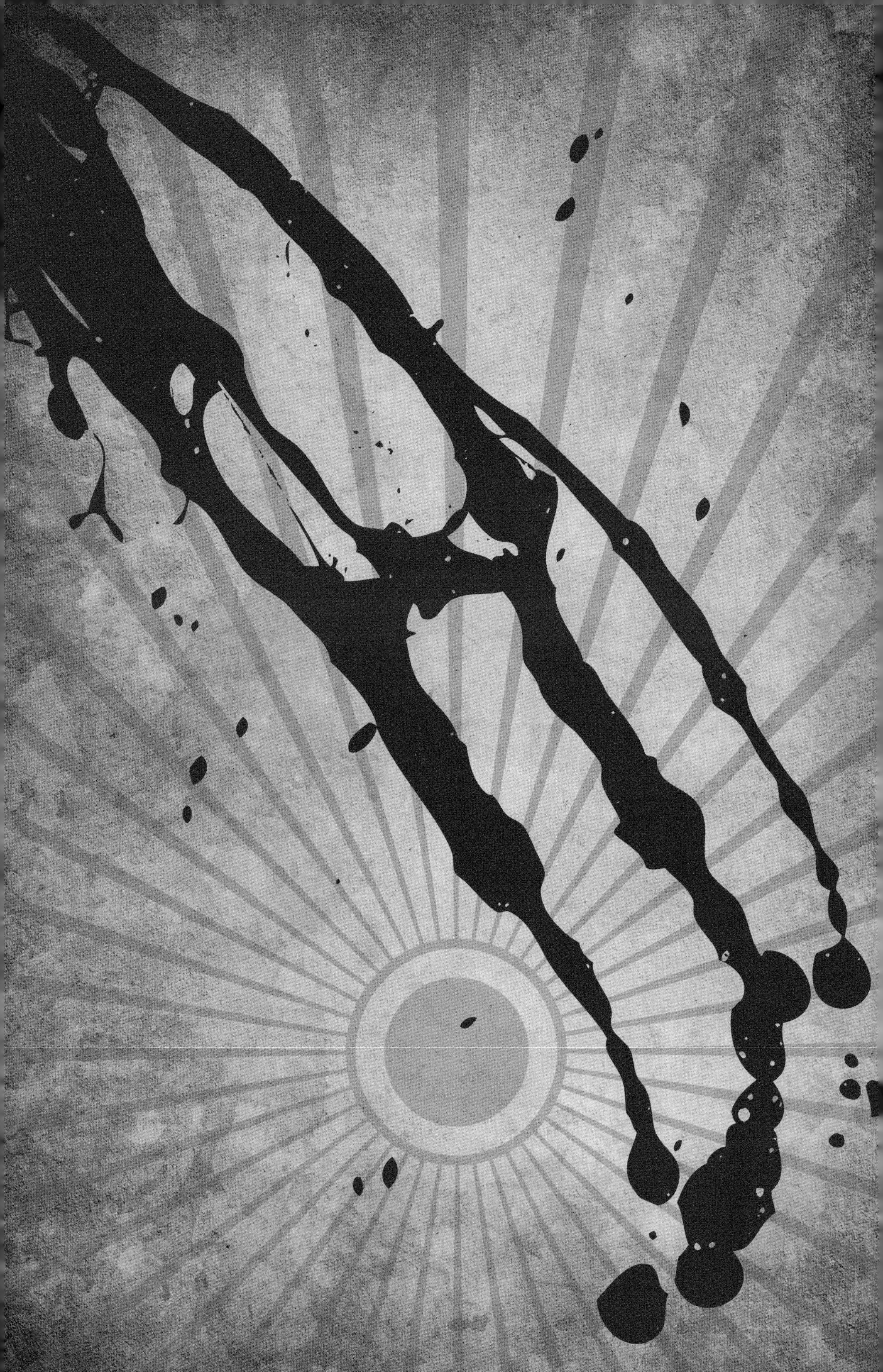